Family Histories of the Irish Revolution

Family Histories *of the* Irish Revolution

Ciara Boylan, Sarah-Anne Buckley & Pat Dolan
EDITORS

OPEN AIR

Set in 11 pt on 13.5 pt AGaramond for
OPEN AIR
an imprint of Four Courts Press
7 Malpas Street, Dublin 8, Ireland
www.fourcourtspress.ie
and in North America for
FOUR COURTS PRESS
c/o ISBS, 920 N.E. 58th Avenue, Suite 300, Portland, OR 97213.

A catalogue record for this title
is available from the British Library.

ISBN 978-1-84682-682-5

Printed in Spain
by GraphyCems, Navarra

Contents

Acknowledgments

The editors would like to thank the Institute for Lifecourse and Society, NUI Galway, for their generous support of this publication. We would also like to thank an tUachtarán Michael D. Higgins for his thoughtful and suggestive Foreword and an t-Ollamh Gearóid Ó Tuathaigh for a characteristically insightful contextualizing chapter, 'The Irish revolutionary decade, 1913–23: voices, narratives and contexts'. Finally, we would like to thank Four Courts Press who have supported and guided the project through to completion.

Foreword

That the staff community of NUI Galway have embarked on a project of ethical remembering of the founding events of our state and its context is surely to be welcomed. The publication of this volume has involved, not only an invocation of the particular, but also it can lead to a sharing of antecedent influences. Volumes such as this one can thus play a vital role in enabling and producing a clear and more inclusive story of the making of the modern form of our nation; one which allows us to view our past in a way that, while avoiding false amnesia, or bogus equivalences, attempts to be inclusive and honest. In doing so, the contributions, taken together, prevent us from such idealizing versions of that past as might, because of the seduction of previous collective versions of the past (often constructed to accommodate apologetic versions of the present), obstruct our capacity to learn from our complex history. The crafting of our future after all can only gain from an inclusive historiography.

For all Irish citizens, the stories of those who fought for freedom are stories of bravery, vision and determination. For their loved ones and dependants, they are also however in addition, stories tinged with sadness, of loss and separation. The human price paid during that seismic period of our history should not ever be forgotten, or underestimated, it should remind us of the great debt of gratitude we owe to all of those who bravely risked their lives, and in so many cases their livelihoods, so that future generations of Ireland could grow up as citizens of a free and independent state. Many who emigrated after independence, for a variety of reasons, were to look at the early history of the state from abroad.

We are all carriers of history, recipients of stories, anecdotes and accounts of the past, many handed on to us by previous generations and often made more palatable or dramatic for the circumstances of their retelling. While they may be stories unique to individual families they are also, in so many cases, a critical part of Ireland's shared social history. These are gifts then to those seeking to achieve an open, wide, inclusive and balanced view of our shared past. It is through the exploration of the different but inter-connecting experiences and individual voices that comprise our past we can achieve a richer understanding of the journey that has brought us to our contemporary moment.

In engaging with the project of ethical remembering during 2016 – a year of commemoration – I often drew on the work of philosophers such as Richard

Kearney and Paul Ricoeur. The important distinction between 'common memory' and 'shared memory' was suggested to me by philosopher Avishai Margalit, in his book *The ehics of memory.* In Margalit's definition, 'common memory' is an aggregate notion that combines the memories of all those people who remember a certain episode that each of them experienced individually.

'Shared memory', on the other hand, is an indirect memory – a memory of memory – which requires communication and seeks to integrate into one version the different perspectives of those who might have directly remembered a given episode. This can never be a finished task. Rather it is a process requiring constant return, the taking account of new evidence, new perspectives.

If we are to set about constructing a shared memory, collections built on the memories of individuals are important. I have no doubt that from the contributions in this collection, of what one might describe as eclectic, common themes and shared revisions may emerge. They also, if left open for addition, will facilitate a wider participation in the production of history, and make an invite for a further gathering of memories in the future. All of which no doubt will bring new perspectives to events of the past into being. We owe a great debt of gratitude to those who so generously share their family stories in their task of remembering, and by doing so, ensure that irreplaceable and historically important memories can now be preserved, archived and made available to all. The staff community of NUIG will, I hope, have come to know each other better in a deeper way. I wish them well in the conversations and elaborations, which will no doubt occur. May we look to these stories of our past and reflect on them in a way that is emancipatory and transformative as we set about constructing the foundations of a new and better Ireland.

Michael D. Higgins
Uachtarán na hÉireann
President of Ireland

Introduction

CIARA BOYLAN, SARAH-ANNE BUCKLEY
& PAT DOLAN

This volume presents a selection of stories from current and retired staff at the National University of Ireland, Galway on how their ancestors participated in the Irish revolution. It captures the ways in which family history and memory are transmitted, and the influence and legacy of these histories. The stories include familial accounts of well-known figures like Peadar O'Donnell, Tom Kettle and Hanna and Francis Sheehy-Skeffington, alongside accounts of men and women unknown or forgotten by the wider historical narrative. Participation in events in Dublin during 1916 and the sectarian tinder box of 1920s Belfast are described alongside the histories of those whose 'revolution' took place in the villages, fields and open spaces of rural Ireland. The stories recounted describe the actions and lives of republican nationalists as well as those who were critical of the events of the period, both as they unfolded and after they had entered the pantheon of nationalist history. Finally, while the focus of most chapters is on the participation of the young in the events of the period, many also recount the impact of those events on that unique generation over their life courses.

The contributions also discuss how family history and memory was imparted and aim to explore the legacy of this on succeeding generations. Some of these family stories and memories have been silenced for generations, such as those of family members who served in the British army during the First World War; of RUC men in rural Ireland; and of the real and personal impact of the Civil War, thus shedding light on the complex politics of memory in post-independence Ireland.

History of family

The volume has been written from a history of family and a life course perspective. As the scholars involved are from a variety of disciplines, this approach allowed a flexibility and diversity in the selection and inclusion of narratives. Methodologically, the editors chose to invite all past and present members of the National University of Ireland Galway (previously UCG) community to share their family stories. Contributors were asked to approach their chapters in three ways – to outline their relative's story from a history of family approach, to apply a life course lens to the narrative and to consider the broader political/economic and social context. Internationally, history of family emerged from debates on the history of demography and later that of childhood, involving scholars such as Michael Anderson, Edward Shorter, Lawrence Stone, Linda Pollock and Hugh Cunningham. Timothy Guinnane's *Vanishing Irish,* published in 1997, is perhaps the most authoritative scholarship using the history of family approach.[1] It has been aided in recent years by work on the history of gender, childhood and youth. This volume takes a 'sentiments' approach – looking at these individual histories, the history of emotions and the impact of external events on the lives of those investigated. In particular, it invokes the work of Michael Anderson, Joanna Bourke and Thomas Dixon.[2] In conjunction with a life course approach, this allows us to bring these histories into the present.

Connecting life course

Life course refers to a multi-disciplinary approach to better understanding the elements and dynamics of an individual's life journey and how this is influenced by socio-economic, political and cultural contexts. By implication the term 'life course' suggests that our past experiences and intergenerational relationships with family (in particular) and community shape who we are. From within these contexts we focus on historic events and how the revolutionary decade (1912–23) impacted in real and human ways. Within life course, there are four key themes, which we see as central to understanding and engaging with our past, ones which are the core rationale for the creation of this volume.

First, healthy lives and well-being may seem an unlikely connection to history, but as will be seen in this volume, for families, engagement in events of the revolutionary period had direct impact on their physical and mental well-being. This is especially evident in contributions that address the Civil War. The second life course theme involves life transitions and life events. Engagement in the various conflicts described, by the ancestors of contributors, not alone impacted at the time, but as will be seen has influenced subsequent generations. Ironically, this influence still occurs despite the common comment by many authors in their chapters that silence prevailed and politics and history were not discussed or passed on by those active in the

1 Timothy Guinnane, *Vanishing Irish: households, migration, and the rural economy in Ireland, 1850–1914* (Princeton, 1997) 2 See Michael Anderson, *Approaches to the history of the western family, 1500–1914*, 2nd ed. (Cambridge, 1995); Joanna Bourke, *Husbandry to housewifery: women, economic change and housework in Ireland, 1890–1914* (Oxford, 1993)

events of the time. The third key life course theme focuses on intergenerational relations, and for many of the contributors the act of engaging with older family members in itself has been a voyage of discovery. Finally, the development of civic participation and engagement is seen as a core positive function within the life course approach. For the generation of contributors to this volume, many grew up on descriptions of those active in the Rising, War of Independence and more contentiously the Civil War, as either those who died for Ireland or gave us our freedom. Two variations to this perception emerge in the various chapters. First, the events were complex, real and stark human experiences for those involved and those they loved, with negative as well as positive outcomes. Second, it could be argued that since the formation of the state, how the subsequent generations celebrated it mirrors how we contributed to it civically, in a somewhat muted and reserved manner. We are now moving to a more expressive form of marking historical events which implies that rather than just acknowledging dying for Ireland (as in the past) we need now to celebrate living for it and contribute to the new multi-cultural society Ireland has become.

Themes

The chapters in this volume describe the lives, experiences and contributions of a representative cross section of Irish society during the revolutionary period, and their stories offer new insights into the experiences Irish women and men lived through during this tumultuous and era-defining period in our national history. Cutting through all of these personal experiences are sub-themes of class and politics. Social class influenced participation in the revolutionary period in a great number of ways, and was as marked as gender in this regard, if not more so. Yet the small farmer, the grocer, the publican's apprentice, the policeman, the well-to-do politician and the British army officer alike all formed part of a unique generation, for whom the independence struggle and the foundation of the Free State was a key factor shaping their experiences and worldviews. Personal politics was also relevant throughout the period and particularly potent during the Civil War period. The volume recounts the lives of a number of republican nationalists; however, alternative views and positions, some of them complex, are also discussed. There are chapters discussing the pacifist Francis Sheehy Skeffington; the Home Rule MP and vocal opponent of the Easter Rising, Tom Kettle; the equally vocal detractor Patrick Shaw, a Cumann na nGaedheal TD who wrote a letter to the King apologizing for the events of Easter week and whose son wrote a notorious 'revisionist' essay on the Rising for the 50th anniversary; and the fierce and unrepentant social radicalism of the veteran republican Peadar O'Donnell who saw nothing 'revolutionary' about his generation.

The ways in which memories and personal histories are spoken about or buried, and the impact this has on the transmission of family narratives, forms a crucial element of all of the chapters below. Many of the authors note that their relative did not speak about the events of the period or their participation in those events. This silence had many causes, from the personal to the political, and it is often only possible to surmise as to why the 'revolutionary generation' recorded, opined upon, ignored or buried their experiences as the case may be. The unreliability of memory – its self-serving or self-effacing tendencies – gives rise to an entirely different set of challenges, as Gearóid Ó Tuathaigh reminds us in his introductory chapter. Nonetheless, the authors of these chapters have done us a service in attempting to recover those family histories using a wide variety of sources. In doing so, they have not shied away from the complexities of the period. Nowhere does the binary simplicities of the older dogmas – a history of winners and losers, rights and wrongs, heroes and villains, bravery and weakness – fall apart quite as obviously as in the personal family stories that make up our collective history. The lived realities of individual lives, embedded in communities, simply don't allow for such binary thinking and as some of the contributors remind us, veterans of the period did not, could not, or would not, keep up old animosities in the post-revolutionary period.

Women and gender

Section one of the volume, Women and Gender, includes the histories of a number of girls and women caught up in the tumult of the revolutionary period, as well as examining the lives of noted contemporary feminists (both men) who engaged progressively with gender issues. The centenary commemorations of the 1916 Rising and revolutionary period have brought new and insightful historical work on the participation of women.[3] Indeed, this integration of women's experience into the historical narrative has emerged as one of the key historiographical developments stimulated by the 'Decade of Centenaries' programme. New and additional research on high-profile female participants in the revolutionary period, such as Constance Markievicz, has formed part of this work; but so too has uncovering the roles played by women

3 See, for example: Liz Gillis, *Women of the Irish revolution, 1913–1923: a photographic history* (Cork, 2016); Cal McCarthy, *Cumann na mBan and the Irish revolution* (Cork, 2014); Ann Matthews, *Renegades: Irish republican women, 1900–1922* (Cork, 2010). See Gearóid Ó Tuathaigh's chapter for more on this historiographical development.

who had previously been ignored or side-lined by the scholarship of the period. However, these scholarly developments are for the most part reliant on the existence of the sources, methodologies and approach of mainstream historical research.[4] This volume, employing the unique tools of family history, has unearthed hitherto-inaccessible stories or added previously unknown insights into the lives of better-known figures.

Pat and Michael Dolan present the extraordinary story of their aunt Eilish Dolan, whose anti-Treaty parents had hidden guns and ammunition in their family home in the Stoneybatter area of Dublin city during the Civil War. The fifteen-year-old Eilish, at the time a pacifist, admitted to hiding the arms in order to save her parents from at best arrest and imprisonment, and at worst the execution of her father. She was subsequently imprisoned for six months. This act of single-minded bravery became the precursor to a singular and eventful life, which led to religious conversion from Catholicism to Methodism, and success as a novelist and playwright. Eilish, at fifteen years of age, showing incredible bravery at enormous personal cost and risk; her story demonstrating both the vulnerability and courage of youth in situations of political and civil conflict, something which continues to have contemporary resonances in civil conflicts around the world.

Prompted by the existence of two family artefacts – a Cumann na mBan pin and family album – Anne and Colm Byrne consider the life of their grandmother Molly Bastible and her siblings. As a young woman Molly was active in Cumann na mBan, was an Abbey actress with The Gaelic Players (Aisteoirí), and a teacher in an all-Irish language school, Scoil Mhuire, in Dublin. Two of her brothers, Chris and Michael Bastible, were interned in Gormanston Camp, Co. Meath. Another brother, Jim, was active in the Gaelic League, promoting Irish language drama and summer schools, the Feis Cheoil, and lecturing for the Gaelic League in Cork and Wexford. These young people – grounded in a belief in the ideology and dynamics of the Gaelic revival, the importance of the national language, and involvement in the revolutionary political independence movement – are part of the story of the search for a new Ireland.[5] The authors discuss the way in which family history has operated, with its omissions and discontinuities, arguing that despite this, stories emerge through artefacts, of those factors – personal, political and ideological – that shaped the minds, attitudes and actions of Molly and her brothers.

Finally, two contributions cover the lives of pioneering activists on behalf of women's causes, who were themselves related through marriage. Micheline

4 Felicity Hayes-McCoy, *A woven silence: memory, history and remembrance* (Cork, 2015). 5 Roy Foster has uncovered the dynamics motivating this generation in his *Vivid faces: the revolutionary generation in Ireland, 1890–1923* (London, 2014).

Sheehy Skeffington, who took a case against NUI Galway to the Equality Tribunal in 2009, writes about the legacy and influence of her grandparents, Hanna and Francis Sheehy Skeffington. Their tireless campaigns for women's votes and against injustice, their abhorrence of hypocrisy and, later, Hanna's indomitable fight to expose the truth about her pacifist husband's murder one hundred years ago in British custody, was, the author argues, an inheritance impossible to ignore. The chapter examines the legacy of this extraordinary family through the stories of Hanna and Francis and the activism and experience of each subsequent generation. This chapter draws on documents from inside and outside the Sheehy Skeffington archive.

Niamh Reilly examines the life of her grand-uncle Tom Kettle, a figure whose reputation has experienced a revival of fortunes during the centenary commemorations, being recognized by President Higgins in a 2014 address as an 'Irish patriot, British soldier and true European' who, in grasping the imperative of reconciliation and friendship across Ireland, with the UK, and among the nations of Europe, remains a relevant thinker today. Kettle, a Home Rule MP who died at the Somme, did not support the Easter Rising and, moreover, having witnessed first-hand and written for newspapers on atrocities by German forces against civilians in Belgium, he had backed the British war effort as a moral imperative. As a result, his wife Mary Sheehy Kettle (sister of Hanna Sheehy Skeffington) and others expended considerable effort in subsequent decades countering the erasure of his reputation as a committed nationalist. While Tom Kettle has rightly been held up as a bridge between nationalist and unionist sensibilities in Ireland, this chapter argues that his range as a progressive and social-democratic thinker has yet to be fully appreciated and still has the potential to inform thinking on contemporary challenges.

1916–21

Section two examines the period between 1916 and 1921, with a number of histories of republican rebels and fighters recounted along with the fascinating story of a British army officer caught up in the events of the Rising and eventually forced to leave his home. The Rising and War of Independence have, of course, been the subjects of renewed and enthusiastic public and academic interest in recent years. There has been some attempt to focus attention on the experience of the 'ordinary' participants.[6] Here again, as with the stories of female participants, family history can shed light on hitherto-untold and inaccessible

6 See, for example, Fearghal McGarry, *The Rising – Ireland: Easter 1916* (Oxford, 2011).

experiences. Class emerges as a key theme in this section – an undercurrent dictating the protagonists life courses and therefore their roles in the independence struggle. It is notable that internal migration from rural to urban Ireland resulted in two young men, from Sligo and Kilkenny, taking part in the Rising in Dublin. Meanwhile, the story of Jack Morrogh, from a wealthy Cork family, educated at Castleknock College and commissioned as a British army officer after training at Sandhurst, led to a very different experience of that same pivotal event. Internal migration, as much as emigration, is an often-overlooked demographic determinant that shaped modern Irish history in a number of ways, not least at the personal level of family history.

Róisín Healy examines the story of her grandfather Richard Healy. Born in 1894 and from a farm in Kilcollen, Conahy, Co. Kilkenny, he was one of just two men from Kilkenny in the GPO in Easter week. A committed nationalist through his keen interest in hurling and the GAA, he had moved to Dublin in 1910 to be apprenticed as a barman at a public house belonging to his uncle, located at the corner of Parnell Street and Marlboro' Street. A favourite meeting place of revolutionaries, Healy's pub became known as the 'War Office'. Richard became a Volunteer and IRB member, and after serving in the GPO during Easter week he was subsequently arrested and interned for three months in Frongoch. He later fought in the War of Independence, but not the Civil War. In her chapter, Healy discusses how researching her grandfather's life for a Leaving Certificate project marked an early, but important, step in her career as a professional historian, while his remarkable courage and commitment to the principles of the Proclamation of the Republic left an inspiring legacy.

Angela Savage writes about her grand-uncle Martin Savage, one of thirteen children, who left a small farm in Ballisodare, Co. Sligo, in 1915, at the age of sixteen to move to Dublin to work as a grocer's assistant. From a nationalist background, he became a member of the Keating branch of the Gaelic League and D Company, 2nd Battalion of the Dublin Brigade. He fought in both the GPO and the Four Courts during Easter week, was detained in Richmond Barracks and deported to Knutsford Detention Barracks. Following his release, he was a Lieutenant in 2nd Battalion of the Dublin Brigade and was killed in a failed ambush on Lord French on 19 December 1919. Martin Savage was one of the many poor but highly motivated young men and women who became involved in the Easter Rising.

Two chapters in this section relate to the revolution as experienced outside Dublin. Enda Fallon, Daithí Fallon and Cian Ó Néill's chapter looks at the activities of Commandant Pat Fallon who was mobilized during Easter week, took part in an action in Balla, Co. Mayo, and was imprisoned in Richmond

Barracks in the aftermath. He participated in the majority of actions carried out by the South Mayo Brigade Flying Column and was involved in gun-running activities in England, accompanying Dick Walsh, the organizer of the IRA in Co. Mayo. Fallon took the republican side during the Civil War, was captured and interned first in Athlone where he witnessed the aftermath of the January 1923 executions. He spent the remainder of 1923 in Tintown. He joined Fianna Fáil at its foundation but continued his friendships with former comrades of all shades of green in post-independence Ireland and adopted a conciliatory role in local events to ensure that tensions and political differences did not spill over into violence. As a result of the self-imposed vow of silence taken by combatants, the authors note, it is difficult, if not impossible, to fully understand what caused Pat Fallon to take the decisions he took regarding physical force or how he felt about the choices he made. However, what is clear from talking to people who knew him is that he was not motivated by, and did not take satisfaction in, the violent activities he was involved in. Fallon's story points to the silences that have affected intergenerational understanding of the period and the bloody foundation of the state.

Bernadine Brady outlines the story of her grandfather, Bernard Brady, born in 1893 in Virginia, Co. Cavan. Some years ago, the family came across a typed statement regarding his activities from 1913, when he was twenty years of age, up to the Truce in 1922 when he led a company of Irish National Volunteers and a Sinn Féin club in Virginia. In it he describes various efforts including mobilizing against conscription in 1918, support for the election of Arthur Griffith as Sinn Féin candidate in the 1918 by-election in Cavan, and the establishment of a network of Sinn Féin clubs throughout Cavan. Bernard Brady later joined the Free State army with the rank of commandant. Her chapter draws on his statement and the reflections of family members to build a profile of the man and his political activities and how these stories have been preserved or lost through the generations.

Finally in this section, Tony Wheatley presents the history of his great-uncle, John (Jack) Morrogh. Morrogh was born into a wealthy Cork family, and after being accepted into Sandhurst Military Academy, was commissioned in 1902 and joined the Royal Irish Regiment in 1903. Having served time in India, he returned to Europe in 1914. Wounded at the 2nd battle of Ypres in May 1915, he was sent home to Cork to recuperate and in the spring of 1916 he was transferred to a Dublin battalion. When the Rising began, he was called up for active service and led a group of men around the GPO. It is reported in the regimental history that his men wounded James Connolly and later killed The O'Rahilly. He and his men also captured the flag over the GPO. All of this information is in the public domain. What has not been made known but has been kept within his family is that Jack was believed to have been given the task of informing James Connolly of his execution and escorting Connolly to Kilmainham Gaol on the day of his execution. After the Rising, Jack returned to the Western Front and came back to Cork at the end of the war. However, during the War of Independence the IRA broke into his house and warned the family that they were in danger. Eventually, Jack thought Cork too dangerous and took his family to Argentina. Family folklore has it that he returned to Cork in the late 1920s or early 1930s. Once again the IRA warned him off and he left the country for good.

The Irish Revolution and beyond

Section three examines the period from the War of Independence to the Civil War and beyond, covering the confusions and trauma of the internecine conflict that followed the founding of the state and the challenges faced by that first generation living in post-independence, post-partition Ireland.

Liam Ó hAisibéil uncovers the history of Patrick Maher from Knocklong, Co. Limerick, who was one of a group of Volunteers now known as 'The Forgotten Ten' who were executed in the summer of 1921 by British forces. Patrick was wrongly accused of taking part in an ambush at Knocklong railway station in the successful attempt to free an IRA prisoner. Edmond Foley and approximately seven other Volunteers took part in the rescue during which two members of the RIC were killed. Patrick was arrested during subsequent searches of the countryside and was put on trial in Dublin over a year later. Both Edmond Foley and Patrick were tried on two occasions for the murders of the RIC officers but the juries could not agree a verdict. On the third occasion, at a military court martial held on 15 March 1921, they were both convicted of murder and sentenced to death by hanging. In 2001, the Irish government held a state funeral for The Forgotten Ten. The injustice suffered by Patrick – the lack of reliable evidence from the prosecution, his trial and retrial until conviction, the lack of proper representation and rejection of appeals for clemency, along with the hopelessness of his situation while imprisoned in Mountjoy – all paint a picture of a country suffering state-perpetrated injustices in the final stages of a bitter conflict.

Two chapters point most obviously to the tenacious hold of history on the present day with references to issues that continue to cast shadows over the island. Chris McNairney's chapter examines the life of Dan McCann, born into a republican family in the Markets area of Belfast, a nationalist enclave in the staunchly loyalist heartland of east Belfast. Dan joined Bulmer Hobson's Na Fianna Éireann and remained a committed republican until his death in

1933. Following the assassination of unionist politician William Twaddell by the IRA in May 1922, Dan was arrested and interned and along with some 500 other republicans was held in dreadful conditions on the prison ship HMS *Argenta.* In protest against the prison conditions, Dan and some of his colleagues embarked on a hunger strike. On his release, he re-joined the republican grouping in Belfast and died in 1931 as a young man, largely as a result of consequences of his hunger strike and perhaps what might today be termed post-traumatic stress disorder. Chris McNairney, growing up in Belfast in the 1960s, describes his family's awareness of their republican background and of Dan's legacy, and reflects on the impact of recurring history in the nationalist community and the realization that peace is not just the absence of violence but is something that must be worked for and nourished continuously.

Tom Boylan's chapter on the well-known republican socialist Peadar O'Donnell points to other issues from our recurring history which continue to provoke us almost a hundred years after independence. O'Donnell's career, apart from military activities during the revolutionary period, included that of teacher, trade-union organizer, political agitator, socialist revolutionary, literary figure and social critic until his death in 1986 aged ninety-three. His career over the revolutionary period was intense and varied. Abandoning a teaching career, he was by 1919 a leading trade union organizer for the Irish Transport and General Workers' Union (ITGWU). He joined the IRA which involved an active career during the War of Independence (1919–21). In 1921 he became commander of the 2nd Brigade of the Northern Volunteer Division of the IRA, who had to evade, in the spring of 1921, a sweep of Co. Derry by over 1,000 British troops. O'Donnell opposed the Treaty and, in March 1922, was elected one of the two Ulster representatives of the anti-Treaty IRA's Army Executive. The following month he was among the anti-Treaty forces who took over the Four Courts in Dublin, initiating the Civil War. At the end of the Civil War he participated in a mass republican hunger strike and remained on hunger strike for forty-one days. In 1924, following his release from internment, he became a member of the Executive and Army Council of the anti-Treaty IRA. He later parted company with the IRA after his failure to persuade them to become a serious socialist organization. O'Donnell went on to become, over the next fifty years, a major voice of the political left in post-independence Ireland. As Tom Boylan recounts, to encounter Peadar O'Donnell was to experience a genuine and relentless radical, who was completely devoid of any intellectual or political pretence or preparedness to compromise his principles. He argues that contemporary Ireland would do well to remember his searing critique of inequality and his contempt for conservative political leadership that eschews meaningful change.

Two further chapters in this section present challenges to our notions of the heroic. John Canavan, Dorothy Ní Uigín and Jim Higgins discuss the burying of extraordinary experiences beneath the protective folds of the ordinary life in their chapter on Michael Canavan. Michael, from Corrandulla in Co. Galway, was arrested and imprisoned in 1923 for his part in the activities of anti-Treaty forces during the Civil War, spending time in both Galway Gaol and the Curragh. Despite his participation in the tumultuous events that marked the beginning of the modern Irish state, for his children and grandchildren the extended family narrative did not reference this extraordinary experience. He did not talk to his children about his experiences of this time, did not attend commemorations, and did not accept any pension or other form of recognition for his contribution. Instead, his life was remarkably ordinary, involving work, marriage and parenthood. This chapter notes the significance of the ordinary and the private in our collective understanding of the Civil War and its consequences. It offers a family interpretation of Michael's story, focusing on a number of themes including private versus public; the heroic in the ordinary; and religious faith and the moral justification of war – framing these within a life course perspective.

Michael Lang's chapter challenges notions of heroism in a different way. During the 'Decade of Centenaries', he notes, most of the focus has been on those who took up armed struggle against crown forces a century ago. In contrast, relatively little attention has been paid to the stories of the Royal Irish Constabulary (RIC), the majority of whom were ordinary, decent men from rural homesteads who joined the police force during peaceful times. These men found themselves caught in the middle of a conflict, forced to reconcile their political loyalties and family obligations with the call of duty. This chapter therefore examines an alternative tradition to the lauded, revolutionary experiences. It discusses the different trajectories of two men – Head Constable John Dillon who resigned from the RIC during the War of Independence and Sergeant Michael Lang who remained in his job. In this chapter Michael Lang discusses the politics of family memory when one's family narrative does not conform easily to the heroic nationalist one of the period.

After independence the state embarked on a process of nation-building. This forward momentum was built upon a heroic history fired with a sense of righteous moral outrage: a long struggle against oppression and injustice that culminated in the manifest destiny of the Easter Rising and War of Independence. Those who challenged the nationalist orthodoxies were not common in political or intellectual life. In this context, John and Olga Cox offer a very interesting account of a father and son whose views placed them at odds with the prevailing narratives of post-independence Ireland. Patrick Shaw was a Cumann na nGaedheal TD for Longford–Westmeath 1923–33 who wrote to the King in 1916 to apologize for the Rising while his son Francis Shaw SJ marked the 1966 celebrations with a strongly worded 'revisionist' paper that the journal *Studies* declined to publish until after his death in 1970. This chapter collates family memories of Patrick and Francis Shaw, asking if it is possible to speculate on and explore how Patrick Shaw's views impacted on Frank and the other children in the family. The stories told and the stories silenced are what form the warp and weave of family identity, something the two authors aim to consider along with the influence of the activities of Patrick and Francis Shaw and their views about the Irish Revolution.

The Irish revolutionary decade, 1913–23: voices, narratives and contexts

GEARÓID Ó TUATHAIGH

The historiography of the Irish revolution of 1913–23 has been in a continuous, if irregular, state of change and revision throughout the century since the revolutionary events themselves. This is hardly surprising: our understanding of past events and their significance is constantly subject to revision. Of the many factors that determine such revision, the most influential are the discovery and deployment of new primary sources, the ideological disposition of historians and the extent to which they are affected by changing ideological and intellectual currents in the wider society, and the changing perspective on past events that comes with the simple but invincible passage of time. Significant anniversaries of historical events frequently produce a surge of new research and reassessment of the events themselves and their legacy.

All of these factors have been at play in the changing historiography of the Irish revolution.[1] Thus, for example, we may note the changing ideological climate, as the heavily affirmative nationalist reading of the struggle for independence (including the valorization of the military aspect of the struggle and of the sacrifice of life for the cause of freedom) in the early decades after 1922 gradually yielded from the later 1950s to more critical readings of the fruits of independence, notably in terms of economic and social progress. The economic and social crisis of the 1950s – together with the natural intergenerational shift in political leadership and priorities – demanded fresh thinking and, inevitably, a reassessment of earlier ambitions and achievements of the revolutionary generation.

Again, from the later 1960s and the outbreak of communal violence (commonly described as 'the Troubles') in Northern Ireland, we may trace – in the historiography no less than in the dominant currents of contemporary political rhetoric – a decisive, if frequently controversial, shift in nationalist Ireland's attitudes towards the justification of armed struggle in pursuit of political objectives, however elevated. Over several decades, there emerged a general acknowledgment of the complexity of identity issues within Northern Ireland and an acceptance of the need for equally complex structures of accom-

1 See, for perceptive commentary, Diarmaid Ferriter, *A nation and not a rabble: the Irish revolution, 1913–1923* (London, 2015), pp 17–96.

modation, based on parity of esteem and equal rights as prerequisites for a stable and peaceful polity in the north. This (frequently painful) reassessment of the acceptable means for achieving conflicting political ends in Northern Ireland, and the accommodations needed to end communal violence and move towards a 'shared future', required a thorough reconstruction of strategies and structures, and, more importantly, of the mood and manner of British-Irish relations. It also required major reconsideration of dominant attitudes of various communities within Ireland, North and South.[2]

But this transformation of the landscape of Anglo-Irish relations, and of the ideological and political climate within Ireland itself, inevitably had implications for developments in the historiography of the Irish revolutionary decade and its legacy. The frequently fractious debate on historical 'revisionism' in writings on modern Irish history was one very public manifestation of this phase of Irish historiography, from the 1960s and, more bitterly, from the 1970s to the end of the century.[3]

However, arguably the most potent driver of historical reassessment of the revolutionary decade was the deployment, in successive phases, of significant new primary source material. Some of this material became accessible through initiatives by both the British and Irish governments in opening various official state archives, but the increasing access to private papers was a major contribution to the expanding store of source material available to researchers. One particular category of source material that bears directly on the value of the perspectives represented in this collection of essays is the body of evidence or testimony from those who were actively involved in the revolutionary events, those who were directly affected by those events, and those who witnessed the events and recorded their response to them; together with the narratives of others connected by ties of family, kin or friendship to these historical witnesses to the Irish revolutionary events of 1913–23.

Early first-hand accounts of the revolutionary events, including biographical studies, came mainly from writers who themselves had been involved or had personal acquaintance with the actors and organizations that had made the revolution. Dan Breen's *My fight for Irish freedom* (1924) was an early and popular memoir, while biographical studies of such leaders as Pearse, Connolly, Collins and John Redmond (by Desmond Ryan, Piaras Béaslaí and Stephen Gwynn, respectively), were the work of authors who had the advantage of close acquaintance but were overwhelmingly firm admirers of their subjects.[4] This

2 The common European framework (the EEC later EU) facilitated the process of reconfiguring attitudes and policies in Anglo-Irish relations from the early 1970s. 3 Ciaran Brady (ed.), *Interpreting Irish history: the debate on historical revisionism, 1938–1994* (Dublin, 1994) 4 Desmond Ryan, *The man called Pearse* (Dublin, 1919); idem, *Remembering Sion: a chronicle of storm and quiet*

was also the case with several early biographies of the main Ulster unionist leaders, Craig and Carson.[5]

Personal memoirs by veterans of the independence struggle continued to appear during the 1930s and 1940s, with, for example, Ernie O'Malley's acclaimed *On another man's wound* (1936) and Tom Barry's *Guerilla days in Ireland* (1949) attracting extensive public attention. Throughout these decades there were occasional proposals for the launch of a more comprehensive project to record veterans' accounts of the 'struggle for independence'.[6] In the event, during the 1940s and 1950s significant steps were taken to assemble such an archive. In the first instance, the *Kerryman* newspaper embarked on compiling a series of accounts from surviving activists of the 'Tan war', resulting in the publication, between 1947 and 1949, of four 'Fighting Story' volumes – on the War of Independence in counties Limerick, Cork, Tipperary and Dublin. The heroic note dominated these valuable first-hand accounts.[7]

While the witness narratives contained in the 'fighting story' volumes were valuable, it was widely acknowledged that there was need for a more systematic and extensive collection of evidence from surviving participants. Accordingly, in 1947 the government established the Bureau of Military History (BMH) 'to record the experiences of those who took part in the fight for Irish independence', but excluding the contentious run-up to the Treaty and the Civil War.[8] Throughout the following decade, evidence was gathered by the BMH, principally some 1,773 signed 'witness statements', the final collection coming to more than 30,000 pages. To the dismay of historians, the complete archive was then locked away and would only be opened to researchers following the death of the last witness, which event occurred in 2003.[9]

Meanwhile, a leading republican, Ernie O'Malley, had begun conducting interviews and taking detailed notes (initially for his own information) from veterans of the War of Independence and the Civil War, many of whom would have been reluctant or unwilling to participate in any collective project under the direction of or sanctioned by the government: the material from these

(London, 1934); idem, *James Connolly: his life work and writings* (Dublin, 1924); Piaras Béaslaí, *Michael Collins and the making of a new Ireland* (Dublin, 1926); Stephen Gwynn, *John Redmond's last years* (London, 1919); Denis Gwynn, *The life of John Redmond* (London, 1932). An early female activist's account is Margaret Skinnider, *Doing my bit for Ireland* (New York, 1917). **5** Ian Colvin, *Carson, the statesman* (New York, 1935); St John Ervine, *Craigavon: Ulsterman* (London, 1949). **6** See Gerard O'Brien, *Irish governments and the guardianship of historical records, 1922–72* (Dublin, 2004), pp 130–53. **7** Republished – under the general editorship of Brian Ó Conchubhair – in recent years: for example, *Limerick's fighting story 1916–21: told by the men who made it*. Introduced by Ruán O'Donnell (Cork, 2009). **8** Gerard O'Brien, op. cit. Also Ferghal McGarry, *Rebels: voices from the Easter Rising* (London, 2011), pp xii–xxi. **9** Individual witnesses were provided with a copy of their own personal statements.

informants would not be published until much later.[10] The flow of publications of first-hand accounts by participants in the revolutionary era scarcely exceeded a trickle in the 1940s and 1950s, though a clutch of engaging autobiographical works in Irish – by Colm Ó Gaora, Liam Ó Briain, Earnán de Blaghad and Séamas Ó Maoileoin – merited more attention from historians than they have often received.[11]

By the mid-1960s, however, the beginnings of a decisive shift in the historiography of the revolution were already discernible. The intergenerational shift in political leadership removed key foci of earlier polemical and partisan positions. New primary documents began to be published, albeit limited in scope and with a clearly corrective intention; F.X. Martin's edition of documents on the Irish Volunteers and on Eoin Mac Neill belongs in this category.[12]

Commemorations surrounding the fiftieth anniversary of the Rising in 1966 generated a substantial crop of academic publications, some of which drew on newly released primary source material. Direct witness accounts, from state and private sources, proved particularly valuable: for example, Breandán MacGiolla Choille's *Intelligence notes: 1913–1916* (1966), an edited digest of police reports from around the country provided to Dublin Castle in the crucial years before the Rising. Likewise, León Ó Broin's studies of the role (and response) of key personnel in the Dublin Castle regime during the revolutionary upheaval drew on rich primary sources and offered a challenging new perspective to existing narratives on the Rising.[13] A series of essays published in the *Capuchin Annual* of 1966 contained valuable accounts of the events of 1916 in different parts of the country. Editions of hitherto-unpublished documents began to appear with increasing frequency, facilitated from the 1970s by a progressive easing of access to state archival records, initially on the British side but later, and gradually, by the Irish government. Already by the 1970s private collections of papers from key activists in the independence struggle and the foundation of the state were being deposited in university and other archives accessible to researchers, a process that gained momentum during the following decades.[14]

10 Cormac K.H. O'Malley and Tim Horgan (eds), *The men will talk to me: Kerry interviews by Ernie O'Malley* (Cork, 2012); Cormac K.H. O'Malley & Cormac Ó Comhraí (eds), *The men will talk to me: Galway interviews by Ernie O'Malley* (Cork, 2013). **11** Colm Ó Gaora, *Mise* (1943); Liam Ó Briain, *Cuimhní Cinn* (1951); Earnán de Blaghd, *Trasna na Bóinne* (1957); Séamas Ó Maoileoin, *B'fhiú an Braon Fola* (1958). See, also, Máire Nic Shiubhlaigh (with Edward Kenny), *The splendid years* (Dublin, 1955). **12** F.X. Martin (ed.), 'Select documents: Eoin Mac Neill on the 1916 Rising', *Irish Historical Studies*, 12 (March, 1961), pp 226–71; *The Irish Volunteers, 1913–1915: recollections and documents* (Dublin, 1963). **13** León Ó Broin, *Dublin Castle and the 1916 Rising: the story of Sir Matthew Nathan* (Dublin, 1966); idem, *The chief secretary: Augustine Birrell in Ireland* (London, 1969). **14** The

Not surprisingly, the improving access to official archives and personal papers contributed to the growing volume and originality of the scholarly output, even as the ideological climate within which historical debate was conducted became more fraught, and at times fractious, under the dark shadow of the northern conflict from the 1970s to the close of the century.

Later biographies from the 1970s – mainly by academic or independent scholars – increasingly deployed fresh primary source material (letters, diaries, unpublished writings). In general, these works were not only less reverential towards their subjects than earlier biographers – a number were aggressively critical – but were also securely contextualized in the light of a developing historical scholarship.[15] Moreover, the increasing availability of primary documents not only generated new interpretations of, and perspectives on, the more familiar leading figures of the revolutionary era, but also contributed to a striking expansion of serious biographical studies of many 'second order' figures from all sides of the political struggles of the revolutionary decade. Nor was the expanding arc of biography confined to the politically active: cultural activists, trade unionists, journalists, policemen and officials, the spouses, siblings and associates of the 'active' cohort attracted attention, if they left a record of their experiences for posterity.[16] In addition to the expanding gallery of individual portraits (or editions of primary narratives – diaries, letters), family experiences of the revolutionary decade were explored, a splendid example of which is Deirdre McMahon's edition of the letters of the Moynihan family of Kerry during the years 1909–18.[17] Among a clutch of collective profiles of the revolutionary generation, based upon primary source material, Roy Foster's ambitious group portrait of the revolutionary generation is especially stylish and satisfying.[18]

National Library of Ireland and University College Dublin were the principal depositories of choice for such collections. To compare the range of primary sources available in 1966 to the then leading scholars of the revolution, with the range of primary material listed in the bibliographies of recent studies of the revolutionary period by, for example, Foster, Ferriter and Townshend, is to be struck by the transformation that has taken place in the past half-century in the accessibility of source material on the Irish revolution. **15** For an early and influential example of rich source material interpreted from a sharply critical perspective, see Ruth Dudley Edwards, *Patrick Pearse: the triumph of failure* (London, 1977). **16** Examples of narratives of a range of contemporary 'witnesses' published in recent decades include: S. and A. Warwick-Haller (eds), *Letters from Dublin, Easter 1916: the diary of Alfred Fannin* (Dublin, 1995); Michael Hopkinson (ed.), *Frank Henderson's Easter Rising* (Cork, 1998); idem, *The last days of Dublin Castle: the Mark Sturgis diaries* (Dublin, 1999); Keith Jeffery (ed.), *The Sinn Féin Rebellion as they saw it: Mar Louisa and Arthur Hamilton Norway* (Dublin, 1999); Timothy G. McMahon (ed.), *Pádraig Ó Fathaigh's War of Independence: recollections of a Galway Gaelic Leaguer* (Cork, 2000); Joost Augusteijn (ed.), *The memoirs of John M. Regan, a Catholic officer of the RIC and RUC, 1909–48* (Dublin, 2007); Clara Cullen (ed.), *The world upturning: Elsie Henry's Irish wartime diaries, 1913–1919* (Dublin, 2013); Thomas J. Morrissey (ed.), *From Easter week to Flanders Field: the diaries and letters of John Delaney SJ, 1916–1919* (Dublin, 2015). **17** Deirdre McMahon (ed.), *The Moynihan brothers in peace and war, 1909–1918: their new Ireland* (Dublin, 2004). **18** R.F. Foster,

The incremental advance (notwithstanding occasional setbacks) during the 1990s towards a cessation of violence and political accommodation in Northern Ireland created a more open climate for research and reflection on many contentious aspects of Irish history, including the revolutionary era within which the partition settlement and the two jurisdictions in Ireland had been established. The new political atmosphere, as the peace process took firmer hold, proved hospitable to a more relaxed and empathetic consideration – in general public discussion no less than in academic debate – of alternative perspectives and of the recorded experience of a wide range of witnesses to the Irish revolutionary period. From the turn of the century, a perceptible quickening of interest in major upcoming centenary anniversaries was a further stimulant to research and publications. In particular, as the centenary of the outbreak of the Great War hove into view, the central role of that calamity in shaping the course of events in Ireland during its own revolutionary decade became widely acknowledged and explored.[19] The sheer scale of Irish participation in the military campaigns and, pervasively, in the 'home front' effort, ensured the emergence of a strong flow of Irish narratives of the war experience, narratives that had been largely ignored or concealed in the prevailing ideological climate of earlier decades. Shared public ceremonials of commemoration – at official and local level – served to endorse the exploration of the Irish experience in the Great War, not only in historical and biographical works, but also in popular media and fiction.[20]

The growth in popular interest in the Great War (its impact on belligerents and on the general population) was fuelled by rising interest in family history, facilitated by ever-increasing electronic access to archival sources through digitization. Irish 'voices' of the Great War came to share an audience with narratives of the independence struggle. The complex loyalties and shifting allegiances that marked the Irish experience of the years between 1913 and the aftermath of the 1916 Rising were explored in a wider, shared context of war and upheaval.[21]

Reflecting developments in wider historical scholarship, a striking feature

Vivid faces: the revolutionary generation in Ireland, 1890–1923 (London, 2014). **19** Keith Jeffery, *Ireland and the Great War* (Cambridge, 2000); John Horne (ed.), *Our war: Ireland and the Great War* (Dublin, 2008); John Horne and Edward Madigan (eds), *Towards commemoration: Ireland in War and Revolution, 1912–23* (Dublin, 2013): the bibliographies of these works highlight the developing historiography of the impact of the Great War on Ireland. **20** In addition to a busy programme of television documentaries coinciding with centenary anniversaries, Frank McGuinness and Sebastian Barry were among the creative writers who turned to the Great War and its aftermath for themes. **21** Public ceremonial (at national and local level) and debate on historical events may become more problematic from 2019, as the centenaries of the War of Independence and the Civil War occupy centre stage in the commemoration calendar.

of this explosion in recent decades of new 'narratives' based on primary source material is the emphasis on recovering the long-neglected experience of women in the revolutionary era. The testimony of women from a wide variety of social and political backgrounds has informed a growing body of biographies and studies of dedicated women's organizations and networks. The impact of these new perspectives has greatly enhanced our understanding of the lived experience of a broad swathe of Irish people during the revolution.[22]

Undoubtedly, the belated release in 2003 of the material collected in the 1947–57 period by the BMH heralded a decisive shift in studies of the military dimension of the campaign for independence. Described by Fearghal McGarry as 'one of the richest and most comprehensive oral history archives devoted to any modern revolution',[23] the BMH material, notably the witness statements, quickly became the core resource for a stream of new publications – including local and biographical studies – on the Irish independence struggle.

Early 2014 saw the release by the state of the first two tranches of material from the Pensions Files. These files, comprising applications for pensions made to the Irish state from the 1920s to the 1950s in respect of 'national service' during the revolutionary period, contain not only the formal application for a pension but also supporting documentation, the whole constituting a rich body of evidence that, when fully available, will come to some 300,000 files. The Pension File material, together with the witness statements of the BMH and other archives,[24] constitutes a body of evidence – a trove of voices and narratives of revolutionary experience – of extraordinary value.

The opening of the rich store of personal testimonies in the Bureau of Military History, and the ongoing improved accessibility of the documentary evidence of the Pension Files, had already by 2017 transformed most recent new writings on the revolution – whether general accounts, specific local and biographical studies, or particular interpretative or theme-focused accounts. The value of these recently accessible sources hardly needs to be explained at length or in detail: the size and spread of the 'sample' and the opportunity it offers for cross-checking are readily apparent. Moreover, the detailed supporting documentation in the Pension Files provides enhanced corroborative evidence for the claims of witnesses in their individual testimonies.

22 A sense of the explosion of writings on the role of women in the revolutionary era can be gleaned from Sinéad McCoole, *No ordinary women: Irish female activists in the revolutionary years, 1900–1923* (Dublin, 2003); Ann Matthews, *Renegades: Irish republican women, 1900–1922* (Cork, 2010); Senia Paseta, *Irish nationalist women, 1900–1918* (Cambridge, 2013); Cal McCarthy, *Cumann na mBan and the Irish revolution* (Cork, 2007). **23** Fearghal McGarry, *Rebels*, p. xii. **24** In addition to the BMH and Ernie O'Malley witness statements, Fr Louis O'Kane collected material from veterans of the revolutionary years resident in Northern Ireland after partition. Now accessible at the Cardinal Tomás Ó Fiaich Library in Armagh; for details, see: www.ofiaich.ie.

But a word of caution on the witness statements, in particular, may not go amiss. For the most part, these accounts by witnesses were recorded between thirty and forty years after the events described: inevitably, they were influenced (in emphasis and omission) by what had happened – in Ireland and in the life-experience of the narrators – in the intervening period. How life had 'turned out' for Ireland and for the narrator was the canvas against which even the sharpest memory or the most scrupulous recollection shaped its narrative of earlier events. Furthermore, it is worth noting that the witness statements for the Bureau of Military History were recorded during a decade of exceptional political volatility in Ireland – in political loyalties, party prospects and changes in government – and of severe social dislocation, with economic crises and an emigration haemorrhage from the state of more than 400,000 during the 1950s. This immediate context of national crisis (to say nothing of the wider European and global ideological and political climate in the aftermath of the Second World War) demands attention from all those who aspire to extract full value from the witness statements of the BMH.

However, beyond the issues that arise from the immediate context of the recording of the witness statements for the BMH project, there is the underlying question of the relationship between 'history' and memory. The novelist and critic, Julian Barnes, addressing this issue in the opening to his 2011 Booker Prize-winning novel, *The sense of an ending,* confessed that:

> We live in time – it holds and moulds us – but I've never felt I understood it very well … I'm not very interested in my schooldays, and don't feel any nostalgia for them. But school is where it all began, so I need to return briefly to a few incidents that have grown into anecdotes, to some approximate memories which time has deformed into certainty. If I can't be sure of the actual events any more, I can at least be true to the impressions those facts left. That's the best I can manage.[25]

Nor is it only novelists who fret over this dilemma: historians, naturally, have a particular need to engage the issue. Richard White (American born, with maternal Irish ancestry), in his classic *Remembering Ahanagran* (1998), addressed directly the issue of how a trained historian, with a scruple for verifiable evidence, engages the stories (in effect, oral history) that his mother told of her youth and early upbringing in Ahanagran, a townland outside the village of Ballylongford in north Kerry, in the 1920s/early 1930s.

25 Julian Barnes, *The sense of an ending* (London, 2011).

> I once thought of my mother's stories as history. I thought memory was history. Then I became a historian, and after many years I have come to realize that only careless historians confuse memory and history. History is the enemy of memory. The two stalk each other across the fields of the past, claiming the same terrain. History forges weapons from what memory has forgotten or suppressed. Few non-historians realize how many scraps a life leaves. These scraps do not necessarily form a story in and of themselves, but they are always calling stories into doubt, always challenging memories, always trailing off into forgotten places.

But there are regions of the past that only memory knows. If historians wish to go into this dense and tangled terrain, they must accept memory as a guide. In this jungle of the past only memory knows the trails. …

> [Turning then to the mother's stories that he has 'researched'] …There is nothing my mother has told me that is without some basis in the past. But neither, at least in those cases where I can recover the historical scraps, is there a story that to a historian sifting through the evidence clearly happened as she remembers …
>
> These stories and our collaboration have taught me much about the relation of history and memory. They have made me face in at least a small way the cruelty of recovering what memory seeks to bury or disguise. It is no wonder people prefer memory to history.[26]

Memory is indeed a major preoccupation of our time. It has been suggested that we live in an 'age of reminders': lists kept by people, in offices, in diaries, on mobile devices – to 'remind' them of things to do, appointments to keep. This need for 'reminding' reflects, no doubt, the busy lives we lead and perhaps our distrust of our ability to remember everything on our crowded schedule. But, more darkly, the lengthening life expectancy of people (at least in the developed world) has brought with it anxieties about the failing or the loss of memory – senility, forms of dementia and Alzheimer's – as an issue that has to be dealt with in our own personal lives or in the lives of family and friends.

It is hardly surprising therefore, that individual memory has become such a central preoccupation of our times for a variety of commentators on the human condition. A recent study by Alison Winter explores the controversies

26 Richard White, *Remembering Ahanagran* (Cork, 1998), pp 4–5.

that have congealed around research on memory – from the psychoanalytical approach to more recent neurophysiological studies.[27]

Historians have been wrestling with this issue of the relationship between history and memory for a very long time. For example, Moses Finlay (reflecting on chronology, periodization and the computistical notion of time) remarked many years ago: 'Duration of time is not experienced as a measurable quantity, but as an associational or emotional quality … Memory leaps instantaneously to the desired point and it dates by association'.[28]

These warning notes, on the complex relationship between history and memory, are pertinent to our appreciation of narratives of the Irish revolution.

The testimony of actors who were participants in, or direct witnesses of, major historical events is clearly of immense value. But even here important distinctions must be made between testimony that is contemporary (or virtually contemporary) with the events as they occurred and testimony that is recorded, orally or in written accounts, some time afterwards.

The core of this distinction is not difficult to grasp. With contemporary accounts of any historical event or episode the future consequences or outcome of the event remain unknown: later accounts are ineluctably framed with the benefit of hindsight. Of course, later narratives may strive, imaginatively, to restore to past events the uncertainty as to outcome that was present at the moment the events took place. But it is impossible to totally expunge the knowledge and the experience of what will have transpired in the period between the precise historical moment observed or experienced and the later moment when the narrative of the event is put on record.

Insisting on this distinction should not be understood as being, simply or even primarily, born of an anxiety regarding factual accuracy and the danger of its being compromised by memory lapse or by the weakening of the power of recall that comes with the passage of time. Matters of fact, for example, refer to when precisely an order was given, a message received, a meeting held, who was present or participated, the sequence of events in an ambush or a campaign. Such details of fact may be – indeed more often than not are likely to be – amenable to confirmation and corroboration, though this does not exclude the possibility of controversy erupting from time to time, as a result of contested versions of past events recorded by different participants. The continuing controversies surrounding versions of the Kilmichael ambush in

27 Alison Winter, *Memory: fragments of a modern history* (Chicago, 2012). **28** M.I. Finlay, *The use and abuse of history* (London, 1986), p. 23.

Co. Cork during the War of Independence illustrate the hazards of later recollections.[29]

But the nub of the issue is not checking for factual accuracy of detail, but, rather, the way in which memory, understanding and assessment of events in one's earlier life (including involvement in notable historical events) are inevitably mediated by the experiences of later years, the experience of personal growth and development and the experience of a changing world. In short, it is impossible – in reviewing one's involvement in historical events – to escape or suppress the knowledge of 'how things turned out'. It is this dilemma that disposes historians to confer special value on those contemporary sources that give an insight into the 'unknown futures' contemplated or envisaged by historical actors at the time.

While such cautions may seem to apply with special force to narratives by activists in decisive historical events of the revolutionary decade, they also have wider relevance. What is striking about the developing historiography of recent years on the Irish revolutionary era is the expanding diversity of narratives, extending well beyond those of participants in revolutionary action of a political or military kind; beyond the testimony of volunteers in the Irish revolutionary struggle or of the crown agents (military or political) on the opposing side. Soldiering – on whatever side or in whatever cause – was, of course, a central theme of the narratives, but it was not the whole story. The civilians affected by the revolutionary episode also had stories that merited an audience: the casualties of military action – bystanders caught up in the struggle, civilians (including children) in the wrong place at the wrong time; the victims of reprisal or intimidation during the guerilla war of 1919–21. The bereaved no less than the belligerents had stories to tell.[30]

The role of women in history – for decades a seriously neglected dimension of Irish history (and not only of the revolutionary era) – began to be explored by a growing cohort of scholars. Increasingly, narratives emerged of local communities, social networks and of various institutions of associational culture during the revolutionary period. More and more the historiography became that of 'Ireland in a time of revolution' rather than the more restricted narratives of the *dramatis personae* of direct revolutionary struggle. Moreover, while there can be no doubt regarding the extent to which the mining of these

29 The controversy originated with Peter Hart's *The IRA and its enemies: violence and community in Cork, 1916–1923* (Oxford, 1998); participants in the controversy are noted in Eve Morrison, 'Kilmichael revisited' in David Fitzpatrick (ed.), *Terror in Ireland, 1916–1923* (Dublin, 2012), pp 158–80. **30** Joe Duffy, *Children of the Rising: the untold story of the young lives lost during Easter 1916* (Dublin, 2015). Several categories of casualties are discussed by various contributors to David Fitzpatrick (ed.), *Terror in Ireland, 1916–1923*.

recently-accessible sources has greatly enriched the writing of works of synthesis and the analytical and interpretative studies of the Irish revolution, the very plurality of perspectives and narratives (in diaries, letters, memoirs and similar testimony) of the 'lived experience' of witnesses affected by the revolution constitutes a formidable shield against any attempt to devise or insist upon a single official or authoritative version of the revolutionary upheaval and its significance.

Furthermore, the value of attending to the voices of those contemporaries who may not have been directly involved in military episodes of the Irish revolution but whose lives were altered, many fundamentally, by it, is underlined by consideration of the strikingly concentrated geographical spread of significant military actions during the revolutionary decade. Whatever the strength and geographical distribution of the Irish Volunteers (MacNeill's minority) before 1916, the Rising was overwhelmingly a brief metropolitan episode, with purposeful mobilization outside of Dublin confined to Galway, Enniscorthy and the Ashbourne ambush. Elsewhere, partial and aborted mobilization was marked by confusion and indecision, generally followed by regret and recrimination. But even later mobilization and volunteer activity in the War of Independence and the Civil War was markedly uneven in geographical spread and intensity. As Mike Cronin has stated: 'the War of Independence (1919–21) was responsible for approximately 1,400 deaths; sectarian violence in the North between 1920 and 1922 accounted for 557 deaths; and the Civil War (1922–23) took some 1,300 lives'. But, 'the killing was highly localized, with half of the total deaths occurring in the cities of Dublin, Belfast and Cork. A quarter of all deaths took place in Limerick, Kerry, Tipperary and Clare ... The Irish wars were primarily focused on the three main urban centres on the island, and on Munster'.[31]

There was also a distinct geographical distribution of labour disputes (including strikes) and of land-related incidents during Ireland's revolutionary years.[32] Nevertheless, while direct military action or conflict, and its attendant casualties, may have been more sporadic and occasional in other parts of the country than in the core conflict zones, the pervasive climate of division, suspicion, surveillance and tension affected most communities and left them with their own vivid narratives of the revolutionary years. And, all the while, the toll of the Great War being waged at a distance came home to many communities

31 Mike Cronin, 'The GAA in a time of guerilla war and civil strife, 1918–23' in Gearóid Ó Tuathaigh (ed.), *The GAA and revolution in Ireland, 1913–1923* (Cork, 2015), p. 155. Also, Peter Hart, 'The geography of revolution in Ireland, 1917–1923', *Past & Present,* 155 (May 1997), pp 142–76. 32 Emmet O'Connor, *A labour history of Ireland, 1824–1960* (Dublin, 1992), pp 94–116; David Fitzpatrick, 'Strikes in Ireland, 1914–1921', *Saothar,* 6 (1980), pp 26–39.

and families all over Ireland, up to the end of 1918; and, thereafter, its legacy continued to impinge deeply on many of the maimed and the now marginalized: demobilized soldiers, their families and friends.

The relationship between memory and history comes into sharp relief in the writing of family history, a branch of historical writing that has experienced major growth in recent decades. Among the developments that have powered this surge of interest in genealogy and family history, the role of technology (notably digitization) has been crucial in facilitating wider access for the general public to categories of primary source material (census and other official data, records of institutions, societies and corporate bodies, private papers) hitherto accessible principally to a limited cohort of professional researchers in specific archival locations. But while technology may have facilitated improved access to primary sources (a 'democratizing', as it were, of the practice of historical research), the growing interest in family history probably needs to be related to wider and more complex currents of cultural change: specifically, the relentless advance of an urbanized society across both the developed and the developing world, with the disruption of 'traditional' communities; increased mobility, extensive family dispersal (globally, in the case of the Irish diaspora), insecure or unstable employment prospects, and changing patterns of cultural consumption and socialization.[33] It is hardly fanciful to see the urge to trace family roots and connections, to establish (not least through powerful narratives) inter-generational links that constitute forms of emotional bonding, as a form of reaction to the seemingly dominant culture of fracture, dislocation and social isolation. The lengthening life expectancy (and its demographic and social consequences) throughout the developed world provides a further spur to forging new and firm inter-generational links. In short, family history provides an enabling framework for sociologists, psychologists and other social scientists concerned with investigating the evolving nature and determinants of social cohesion and social solidarity over time.

These considerations apply – in different degrees – to the collection of essays in this volume. Engagement with the revolutionary decade through the lens of family history presents its own challenges: there are hazards as well as rewards. The circumstances that prompt or trigger such engagement are crucial to the outcome; that is, to the emergence of the kind of narratives that comprise this volume. Does the exercise tackle a well-rehearsed family story that invites re-examination, or a dormant or concealed chapter of family

33 The ambiguous nature of new social media, as vehicles of socialization and creators of 'virtual' communities, demands more detailed discussion than can be attempted here.

history that demands excavation and recovery? At what point did the narrator become aware of the direct family connection with the historical episode? How was curiosity aroused, why and how was it pursued? What attempts at family research, or a search for corroborative evidence, were possible or undertaken? How extensive or rich was the available evidence? These are some of the questions addressed, in various ways, by the contributions to this volume.

But, beyond these practical, procedural questions, there is the more complex, engrossing issue of what is the particular emotional charge in the narrative in each case that inheres in the family connection: what particular tone and empathy does the family connection confer on the narrative? The contemporary values and perspective of the narrator must seek to come to terms with the world and the actions of a family member of an earlier era. Clearly, seeking to understand what that earlier family member thought and did in the context of his/her own time demands an intellectual disposition and an empathy that is essentially historical. But the more subjective dimension of the narrative – admiration, approval, endorsement of the attitudes and actions of the earlier family member, or, on the other hand, doubt, unease or disapproval of them – may be explicitly declared or voiced more discreetly in the narratives: in exceptional cases, it may be altogether subordinated to the imperative of understanding just why the earlier relatives followed the course that they did. But for each essayist the challenge has been to find the tone that best captures the degrees of empathy and distance that have informed their encounter with a seismic decade in the Irish past and with an intimate alcove in the past of their own family.

There is, therefore, in this collection of family narratives relating to the Irish revolutionary decade, a rich assembly of inter-generational dialogues: with a refreshing variety of perspectives and a wide breadth of emotional engagement. The historiography of the Irish revolutionary decade continues to expand, to develop and to pose new challenges.

Our aunt Eilish's untold story of rebellion, romance and religion

PAT DOLAN & MICHAEL DOLAN

As small children, we, the authors, were led to believe that our heroic aunt Eilish was a revolutionary who lived an amazing life through the 1916 Rising, War of Independence, Civil War and the Second World War; a life filled with drama and mystery. But we never knew the actual facts behind her story. In researching this chapter on our journey to rediscover our aunt we not alone managed to access the details but also uncovered the drama. Eilish Dolan was born into a strong republican household in Manor Street in the city centre of Dublin on 15 July 1907.[1] Her mother Mary Anne Dolan (nee Cowley) was an ardent nationalist and member of the Gaelic League; her father James Dolan a somewhat less fanatical republican than his wife, was a drayman with Guinness brewery. Eilish's uncle Michael Cowley was a high-ranking member of the IRB (Teeling Circle) who swore Sean T. O'Kelly into the organization.[2] He fought with P.H. Pearse's E. Company, 4th Battalion Dublin Brigade in the GPO during Easter week 1916, participated in the War of Independence, but did not engage in any way with the Civil War.[3] Although rightfully our grand-uncle has had some recognition for his participation in the Easter Rising, this chapter focuses on the untold and fascinating story of his niece, Eilish.

At the outbreak of the Rising on Easter Monday 1916, Eilish Dolan recalled the events as follows in her memoir written in 1932:

> One glorious Easter Monday when Dublin basked in the spring sunshine, my sister and I and some little playmates were playing in the garden at the back of our home when we paused to listen to strange and eerie sounds. We had never heard rifle-firing before, nor the boom of big guns, so naturally we wondered what it was all about. At length we were called indoors, and we felt at once that something terrible had happened. My father and mother looked so grave and my grand-mother wept uncontrollably, crying at intervals – Oh my son what is to become of those foolish boys – The rebellion of 1916 had

1 Eilish Dolan married and became Eily Horan and later remarried and was known as Elizabeth Brennan – all three names are used interchangeably in this chapter, but all relate to the same person. 2 Marnie Hay, *Bulmer Hobson and the nationalist movement in twentieth-century Ireland* (Manchester, 2009). 3 Jimmy Wren, *The GPO garrison Easter week 1916: a biographical dictionary* (Dublin, 2015).

> commenced and my uncle (Michael Cowley) … was not expected to escape alive.[4]

Although not radicalized by the experience of the Rising, in her formative years Eilish was influenced by, and was a great admirer of, Padraig Pearse for his artistic and poetic prowess rather than for his military leadership. As a young girl she was more interested in art, music and literature, an interest that remained with her all through her life. During the immediate aftermath of the War of Independence, Eilish's mother Mary Anne was a close friend of Sinéad de Valera (neé Flanagan) who was a regular visitor to Manor Street for tea. Mary Anne also attended Gaelic League meetings and republican open-air demonstrations headed by Mary McSweeney, Maud Gonne McBride and others. However, as Eilish refused to attend these meetings her mother scolded her and called her a 'shoneen maid', i.e., a lover of all things British. Despite this reluctance, Eilish's mother wanted all her children including Eilish to learn the Irish language and she had heard of a young teacher who was a fluent Irish speaker by the name of Padraig O'Horan. Padraig, who was from inner-city Dublin, was an IRA volunteer who had fought in the War of Independence and like Mary Anne Dolan was an ardent republican. Subsequently, he was hired to give Irish lessons to the Dolan children in their home every Saturday afternoon.

One Saturday after the lesson had finished, Eilish was going into the city centre on an errand and Padraig accompanied her. At the time he was nineteen years old and Eilish was just under fifteen years. It was the first of many shared walks together and romance blossomed. During these walks they discussed poetry, literature and music, but mostly Padraig spoke about his vision for a future independent Ireland and the hopes he treasured for Eilish and their future together.

However, these happy and peaceful days were suddenly brought to an end by the onset of the Civil War. On the morning of 28 June 1922, anti-Treaty forces who had taken occupancy of the Four Courts, which is situated very near Manor Street, were attacked by provisional government forces. Eilish recalled the event as follows: 'Free state soldiers in armoured cars opened fire on the occupied buildings and once again war and hate held sway in the streets of Dublin'.[5] On that day Padraig rushed to be with his anti-Treaty comrades but on his way called to her home to say goodbye to Eilish. She was not there but he left a message saying that if at all possible he would risk coming to see

4 Eilish Horan, *Through the gates of Babylon: the story of a conversion* (Belfast, 1932), p. 16. 5 Ibid., p. 28.

her before nightfall. Despite the danger, he subsequently met Eilish later that evening and Eilish described him as looking pale and drawn but smiling and cheerful although he knew he was going to face possible death. Eilish explained: 'I cannot describe our conflicting emotions. I felt that the whole world was dead and that life was grey and bitter. I felt, too, that the whole thing was utterly wrong. Yet I would not have it otherwise but that Padraig should "stand by the boys" as he expressed it'.[6] Padraig left the house that evening and as events unfolded he would not see Eilish again until six months after the Civil War had ended.

During the Civil War, Eilish experienced the first few days of fighting around her home as terrifying, to the extent that she even questioned her belief in the existence of God. At the end of that first week of fighting a note was delivered to Manor Street for Eilish from Padraig. Scribbled on a scrap of paper he told her that he was uninjured and that he hoped to get through the ordeal. He urged Eilish not to worry and keep a courageous heart. The note was written from one of the last occupied buildings by the anti-Treaty Volunteers, a store in North Earl Street. Just previous to this Padraig had seen action in the Hammam Hotel, 11–13 Upper Sackville Street and volunteered to assist in the escape of anti-Treaty headquarter staff including Eamon de Valera. Padraig was one of eight volunteers who caused a distraction by making a dash from the hotel into Cathedral Lane.[7] He was subsequently arrested by Free State forces and was held prisoner for a year-and-a-half. However, all through this time he kept up regular written correspondence with Eilish.

Eilish and her family were also about to have a very direct experience of the Civil War. In early April 1923, some members of the anti-Treaty forces called to Manor Street to ask Eilish's mother to hide some firearms and ammunition in the house and said that they would collect them some time later. Although very strongly anti-Treaty and very sympathetic to the republican side, Mary Anne Dolan was at first reluctant to agree to hide the arms, because she feared the disastrous consequences if the arms were discovered. It should be noted that her fear was very well justified as the previous October (1922) the Public Safety Bill had come into law. This legislation allowed for the execution of men found bearing arms against the state forces. By agreeing to hide arms, this in effect put her husband directly at risk.

On the night of 17 April 1923 Eilish was asleep in an upstairs bedroom she shared with her younger sister Christina when the following life changing event unfolded for Eilish. She described what took place in detail as follows:

6 Ibid., pp 28–9. **7** Padraig K. Horan, *In Kilmainham jail* (London, 1927).

> Suddenly I was awakened by the loud knocking on the hall door down stairs and the sound of men's voices demanding that the door be opened. Everywhere was confusion and the next thing I knew was that a flashlight was playing on my face, and I could see the glitter of brass buttons on a green uniform. My sister was terrified, and clung to me; but curiously enough I felt quite calm and unafraid because I knew what I had to do. We were told to get up and come down stairs at once. The door was then closed upon the intruders and two of them were placed outside on guard. We could hear them talking as we dressed. Other soldiers were moving all over the house, upstairs and down. We heard doors being opened drawers pulled out, and furniture being pushed about in the search.
>
> My sister wept with fear, but I did not feel anything except a dead weight on my heart and I was almost glad it had come at last, because for so long before I had guessed this would happen. We were escorted downstairs by the soldiers and found the sitting room in a state of topsy-turvy-dom. Pictures were torn down, the carpet was rolled up and some of the floor boards were broken. The piano was taken to pieces. Every corner in the house underwent a searching examination. At length, of course, the hiding place of the firearms and ammunition were discovered, and I at once took on the responsibility for them, because if I did not my father or mother would be arrested. I was only 15 at the time but was quite fully-grown and possibly looked somewhat older than I really was. At any rate, hundreds of women and girls had been arrested throughout Ireland, especially in Dublin. It was therefore, no uncommon thing, and so my arrest caused but little wonder when the news was heard by neighbours and friends next morning. I was just another republican girl arrested to be imprisoned for a few months.
>
> I received a severe lecture from the officer for my supposed folly and treachery, and was immediately placed under arrest. I was allowed a few minutes to dress for out-of-doors and was taken by the soldiers to the waiting lorries.[8]

It should be noted that at the time of the discovery of the arms her father (our grandfather), who had no knowledge of the hidden arms, was being led away at gunpoint when Eilish confessed to being responsible for the arms even though this was not the case, but her actions in all probability saved her father's life.

8 Horan, *Through the gates of Babylon*, pp 31–3.

On the night of Eilish's arrest she was taken into custody at Richmond Barracks and the next day transferred to Kilmainham Gaol and while there she was questioned on arrival but refused to speak. She described her questioning as follows:

> I was brought into an office where I was questioned minutely concerning the things found in the house. A revolver was held to my now wildly beating heart, and all sorts of threats were poured into my ears, but I refused to speak. I knew quite well, however, that this was the usual procedure after an arrest of a prisoner in those days. They did not really expect to be told anything.[9]

Eilish's prisoner number was 3293 and her date of detention was 18 April 1923. She was transferred to North Dublin Union on 27 April 1923. Eilish was charged for being in the possession of the following arms and ammunition: one .45 revolver; one .23 revolver; six bomb detonators; and six rounds of ammunition for a .45 revolver.

During her imprisonment in Kilmainham, Eilish made friends with fellow inmates and signed autograph books for them, which was the custom among prisoners at the time. Among the friends she made and whose autograph book she signed were Sadie Dowling, Mary Street, Dublin; Kathleen Campbell, Railway Avenue, Inchicore, Dublin; Mary Doyle Gracepark Gardens, Drumcondra, Dublin; and Kathleen Guilfoyle, Sea View, Clifden, Co. Galway.[10] During her imprisonment, Eilish remained a nationalist as evidenced from her drawing of Róisín Dubh, a drawing that is also cited by McCoole in *No ordinary women* (2008).[11] Having spent ten days in Kilmainham Gaol, Eilish was then transferred to the North Dublin Union, just a three-minute walk from her Manor Street home. She was finally released on 29 October 1923, having spent a total of six months in prison, sadly spending her sixteenth birthday under lock and key.

Meanwhile, during his eighteen-month incarceration Padraig became completely disillusioned with the Catholic Church. Over this period he came to the conclusion that the republicans had been betrayed by the Catholic hierarchy.[12] At a meeting of Catholic bishops in Maynooth towards the end of April 1922 a statement was issued resolutely in support of the Treaty, and condemned anyone who would take up arms against the new state.

9 Ibid., p. 34. 10 Kindly sourced from Aoife Thorpey, Curator, Kilmainham Gaol, Dublin. 11 Sinéad McCoole, *No ordinary women: Irish female activists in the revolutionary years* (Dublin, 2008). 12 Robert P. Roddie, 'Padraig and Eily O'Horan: a story of rebellion and redemption', *Dublin Historical Record*, 55:1 (Spring 2002), pp 75–87.

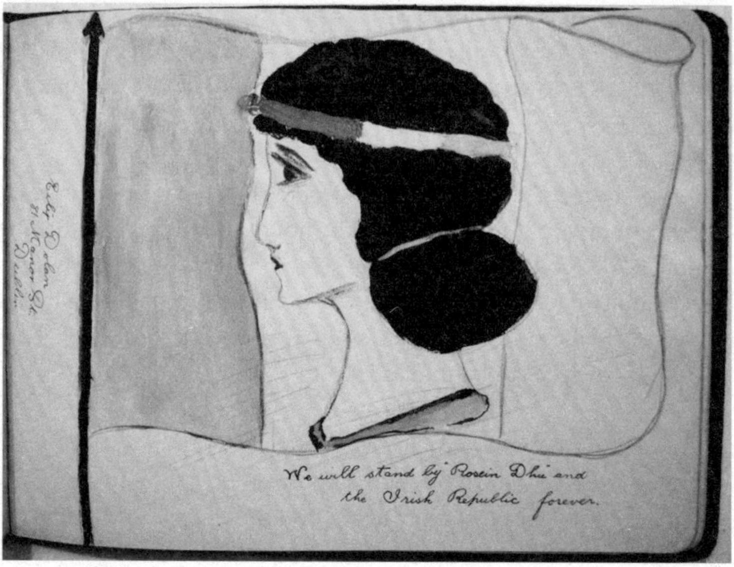
We will stand by "Rosein Dhu" and
the Irish Republic forever.

Autograph book drawing by from Eilish Dolan while imprisoned
(courtesy of Kilmainham Gaol Library).

Importantly, Eilish also began to notice this radical transformation in Padraig from the letters she received from him at that time. Padraig O'Horan was released from Gormanstown Internment Camp just after Eilish and just before Christmas 1923. He, along with several other former republican volunteers imprisoned in Gormanstown Camp, were attracted to the Methodist Mission in Georges St, Dublin. Padraig was now converted to the teaching of Revd Lindsay H. Cullen.[13]

With Padraig's release from prison one would have assumed that his reunion with Eilish would have been a joyous occasion, but it did not turn out that way. When he called to Manor Street to see Eilish he had changed drastically. Gone was his staunch republicanism; gone also was his unquestioning faith in the Catholic Church. Eilish's parents were astounded at the change in him. Her mother refused to listen to Padraig and asked him to go, leaving Eilish heartbroken as she believed she would never see him again. Months passed and then one evening in the summer of 1924 Padraig returned to Manor Street. He began to talk to Eilish's parents about his newfound evangelical faith. He took from his pocket a book of Scripture and began to read from it. Eilish's mother interjected and told him to stop – according to Eilish's account her mother said, 'please close that book, it is a Protestant bible'.[14] And then she went on to say that, as he had become a heretic and renounced his holy faith,

13 Ibid. 14 Horan, *Through the gates of Babylon*, p. 41.

the Dolan family must discontinue all friendship, and she must ask him to leave.[15]

This situation left Eilish in turmoil, but despite her mother's protestations she was determined to read the version of the New Testament that Padraig had given her. Eilish read the book without her parents' knowledge and would read it every lunchtime in an art gallery in Harcourt Street. In actual fact Eilish indicates that she found great comfort in this activity. She then tried to explain her new religious outlook to her parents who reacted badly. Eilish describes it as follows: 'I spoke my thoughts aloud thereupon a little Gospel by St John which I greatly prized was taken from me and burned before I had time to realize what was happening'.[16]

Ultimately and much to the upset and distress of her parents she took an informed decision to leave the Catholic Church and become a Methodist. Once she had told her parents of her final decision they tried to dissuade her to the point where she was given a period of a week to change her mind by her father. This she did not do. A week later a very saddened and penniless Eilish left for London with Padraig to start a new life together. It might be noted here that at that time a change of religion from Catholicism to Methodism was not alone very unusual but totally unacceptable to most Catholics. This must have been a huge strain on Eilish at such a young age.

On arrival in London Eilish found life there very different and difficult with employment hard to come by. Subsequently, she and Padraig moved to Belfast where Padraig was appointed to Doncloney parish, Co. Down. Padraig and Eilish were married at Knock Methodist Church, Belfast, on 2 July 1928. Before their marriage Padraig wrote a love poem to Eilish (Eily), which reads:

Eily Mine
Little rowan-berry mouth,
Soft starlight of all my skies
Song and praise for thee were meet
My love – unutterably sweet!
Eily Mine

Warm winds from the songful south
Bear a lay of loveliness;
And lovelier still my little Queen –
My fairest flower of tenderness
Eily mine

15 Ibid. **16** Ibid., p. 47.

Light and lilting on my way
My soul's sweet song and earliest psalm.
More precious then the wealth of worlds –
Thy shy caress and kisses balm
Eily Mine![17]

Eilish embraced her new life and newfound religion and became known as Sister Eileen – Deaconess-Evangelist of Grosvenor Hall. She was in constant demand as a good public speaker and according to Roddie she was well received and became somewhat renowned in the Northern Evangelical Circuit.[18] In 1930, Eilish and Padraig moved to England and converted to the Church of England as a result of some reservation that they had in respect of the Methodist faith. Padraig was subsequently appointed as an Anglican priest serving first in Bath and Wells in 1932. Various appointments in the south and west of England followed, which meant that Eilish and Padraig moved location constantly. For a period they settled in Twerton and found themselves actively serving and supporting the local community. They also adopted a son.

During the Second World War, Eilish (who now found herself once again experiencing a war) was very involved in a leadership role in the local community and demonstrated a gift for producing plays and hosting 'old time' dance nights in a local school with blacked out windows. A close friend from that period Kathleen Young recalls how Eilish mentored her interest in reading and introduced her to the works of philosophers such as Teilhard de Chardin.[19] In her memoir Kathleen Young also recalls that on VE Day when the Second World War ended, Eilish with Padraig in his role as the vicar of the village of Priddy, rang the church bells in celebration.[20] Soon after that time, and somewhat to the disapproval of Padraig, Eilish also began to lean back towards Catholicism and, in fact, would eventually return to the Catholic Church.

However, life changed drastically when Padraig died suddenly from heart failure in 1951 aged 48 years. He was buried in Holy Cross Cemetery, Sampford Arundale (near Taunton). Eilish had a Celtic cross erected over his grave with the very apt inscription 'Priest and Poet'. After his death Eilish decided to return to Dublin with her son and start a new phase in her life. Thankfully, she had repaired her relationship with her parents some years previously. Once home again Eilish managed to get work with the *Irish Independent* in their Dublin office and at the same time embarked on her career as an author of

17 *Daily Irish Christian Advocate,* 15 June 1927, p. 5. **18** Roddie, 'Padraig and Eily O'Horan: a story of rebellion and redemption'. **19** Kathleen Young, *Green velvet dress: memoirs of sixty years in London and Somerset* (London, 1989). **20** Ibid., p. 72.

novels and plays. In December 1954, she was remarried to a Patrick Brennan in the Church of the Holy Child, Whitehall, Dublin, and held her wedding breakfast in Manor Street with her parents and family, healing old wounds. Later she and Paddy Brennan adopted a daughter.

In her career as a writer she used the name Elizabeth Brennan for all her novels and plays. According to Brady and Cleave her work was well received and she became a successful author. In total she wrote ten romantic novels some of which were translated into several languages.[21] She also had at least one play produced on Radio Éireann (now RTÉ Radio) and she received an Irish Countrywoman's Association award for her novel *Girl on an island* (1984).[22] Apart from her memoir cited consistently in this chapter and entitled *Through the gates of Babylon: the story of a conversion* (1932), she never wrote on the topic of her life again. Eilish moved to the west of Ireland, living mainly in various locations in Co. Sligo and while there had one of her plays, *The parting of the ways*, performed in Tubbercurry. She eventually moved to Tullyallen, Co. Louth, where she died suddenly on 2 October 1993 at the age of eighty-six years.

Eilish's Legacy

As in many other Irish households the Civil War was rarely discussed in our nuclear and extended family. In relation to politics generally and the Civil War more particularly, our mother was adamant that politics was not to be discussed. However, the story of our aunt Eilish (such that we had) was passed on to us via intergenerational family verbal testimony. Having said this, for both of us (the authors) as the youngest of a family of ten children, for many years we operated under the misconception that aunt Eilish was arrested and imprisoned by the Black and Tans and not the Free State army as was the case. This misinformation, which we were led to believe as true, may have resulted from the guilt and embarrassment associated with the Civil War, in that it was actually Irish rather than English soldiers who raided our family home and arrested our aunt. However, we are very fortunate that Eilish wrote a short personal account and testimony of these traumatic events in her life. We only discovered this written account later as part of the research for this chapter.

We did not know aunt Eilish well and our face-to-face contact with her was rare. This may have been because our aunt lived much of her life in England and then outside of Dublin when back in Ireland when we were

21 Anne Brady and Brian Cleeve *A biographical dictionary of Irish writers* (Mullingar, 1985).
22 Elizabeth Brennan, *Girl on an island* (London, 1984).

Eilish Dolan (aka Eily O'Horan and Elizabeth Brennan), courtesy of Michael O'Horan.

younger. This, coupled with the fact that Micheal Dolan our father and her brother died tragically in 1958 aged 44 when we were both very small children, meant that any of his memories of her were lost and obviously could not be passed on to us. However, in her later years both of us had at least one occasion to meet with aunt Eilish separately and both now also regret not having used these occasions to discuss her amazing life story with her.

Now, over a century since Eilish dramatically recalled witnessing the start of the Easter Rising from her back garden and what went on to be her most eventful life, what lessons can we learn from her? Certainly, she lived through a very unique time in the history of Ireland and was directly entangled in events that led to the formation of the state. It is our view that by taking the blame and falsely confessing to hiding arms from the Free State forces in order to protect both her parents and her father in particular, Eilish Dolan at fifteen years of age demonstrated incredible bravery at enormous personal cost and risk. She did this as an act of mercy to save her parents. She seemed to accept this burden very pragmatically and, as we noted, her testimony described it as 'doing what I had to do'.

At this very basic level of humanity and altruism, the untold and heroic role played by many young Irish women like Eilish have been kept silent in terms of public attention. For example, in two cases both involving nurses who were very active and involved in the Easter Rising, one up to recently has been totally unknown while the other has been literally 'airbrushed' from history. First, Nurse Linda Kearns from Sligo demonstrated great bravery and humanity by converting a house into a makeshift hospital to treat the injured during the turmoil of Easter week.[23] Second, Nurse Elizabeth O'Farrell, facing danger at Pearse's side during the surrender at the end of Easter week, was airbrushed out of the very famous surrender photograph.[24] The participation of many young people, like Eilish, in the decade of revolution remains unacknowledged.[25]

It is clear that throughout her life Eilish demonstrated enormous resilience in the face of adversity, from coping with imprisonment to overcoming separation from family as a result of her changing religion. Additionally, she coped well as a previously Catholic southerner with moving to live in a staunchly loyalist community in Northern Ireland and at such an incredibly delicate period in Irish history. She further overcame the sudden death of her husband and a subsequent relocation back to Ireland to urgently seek employment and security for herself and her son. Not alone did aunt Eilish bounce back and cope with these challenges, she thrived and went on to have a very successful writing career.

Finally, while it is easy and more straightforward to celebrate and commemorate both the 1916 Easter Rising and subsequent War of Independence, we are all well aware of the fact that the Civil War poses a far more difficult challenge. As has been said by many including President Michael D. Higgins in his address to the Béal na Bláth 2016 Commemoration event, 'how do you mark a conflict of and between families and communities?' Perhaps at least we can all take some solace from Eilish's story and other similar stories of personal bravery. At last, rather than condemn the memory of those

23 Donal Fallon, 'The great escape – nurse Linda Kearns' (2010) https://comeheretome.com/2010/04/17/the-great-escape-linda-kearns/, accessed, 15 July 2016. **24** McCoole, *No ordinary women.* **25** Pat Dolan, 'Children's rights in Ireland: a current perspective on implementation, from a past lens with a view to the future' in Donncha O'Connell (ed.) *The Irish human rights law review* (Dublin, 2010), pp 177–91.

involved in the Civil War to the realm of unspoken silence, we can now move to an acknowledgment and celebration of lives led on both sides of the conflict. In the case of Eilish Dolan who was essentially a pacifist caught in a republican family and a romantic relationship at a time of civil war, the severe personal choices and challenges she endured both during and after the War were all faced by her without hesitation. Once she had overcome each challenge she never looked back; she didn't dwell or live in the past and kept moving forward. More importantly, we know from her later fictional work that she valued the simple wonder and romance of daily living and undoubtedly Eilish Dolan lived out her life to the full.

Acknowledgments

We are particularly thankful to our cousin Michael O'Horan, aunt Eilish's son, for his recent enthusiastic support, kindness and cooperation in bringing this story to light. We also wish to acknowledge all of the Dolan family who are 'collective keepers' of Eilish's memory and to acknowledge especially initial research by Theresa and Monica Dolan. Finally, the authors are indebted to Robyn Roddie for his work on this topic and for his advice and support in leading us to find aunt Eilish's actual written testimony.[26]

26 Roddie, 'Padraig and Eily O'Horan: a story of rebellion and redemption'.

Family stories and secret keepers: who is Máire Bastabal?

ANNE BYRNE & COLM BYRNE

I observed the commencement of the 1916 centenary events at a remove; while professionally interested in what new versions of the taught history of national sovereignty might unfold during 2016, I had no personal interest in 'The Centenary Conversations'. My connection with the symbols and activities of what it means to be 'Irish' is weak. As a student of the 1970s and 1980s, I am more interested in becoming 'European'. I am not a follower or fan of Gaelic football or hurling. I speak Irish without confidence. I work hard to develop my appreciation for the rhythms and melodies of Irish music. Until recently I understood this disinterest or reticence as a personal preference. Growing up with the conflict in Northern Ireland forces another perspective. I am drawn to understanding the causes and consequences of conflict. I feel the profound weight of strong ideologies such as nationalism, republicanism and feminism. But apart from the excitement of feminism and its promise of radical change, these other histories, these other politics, have nothing to do with my family or me. Or so I thought.

Artifacts hold stories. I have two – my grandmother's Cumann na mBan brooch and a family album of photographs and press cuttings, documenting the life of the Barry and Bastible families from Cork. Given to me recently by my uncle, both these artifacts are over 100 years old. Family stories about the Bastible[1] siblings, George, Mary Pauline (Molly), Michael, Christopher, Hannah (Nora) and James (Jim), no longer circulate but fragments of stories linger in memory. Conversations with Caoimh, Molly's son, about our forbearers bring me back to the young women and young men that I knew in their old age and my childhood. This chapter considers the life of Molly Bastible, my grandmother, as a young woman, active in Cumann na mBan, an actor with Na hAisteoirí (The Gaelic Players) and a teacher in the first all-Irish language school in Dublin, Scoil Mhuire. Two of her brothers, Chris and Michael Bastible, were interned in 1922. All of the family members were active in the Gaelic League, promoting the Irish language through drama and lectures while participating in summer schools and Feiseanna Cheoil.

These young people are part of the story of the search for a new Ireland,

1 The family surname has a diversity of spellings; 'Bastible' is the contemporary spelling.

joined in their shared belief of the ideology, dynamics and promises of the Gaelic revival, in the importance of the national language, and in revolutionary political independence. Their political and cultural activism was fired in the nexus of family and society in the first three decades of the twentieth century. Omissions and discontinuities emerge in family history, familiar to those with secrets to keep. Molly, Chris and Michael's stories were not passed on, nor taken up by the following generation. Lizzy, their mother, my great grandmother, did not speak. The not telling may not be deliberate. Societal forces were at work to draw attention away from the conflicted and difficult period of the formation of the new Irish Free State, particularly post-1923. The storytellers may have been more concerned with their own futures rather than the past, and so the legacy or family history was not passed on.

Despite this, stories are held in the artifacts, forcing a telling of those factors, personal, political, and ideological, that shaped the minds, attitudes and actions of the first citizens of the Irish Republic. In keeping these mementoes, preserving the family album and her Cumann na mBan brooch, Molly (or somebody else) did not forget, did not fully conceal. This is their story, put together from family fragments and artifacts, a telling made possible in the post-centenary commemorations of 1916.

The brooch

It is a small object, oval shaped, measuring 3x2 cm, bordered in gold-coloured metal with a green and white centre. It is my sixtieth birthday and my uncle and aunt give me this present. The words 'cumann na mban' and the date '1916' encircle the green enamel in gold Irish script. In the centre is a crossed pike and rifle. Fragments of family stories surface. Is this really Molly's? Was my grandmother a member of Cumann na mBan, and why am I not aware of this until now? The silence of the generations disturbs me. I recall brief and infrequent mentions that maybe some of the forebears had 'something to do' with Irish independence. Or a thread is dropped into a conversation but not pursued. Or a reference is made to a protest outside a jail in which a family member is held in poor conditions. Was it Molly? And why don't I know this story of Máire Uí Beastabl, my grandmother, affectionately known as Molly?

Her Cumann na mBan membership (Cork 1 Brigade Area) is confirmed by a Military Services Pension Collection archive document for 11 July 1921.[2]

2 Military Archives/Military Service Pensions Collection/CMB/2, p. 38. The other Officers listed are President Mrs M.E. Hegarty, Treasurer Mrs Murphy, Captain Miss M. Aherne. See also http://farmgatecork.ie/womenofthesouth/cumann-na-mbn-roll-call/ accessed 14 June 2017.

'Miss M. Bastible' is listed as an Officer and Secretary. The witness statement of Miss Margaret Lucey, Treasurer, Cork City Cumann na mBan, recounts that over a hundred were present at the first meeting in 1914 in Cork City Hall convened by founder member Miss Mary MacSwiney.[3] Was Molly there? The 1915 exit of those in favour of John Redmond's home rule policy left remaining members (about fifty) engaged in 'weekly parades' and 'occasional concerts and ceilidhe' to raise funds as well as becoming 'proficient in first-aid treatment … a scheme financed by the British government'. Lucey writes that 'practically every one of us qualified for the required certificate and was awarded the grant which we passed on to Cumann na mBan funds'.[4]

Lucey's statement attests that Cumann na mBan members were aware that 'some months prior to the 1916 Rising something "big" was going to happen. We were instructed to get ready first-aid outfits, bandages were cut, supplies of gauze, iodine and safety-pins were got together, each girl keeping her own supply. We made public collections for Volunteers arms' funds, organized whist drives, dances and jumble sales, all with the same object'. On Easter Sunday 1916, when the Cork Volunteers left for Macroom, was Molly one of those instructed 'to remain and be alert for any happenings, such as reporting movements of enemy troops, receiving and passing dispatches and generally acting as a link between the Volunteers and the City'? There was no military action taken by the Cork Volunteers, though members of Cumann na mBan were arrested by the British – a 'Mrs Martin and three or four others'.[5] Members of the Cork Volunteers were also arrested and Cumann na mBan members became involved in raising funds for the National Aid Association 'to provide some measure of relief for imprisoned Volunteers and their dependants'.[6]

Further evidence of the involvement of Miss M. Bastible in the Cork Branch is provided in Margaret Lucey's account of the reorganization of the Cork City Cumann in 1917 into 'Craobh Poblachtach na hEireann' (58 members) and Máire/Molly is listed as Secretary of the 'Cork Branch' (40 members). What were the duties of the Branch Secretary? The Constitution of Cumann na mBan lists Branch 'Rules' which include the following: 'Each Branch of Cumann na mBan shall be controlled by a Captain, Secretary and Treasurer who shall be responsible for the training and equipping of the Branch. The Secretary shall call a roll at each meeting and shall keep a written record of work done at each meeting. She shall be responsible for all communications to GHQ'.[7] In addition to weekly meetings, Branch Secretaries 'shall

3 BMH WS 1561: Margaret Lucey, pp 1–42. **4** Ibid., p. 2. **5** BMH WS 1561, p. 3. **6** Ibid., p. 4. **7** L. Conlon, *Cumann na mBan and the women of Ireland, 1913–25* (Kilkenny, 1969), p. 306.

submit to each District Council meeting a written report of the Branch with regard to number of meetings held, numbers of members present, work done'.[8] In addition to 'efficiency' being the sole test for the election of the Secretary to a Branch, further instructions are listed in Leabhar na mBan. 'The most capable and energetic worker must be chosen. Initiative, tact, common sense, promptitude and business instincts all go to the making of a good Secretary … a good Secretary will be grateful for cooperation and counsel'.[9] This is directed at those members who might 'make her life a misery with petty criticisms and continual checks' or 'of leaving her to do all the work alone till she develops into an autocrat by force of circumstances'.[10] This appears to be wise advice on avoiding common organizational pitfalls.

I imagine my grandmother, her friends and associates at their voluntary, collegial, collective work, members of a national women's organization 'to advance the cause of Irish liberty'.[11] They pledge 'to become perfect citizens of a perfect Irish nation'.[12] As I read the first Constitution of Cumann na mBan, I am perplexed by my ignorance of her pledge 'to work for the Irish Republic, by organizing and training the women of Ireland to take their place by the side of those who are working and fighting for its recognition'.[13] From the perspective of the present, she might be considered among those we now call 'rebels', 'radicals', 'renegades' or 'revolutionaries'. This is not how I remember her.

Molly (Mary Pauline) was born to Bartholomew Bastable (sic) and Lizzy (Elizabeth) Bastable (neé Barry) in Midleton, Co. Cork, on 13 June 1893. She was sister to George (b. 1892), Michael (b. 1894), Christopher (b. 1896), Hannah (Nora) (b. 1899) and James (b. 1901). Bart (b. 1855), a widower, was employed as a 'cooper' at the local whiskey distillery and married the younger Lizzy Barry (b. 1861 to Michael Barry and Mary Higgins), recently returned from Chicago. Lizzy emigrated to the US in the 1880s with three brothers and a sister but is 'sent' home, perhaps to look after her parents in Castlemartyr. The 1901 Census of 31 March documents that the Bastible family had now moved to No. 15 Eason's Hill, the north-west ward in Cork city, and Molly was three years old. Although the trade in cooperage is declining, there is some prospect of work. Bartholomew's signature and handwriting on the census form is clear, flowing and legible. Lizzy and Bartholomew are Catholic, can 'read and write' and speak 'Irish and English'. Was their knowledge of Irish a consequence of an interest in the language revival movement? Did they read *The Gaelic Journal, Fáinne an Lae, An Claidheamh Soluis* (Sword of Light), or

8 Ibid., p. 306. **9** Cumann na mBan, *Leabhar na mBan* (1919), NLI, Ir 89162, p. 19. **10** Ibid.,. p. 19. **11** Conlon, *Cumann na mBan,* p. 299. **12** Cumann na mBan Constitution, Corughadh, 21 Jan. 1921. **13** See C. McCarthy, *Cumann na mBan and the Irish revolution* (Cork, 2014) for a comprehensive account of the organization and activities.

Molly Bastible's Cumann na mBan brooch.[14]

an tAthair Peadar Ua Laoghaire's (Fr Peter O'Leary) serialization of *Táin Bó Cúailnge* in the *Cork Weekly Examiner*? I am interested in these details and what it means in 1901 to speak 'Irish' at a time of language decline and when Douglas Hyde highlighted the need to reverse the anglicization of the Irish people through the Irish language movement. But none of this was of concern to Lizzy in April 1901. Ten days after Bartholomew completed the census form for his family, he does not come home in the evening nor is there any sign or message from him for the next week. Lizzy's baby, James, is one month old, her eldest George is nine years old. Her anxiety about the whereabouts of her husband, the circumstances of his disappearance, and the people who help her to search for him are unknown to me. Bartholomew is 'found drowned' on 17 April off Lavitt's Quay in the river Lee in Cork city, according to the death certificate and newspaper report.[15] Lizzy is now a widow in her late thirties with six children and no visible means of financial or family support. Her mother, Mary Higgins, died in 1899, and though Lizzy had eight brothers some had

14 There are a few examples of the oval Cumann na mBan brooch that are documented. The display note for the brooch in Kilmainham Museum donated by Mrs Kathleen Merrigan reads: 'This badge was struck for the Easter Commemoration in 1917 and was given to Cumann na mBan members who had served in the 1916 rising'. See illustration in Sinead McCoole, *No ordinary women: Irish female activists in the revolutionary years, 1900–23* (Dublin, 2003), p. 47. Material on the activities and organization of the 1917 commemoration by Cumann na mBan remains to be investigated. **15** *Skibbereen Eagle*, 20 April 1901.

migrated to the US and perhaps South Africa at this point. The family story is that she was assisted by the Bastibles and Barrys from Midleton to open up a 'huckster shop', selling confectionary and newspapers in the Sunday's Wells area of Cork city.

Founded in 1900, the North Parish Gaelic League provided Irish language and other tuition classes at Eason's Hill schools – boys and girls, every Tuesday and Friday at 8 p.m.[16] The League advertised Irish-language classes and 'Students prepared for all examinations'.[17] The branch was renowned for being vibrant and ambitious.[18] The faded blue-green front cover of *Craobh na Paróiste Thuaidh* booklet (1904) is illustrated in Celtic script and lists two pages of advertisers with the appeal 'We would respectfully ask all Gaelic Leaguers and all sincere sympathizers of the Irish Revival to patronize our undermentioned friends, whom we have great pleasure in recommending as practical supporters of the Language Movement and to whom we hereby tender our most sincere thanks for the manner in which they helped us'. An extensive list of businesses and services are advertised, including John Barry, 'importer of tea and manufacturer of superior bread'. Poems in Irish, notes on Irish names, a list of Gaelic League publications, as well as detailed notes on the 1904 dramatic production *Creideamh agus gorta* (Faith and hunger, 1901), penned for the League by an tAthair Pádraig Ó Duinnín (Fr Pat Dineen), are provided. The play is based on the 'well authenticated incident of the Famine period' in which the children of the widow-woman, Cáit, die of starvation rather than take food from the English Sinclair family, unwilling to forfeit allegiance to the Catholic Church, the Pope and the Blessed Virgin Mary. Máire plays the part of the daughter of the wealthy Sinclair family while Seóirse is one of the hungry but devoted sons of Cáit. One of the sons utters the fateful lines, 'Mháire a Mháthair, is fearr an bás' (Mary my mother, death is better).[19] A nationalist stance is being taken by the author in this play, wholly endorsed by the reviewer in *An Claidheamh Soluis* who writes: 'Agus bhí an ceart agus an fhírinne ag an mbuachaill beag' (and the small boy had the right and the truth of it). The children die of hunger and the reviewer notes that this is the will of God, who has reserved a place in heaven for them.[20] A photograph for the *Cork Weekly Examiner* shows the two children, George and Molly Bastible, sitting on the floor by their fictional families.[21] I consider how Dineen's anti-

16 St Mary's national school (1831), the location of the League classes, is adjacent to No. 15 Eason's Hill where the Bastible family lived. **17** *Craobh na Paróiste Thuaidh (*Cork, 1904), p. 1. **18** T. Ó Riordáin, *Conradh na Gaeilge i gCorcaigh, 1894–1910* (Baile Átha Cliath, 2000), p. 47. **19** *Craobh na Paróiste Thuaidh,* p. 13. **20** Ó Riordáin, *Conradh na Gaeilge i gCorcaigh, 1894–1910,* p. 222. **21** The cast included Treasurer of the Gaelic League, W. O'Callaghan, teachers E. O'Donoghue, M. Lucey and P. Horgan. *Craobh na Paróiste Thuaidh,* p. 1.

Cast of *Creideamh agus Gorta*

colonial, religious play might carry some weight in the recently widowed Bastible household. Ó Riordáin observes that *Craobh na Paróiste Thuaidh* not only contributed to the development of theatre in Ireland with this first performance of a play with nationalist overtones, but in placing children on stage for the first time in the company of adults. *An Claidheamh Soluis* reviewer praises the children and mentions the good performances of Seóirse Bastible, Pádraig Ua Duinín and Séamus Beag Ua Coisdealbhaigh.[22]

How Lizzy or her children survive the next decade can only be surmised. The opportunity of education, the Irish-language classes, and involvement in performance and theatrical works of *Craobh na Paróiste Thuaidh,* clearly offer significant community support to Lizzy, sole parent of six children. This support from the language revival movement also promotes a republican politics for which Lizzy might have had some sympathy.[23] Crucially, the Gaelic League was one of the first national associations that welcomed women as members when the public segregation of men and women was the normative

22 Ó Riordáin, *Conradh na Gaeilge i gCorcaigh, 1894–1910,* p. 223. **23** In her early twenties, Lizzy is reputedly a member of the Ladies Land League in Midelton, Co. Cork.

standard. The 1911 Census return for the family documents some of the changes that occur since the onset of her widowhood. The form is completed in Irish and Bastible is written Bastabl (m) or Bhastable (f). The term 'Ceannuidhe' is used to indicate that Eilís (Lizzy) is head of household as well as 'Bean an Tighe'. Instructions clearly indicate that 'No entry should be made in the case of wives, daughters or other female relatives solely engaged in domestic duties at home'. She signs her name as Eilís, Bean Uí Bastable. Seóirse is eighteen, Máire Póilín (Molly) is seventeen and Mícheál at sixteen secures employment as a census enumerator in the Irish language. The occupation of all sons and daughters is recorded as 'scoláire' (scholar) and they continued to live in Eason's Hill, moving next door to No. 16.[24]

The album

A large, hard-backed and well-worn family album lies before me. Eight red lily-type flowers with golden vines and leaves grace the green cloth cover featuring a fairy tale castle and the word 'Album' in capital letters. Each page comprises faded brown card, discolored, and the edges fray and break with every opening. Family and studio photographs, excerpts from school reports and theatre programmes, letters, postcards and newspaper cuttings document the lives of the Bastible and Barry families over ninety pages from 1900 to the mid-1940s. The collection of documents has some sense of a chronology, disrupted by later insertions as the album becomes crowded and full. Material from the early 1900s lies alongside a newspaper cutting of a 'double wedding' from the 1940s. I don't know how the album came to be in the family, who carefully compiled or guarded it. Perhaps it is the sole occupation of my great-grandmother Lizzy or my grand-aunt Nora, Molly's single sister? Perhaps it is a family affair? A cutting is sent in the post from Chris in Glasgow and Lizzy or Jim glue it into a space on an inner page. They sit in the evening turning the stiff leaves and talk about cousin James Bally's life in South Africa and read again that perplexing letter from Michael. These family 'scrapbooking' albums were popular in the nineteenth century, recording anniversaries and weddings, preserving photographs, correspondence and special events. Such albums were also used to introduce children and the next generations to individual and family histories.

The Barry-Bastible family album is not just a collection of ephemera; it documents in close detail the private and public life of the Barrys and Bastibles. The contents of this carefully preserved album is tangible evidence of the

24 The census return describes this house as 'second class', four rooms are occupied by seven people.

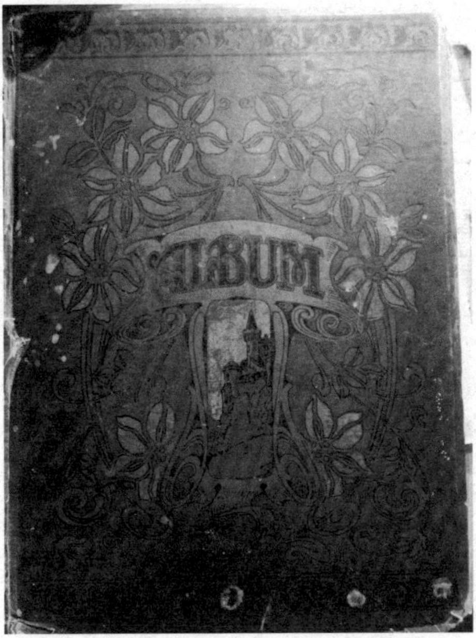

Front cover, Barry-Bastible family album

intention to document the self, social and political identity of Lizzy Bastible and her family, in the foundation years of the state. Three features emerge as key: the significance of education, early involvement in the Irish language movement and theatre and the development of strong political allegiances to an independent Irish Republic.

The Irish language and education

Five certificates of the 'Compántas an Phléimeannaigh' (Fleming Companionship) are pasted into the album for George, Máire (Molly) and Michael (1904–7), documenting their successes at various levels of competitive examination in Irish.[25] Attending Eason's Hill national schools and the North Monastery Christian Brothers, and their familial involvement with *Craobh na Paróiste Thuaidh* ensured that the Bastibles were not only proficient in Irish but were exposed to the ideals and ambitions of the gaelicization of Ireland from an early age. A newspaper cutting, 'Language revival movement in Cork' marks the occasion of the opening of Cork city branches of the Gaelic League and the Munster Training College by the Very Revd Canon Peter O'Leary.[26] There

25 See Cork Public Museum 1916–21 exhibition (www.corkcity.ie), featuring the Fleming Companionship silver trophy shield and archival documents on the rules of the competitions, 11 June 2017. **26** Family album press cutting, no title, 17 Sept. 1915.

were three branches of the Gaelic League in the cty offering classes in Irish at this time. The Training College, located in Ballingeary, held its winter session in Cork city 'to train persons for the teaching of Irish and granting certificates which would be recognized by the National Board'. In the untitled newspaper cutting, Canon O'Leary castigates the audience (and readers) and reminds them that 'This year of grace would pass away, but 2015 would come in due time, and the people who lived then, who saw all the books that were now being printed in Irish, would ask what sort of fools their ancestors were to leave such a language die'. Seóirse Mac Niocall urges 'that it was their duty as Irishmen to learn it because it was the soul of their nation'. The meeting learns that Irish was being taught well 'in the largest and best schools' and parents should remove their children from schools in which Irish was not offered or taught poorly. The account also notes that the Gaelic League 'had forced the National University to make Irish essential at Matriculation'. The account is read and carefully glued to a page in the album.

Ó Riordáin notes that the Eason's Hill national school and the North Monastery Christian Brothers schools (the schools which the Bastibles attended) dedicated a third more of their time to learning Irish, unlike other schools. *Craobh na Paróiste Thuaidh* set out to develop the language, and a specific educational programme was devised and promoted in the parish from 1902. Prizes were awarded to the best students in each school, and by 1904, Irish was taught in every school in the parish.[27] Living in the parish, the Bastible children were among the first to be educated through the medium of Irish at school and in the community. The importance for the young Bastibles of gaining experience and developing expertise to win competitive examinations was first fostered through the Gaelic League. While initially Cork-based, the scheme expanded to other parts of the country, including Dublin and Belfast. Proposed in 1898 by Donnchadh Pléimionn, 'An Síoladóir' (Denis Fleming), 'Compántas an Phléimeannaigh' (Fleming Companionship) was a scheme to encourage Irish language proficiency, consisting of six progressive 'steps' or grades, certified after written and oral examination, and with awards (e.g., gold medal, silver shield, book prizes). The *Irish Examiner* notes that 'with much ceremony, the youngest Companion, Mr George Bastible, North Parish Branch, was admitted to the Companionship'.[28] In 1907, according to her intricate blue-bordered certificate, Máire/Molly was admitted to the 'Hall of Readers', indicating a high level of competencies in the language. She was fourteen years old.

Two newspaper photographs of the Irish language school in Dingle merit

27 Ó Riordáin, *Conradh na Gaeilge i gCorcaigh, 1894–1910*, p. 87. **28** *Cork Examiner*, 16 Nov. 1905.

one page in the album. 'Professors Fleming, Sugrue, Corkery, O'Grady, O'Connor and O'Flynn' provide Irish language accredited instruction in the summer of 1912. I can only assume that Molly and perhaps her sister attend this and other Gaelic League summer schools such as Ballingeary for trainee teachers. J.N. Allen of the Christian Brothers school, congratulates Lizzy and 'Miss Bastible' on the results of the Scholarship examinations. Allen writes 'It is a pleasure to see success attending those who deserve it and our association with yourself and your most virtuous, talented and amiable children have led us to believe that few could deserve better the blessing of God. You have reason to be glad of the favour of Heaven and proud of your dear children. May they live to do you all the honor you deserve'.[29] Molly attained her Irish language teacher qualification and a teaching post in Blackpool girls national school at about this time.[30]

The album also contains a continuous series of studio photographs, certificates and newspaper reports of the scholarly achievements of the Bastible brothers from 1904 to 1914. 'Exhibitioners', 'Prize Winners', 'Medalists', 'Winners of Special Distinctions', and importantly 'University Scholarship Winners'. The awards bring monetary prizes (ranging from £15 to £20 pounds per annum) and scholarships without which Lizzy could not have provided a third-level medical education for her three sons, George, Michael and Christopher, a teacher education for her two daughters, Molly and Nora, and support for Jim in his ecclesiastical career.

Internment and War of Independence

The preceding account of family struggle and success is fragmentary. Family life was disrupted by the wars and politics of 1916–23.[31] A family story surfaces. Molly and her brothers, Chris, Michael and perhaps Jim, sit around the table in the back room at Eason's Hill. It is late evening. Their books are piled around and the atmosphere is quiet and studious. Examinations loom. The men smoke – George draws deeply on his pipe and there is a packet of cigarettes on the table, open. The ashtray is full. The sounds of a motor, loud banging, roaring and shouting, the sounds of splintering wood fill the street outside. The corridor booms with noise, more shouting and commands. The door bangs against the inside wall. Men, guns, bodies spill into the room and

29 Family album, Allen to Bastible, 14 July 1917. **30** The *Cork Examiner,* 9 Sept. 1925 provides a summary CV for Molly on her subsequent appointment to the Central Model Schools, Marlborough Street, Dublin. 'Having passed through a distinguished training course which served to enhance the early promise of her talent, she was appointed to Blackpool Girl's National School'. **31** See J. Borgonovo, *The dynamics of war and revolution: Cork city, 1916–1918* (Cork, 2013).

Lizzy is restrained by force. Molly sits alone in the room, smoking, reading her texts. After some interrogation, the Black and Tans leave. It is her *sang-froid* that persuades them. Yes, it is unusual for a woman to smoke she agrees, but it is also unusual for a woman to study medicine. No, she has no idea where her brothers are or where they might be. She is alone here with her mother.

This was 1920 – the year of Bloody Sunday, the burning of Cork city and the declaration of martial law in the south. Four to five thousand republicans were interned. Lizzy reads the account of the Labour Commission in the paper and later inserts the cutting into the album. The headline, 'Atmosphere of Terrorism' echoes the findings of the Commission. 'People are afraid that their homes might be burned. They fear that they might be arrested or even dragged from their beds and shot … prisoners alleged to have been fired upon and killed in an attempt to escape, have been shot in cold blood'.[32] The burning of central Cork on 11 December 1920 is deemed to have been 'an organized attempt to destroy the most valuable premises in the City' by the British. The death of the lord mayor of Cork, Terence MacSwiney, following his hunger strike, and the execution of Kevin Barry, can only have heightened Lizzy's concerns for the safety of her sons and daughters. Kevin Barry, a medical student, served in the same Volunteer Brigade as Brendan Barry, her nephew. An image of MacSwiney's death mask has a central place on one of the album pages.

Molly's service with Cumann na mBan continued until July 1921, after which the record is broken and I can find no official trace to pursue. Family stories that circulate since childhood refuse to dissipate. Molly is in prison. She can hardly breathe and her lungs are sore. Outside her mother and other women protest at the incarceration of their daughters, sisters, mothers, aunts and friends. The protest continues for a number of days and eventually the women are released. An obituary for her brother James mentions that 'Máire … was also jailed as a member of Cumann na mBan'.[33] When this is, where she is held and for how long, is currently not known. Cumann na mBan organized vigils outside Mountjoy and other prisons in protest against illegal arrests and imprisonment without trial.[34] Molly's subsequent ill-health was related to her time in prison, a life-long reminder of her time spent there.

What can be authenticated is a raid on 10 January 1921 by the British authorities on the Barry family home in Dublin. Lizzy's brother, James Barry and his son Brendan Barry, age nineteen, Ned Cahill and Jerry Golden are

32 Family album press cutting. No title, 31 Dec. 1920. **33** *The Cork Examiner,* no date, 1987. **34** McCarthy, *Cumann na mBan,* p. 227 estimates that '681 women served time as political prisoners during the Civil War'. The unconfirmed family story is that Molly was imprisoned in Kilmainham Gaol Dublin and/or Cork Prison.

arrested, charged, court martialed and sentenced. The charge was based on their possession of arms and ammunition 'not under effective military control' and in contravention of the Defence of the Realm Regulations. James was sentenced to nine months hard labour in Mountjoy Prison (Dublin) and Perth (Scotland). On 22 January 1921, Brendan was sentenced to five years penal servitude in the English prisons of Portland and then Dartmoor.[35]

The Barry house in Dublin was well known as a place of refuge for men 'on the run'.[36] James was President of the Richard Coleman Sinn Féin Club in Santry from 1916 and Brendan and brothers Brian and Patrick are active in the Dublin No. 1 Brigade of the Irish Volunteers.[37] Jerry Golden was Captain of 'I' company and Brendan Barry was Lieutenant.[38] The arms found at the family home belong to the Dublin Brigade of the IRA. The newspaper reports of the arrest and subsequent charges are once more placed into the family album.[39] July 1921 marks the date of the 'Truce' and the beginning of the negotiations that produced the Anglo-Irish Treaty in December 1921.[40] A provisional government oversaw the transition for a ten-month period and by December 1922 the Irish Free State was created ending British rule in the twenty-six counties. All republican prisoners were released under a 'General Amnesty' including some of the Barry siblings. Brendan Barry joined the National Army Free State forces aligned with the Irish nationalists who supported the Treaty.

35 A family newspaper photograph depicts Brendan Barry on a crowded deck with 137 handcuffed men, 'Irish prisoners' on board the HMS *Valiant*, a transport ship arriving at Plymouth from Portland. **36** Family album press cuttings, 'Mr James Higgins Barry', no title, no date; 'Obituary James H. Barry', *Irish Press*, 1946: reference is made to the Barry house as being 'at the disposal of the IRA', offering refuge to Dick McKee OC of the Dublin Brigade. **37** Personal communication, Jan. 2017, Brendan Barry, grandson of James H. Barry. **38** BMH WS 5022: Jerry Golden. **39** 'A County Dublin find, revolvers, ammunition, bayonets and dagger', headline, report on the Field General Court Martial in the Dublin Union, family album press cutting, no title, no date. **40** Mary McAuliffe, in her address on *Cumann na mBan*, Dublin, 2 April 2014, documents the outcome of a vote on the Treaty. 419 members vote against the Treaty with 63 in favour at the Cumann na mBan convention on 5 February 1922. This prompts a split in the organization and the exit of more 'moderate' members. McCarthy, *Cumann na mBan*, provides an account of the dynamics that drove the split, the formation of Cumann na Saoirse and the divisive and often violent consequences of the Civil War for Cumann na mBan members (McCarthy, *Cumann na mBan*, pp 178–228). Ann Mathews, *Renegades: Irish republican women, 1900–1922* (Cork, 2010), p. 323 argues that the split, the 90 per cent reduction in the number of branches countrywide and the alignment of remaining Cumann na mBan members with the anti-Treaty forces 'lay the seeds of the demise of women in republican politics in Ireland'. She notes that Cork district council were predominantly pro-Treaty (Mathews, *Renegades*, p. 323). See also Borgonovo, *The dynamics of war and revolution: Cork city, 1916–1918*, pp 139–53 for a focus on Cork Cumann na mBan and their contribution to the independence movement.

Internment and Civil War (June 1922–May 1923)

Another round of arrests and internments is documented in the album. The headline of the front page of the *Glasgow Citizen* reads 'Mystery of a Glasgow doctor's arrest'.[41] George and Chris leave Ireland for Glasgow at some point between 1921 and 1922. Perhaps the raid of the Black and Tans or the Auxiliaries on the family home was not the only one? On 14 September 1922, while home on a family visit, Chris is arrested 'on suspicion'. He is held at first in Wellington Barracks in Dublin. George Gavan-Duffy brought the matter to the attention of the Dáil. He is quoted in the *Daily Mail and Record,* 'The Free State government in its exercise of its discretion and without legal authority, had arrested people without charge, without any intention of trial and with the intention of keeping them in prison indefinitely'.[42] In response, Minister Kevin O'Higgins spoke of 'the difficulties of the government standing amidst the ruins of one Administration with the foundations of another still unfinished'.[43] Prisoners could be released on Army Intelligence approval, following agreement to sign a 'statement of good faith as to future conduct'. In his verbatim account of his arrest to the *Daily Record and Mail* Chris recalls: 'They asked me to sign a declaration to the effect that I would not take up arms against the government, nor aid or abet anyone taking up arms nor interfere with private property. I refused to sign this document which I told them was an insult to my self-respect, as it really amounted to bargaining with them for my release'.[44] Chris describes the circumstances of his arrest. 'On the afternoon of Friday September 1, I was at my uncle's house in Ellenfield, Drumcondra, talking to my aunt and cousins, when suddenly the door bursts open and about 30 armed men poured into the room. When we had put up our hands at their command, the spokesman said they wanted Bastible … one of the men shoved his pistol against my stomach and I was hustled downstairs into an open motor lorry …next day I was handed over to the military authorities and conveyed in a motor lorry to Wellington Barracks where I was put into 'the cage' with about 120 more prisoners'. In protest, Chris refuses food and decides to 'hunger strike'. On 7 September, he was transferred to the internment camp at Gormonston in Meath. A letter from Gormonston Camp to Lizzy is folded into the album. The delicate script in black ink flows across the page, front and back, interrupted by the censor's purple crayon. The rest of the pages are missing.

41 *Glasgow Citizen,* 14 Sept. 1922. **42** *Daily Record and Mail,* 15 Sept. 1922. **43** Ibid. **44** *Daily Record and Mail,* 7 Oct. 1922.

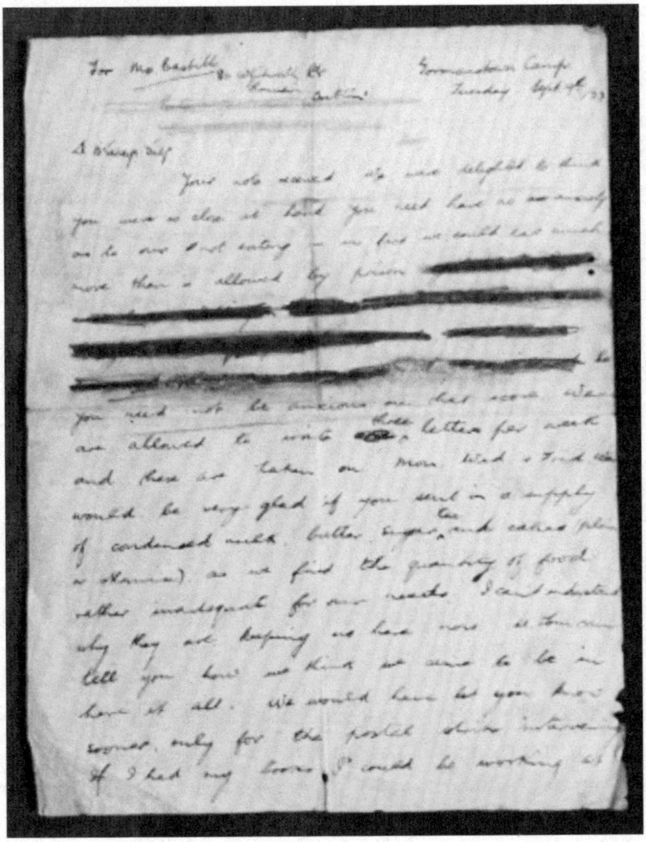

Letter to Elizabeth Bastible, 19 Sept. 1922.

Gormonston Camp,
Tuesday 19 Sept. 1922

For Mrs Bastible, 80 Whitworth Rd Glasnevin Dublin

A mháthair dílis.

Your note received. We were delighted to think you were so close at hand. You need have no anxiety as to our not eating – in fact we could eat much more than is allowed by prison. [4 censored lines follow].

… so you need not be anxious on that score. We are allowed to write three letters per week and these are taken on Mon. Wed. and Fri. We would be very glad if you sent in a supply of condensed milk, butter, sugar, tea and cakes (plain or otherwise) as we find the quantity of food rather inadequate for our needs. I can't understand why they are keeping us here now. U Tom can tell you how we think we came to be in here at all. We would have let you know sooner, only for the postal strike intervening. If I had my books I could be working at them here from time to time. Criostóir is camp MO here. I believe Seán Ua Muirthile is OC of all this area. We have not seen him however. This camp is very clearly [6 censored lines follow] … I suppose we have you to thank for the things we got to-day – cigarettes, fruit, shirts, etc. If so, thanks very much. I left the basket with Eunan, and he sent it on to Wellington along with some things we wanted. I have it here now. I asked him in a note from Wellington to send on the things in my leather bag but he must not have got that note. I had perforce to take the basket then. There are lots of country chaps here who can't get in touch with their people. Why don't Cumann na mBan do something for them? By the way we are very short of reading material. In fact we are lucky if we can borrow a storybook now and again.

PS Perhaps you could forward the other letter addressed to James? M (In pencil and crossed out)

The author of the letter was Michael, also interned in Gormonston. On learning of their internment, Lizzy makes the journey from Dublin to bring food to her sons and to hear news of them. She writes a note that they receive. Her anxiety about not eating, and the possibilities of either of her sons resuming a 'hunger strike', a concern. Both men provided medical assistance to wounded and ill comrades in the camp. Chris was 'liberated' at the end of the month. 'At last on Friday September 29, I was liberated. I was hustled out of captivity as quickly as I was hustled into it. To this day I have no idea why they arrested me. I can only imagine that my coming to Dublin on the eve of the Dáil meeting may have had something to do with it. All I was ever told was that I was arrested on suspicion'.[45] The newspaper account ends with 'Dr Bastible declared that he had never made any secret of his republican sympathies'. Michael escapes by his own devices, smuggling himself into a milk delivery cart with some of his co-internees. The brothers return to Parkhead in Glasgow to resume their medical work. The necessity of residing in Scotland may be a consequence of their alignment with anti-Treaty republicanism. Opportunities for employment for republican professionals are few in the new Irish Free State. Scotland and England are home for at least another decade.[46]

45 Ibid. **46** Lizzy did not own a home of her own; she lived in the houses of her peripatetic family. In the late 1920s or early 1930s, three of the brothers return to Ireland and take up positions as Medical

Back row, left to right, Lizzy Barry Bastible, not known, George Bastible; middle row, Molly Bastible, Michael Bastible, James Bastible, Nora Bastible, Chris Bastible; front row, not known, not known.

Lizzy's album

In the ninety pages of Lizzy's album there are some remarkable omissions. Newspaper reports of the Irish Civil War are scant. This may have been because of the impossibility of an impartial recording or the dangers associated with any partisan documenting of the war. It may also have coincided with a visit to Scotland to be with her sons where she has limited access to the Cork and Dublin papers. As well as omissions, the album contains mysteries; one page is composed of paper currency from Ballykinlar Internment Camp 1921. 'Gaedhil fé ghlas' is stamped on each denomination. Who was interned there and for how long? Two concert tickets are pasted side by side on another page. Who sat in Row G, seats 34 and 25 to listen to the tenor John McCormack on 23 February 1927?

And what of Molly? The album records Molly's move to Dublin in 1927 to work in Scoil Mhuire, the all-Irish speaking Model School at Marlborough Street. Molly and Nora Ashe are the assistant and principal teachers. They pose with their pupils for a press photograph. An Ghaeilge Abú! is written in large

Officers of Health. The fourth secures an ecclesiastical posting in Wexford after time spent in the UK. Lizzy's daughters worked in education until retirement.

script on an blackboard in the foreground.[47] Nora was a sister of Thomas Ashe, a member of the Gaelic League and Irish Volunteer who died while on hunger strike in 1917. The opening of the school is regarded as 'the foundation stone of Irish culture' and in his remarks Richard Mulcahy TD promises 'every assistance to the teachers' and that 'this school would be a star of hope for the future of the language'. The album contains many cuttings on the opening of the school, one of which announces it as 'the most important event in a century' in 'gaelicizing Dublin'. The children are provided with a separate playground to prevent their association with English-speaking children.

Teaching Irish was Molly's passion and life-long profession. Her move to Dublin was also recorded in theatre circles. Having continued to perform with *Fuiréann* Leirithe Craobh na Paróiste Thuaidh for Conradh na Gaeilge from early childhood, her membership of Na hAisteoirí and association with Piaras Béaslaí's company of players is noted. An *Irish Times* reviewer writes:

> Last night the Gaelic Players opened their season at the Abbey Theatre Dublin. An ambitious programme is said to have been arranged for this their third year. Last night's performance had two especially interesting features – the production of a new play by Mr Patrick Brophy, one of the most popular of the players and the first appearance in Dublin of Miss Mary Bastable, a player who has already won a considerable name in Cork, and whose acting was watched with curiosity and delight. It is safe to say that Miss Bastable is a discovery for the Players – her acting is charming and finished and she gives the Gaelic drama the touch which has lent distinction to the work of the Abbey Theatre in English …[48]

The numerous newspaper cuttings and Abbey programme inserts in the album follow Molly's career on stage in Cork and Dublin until 1929.

Piaras Béaslaí (1881–1965) was manager and producer of *Na hAisteoirí Company/An Chomhar Drámaíochta* and a close associate of Molly's. He established the company in Dublin in 1912 to promote theatre performances in Irish. *Na hAisteoirí Company/An Chomhar Drámaíochta* comprise of various branches of Conradh na Gaeilge/the Gaelic League.[49] Béaslaí, an Irish Volunteer, was active in 1916, imprisoned and later became a member of Dáil

47 *Irish Independent*, 13 Jan. 1927. 48 *Irish Times*, 6 Oct. 1925. 49 For an in-depth account of the evolution and contribution of Irish language theatre, see P. Ó Siadhail, *Stair dhrámaíocht na Gaeilge, 1900–1970* (Conamara, 1993), pp 19–94. On the contribution of Na hAisteoirí and An Chomhar Drámaíochta to the production of original plays in Irish, laying the foundation for Irish language theatre such as Taidhbhearc na Gaillimhe, see M. Nic Shuibhlaigh and E. Kenny, *The splendid years* (Dublin, 1955), p. 145.

Eireann. Another founder associate was Leon Ó Broin. Ó Broin aligned himself with the Free State, was an active combatant in the Civil War and later became Minister for Posts and Telegraphs. The Christmas 1928 illustrated poster for *An Chomhar Drámaíochta* features founder-members, authors and actors, Máire Béaslaí, Pieras Béaslaí, Leon Ó Broin, Gearoid Ó Lochlainn, Padraig Ó Bróithe, Pólla Fearghail, Máire Ní Shíocháin, Máire Ní Oisin, Tadhg Mac Firbisigh and Muiris Ó Catháin.[50] Molly's pendant picture is prominent, positioned at the top among the core group of men.

The group shared a belief that Irish-language theatre was not a marginal activity of the Gaelic League but an art form in its own right. A catalogue of thirteen plays in which Molly performs in Dublin from 1925 to 1928 is available on-line.[51] These lists compliment the press cuttings in Lizzy's album. But that accounting is for another time, apart from one play. On 7 November 1927, the company perform Leon Ó Broin's play *An mhallacht* (The curse). Molly is Olenca. The setting as first performed is Warsaw and the plot deals with a 1925 Polish revolt. Ó Broin changes the setting to Ireland, marking one of the earliest performances on stage of kin by kin killing, during the Irish Civil War.[52] The story is told from a pro-Treaty perspective, due perhaps to the political allegiances of the author and other company members. Nonetheless performing and witnessing the costs and consequences of the struggle for independence on stage held a diversity of audiences together for a short period of time. This may have been as brief as the two hours of a performance, but perhaps sufficient for mutual recognition of the importance of solidarities for the future of the country.

Molly's association with *An Chomhar Drámaíochta* in the 1920s can be interpreted in a number of ways. It may have been that she aligns herself with the version of independence as promoted by the Irish Free State and her Barry relatives. This would place her at odds with her brothers' more republican sympathies. Her life-long identification with the Irish language movement, her passion for theatre and the political education and professional expectations for women fostered by the Gaelic League, I imagine must have been keenly felt in navigating a path between a life of her own and the strong political ideologies that divide family, community and society.[53] Continuing with her career as a teacher and Gaelic League supporter, Molly leaves her life of performance and theatre on her marriage to Liam Byrne in June 1929.[54] The album includes a

50 Béaslaí papers, MS 33,953(7), NLI. **51** www.irishplayography.com, Máire Bastabal, accessed 3 October 2016. **52** P. O'Leary, *Gaelic prose in the Irish Free State, 1922–1939* (Dublin, 2004), p. 616, n.323. **53** See Pašeta, *Irish nationalist women, 1900–1918*, pp 17–32, for analysis of the influence of the Gaelic League on women's political education and their subsequent involvement in advanced nationalist politics. **54** The family story is that she was advised to withdraw from her theatrical career on medical advice due to further damage to her health.

list of the wedding guests who include 'Cú Uladh' (Peadar MacFhionnlaoich, president of the Gaelic League). Only Irish is spoken in her home.

Slowly the realization begins to form. I too have spent a life in education and activism. Identity, gender and equality contour my research, writing and politics. I have not left the island that became a Republic. The lives of Lizzy and her family are vividly, visibly and purposefully documented in the family album. They were not secret keepers but storytellers whose histories were muffled by subsequent generations and by the new state. Until now.

Acknowledgments

Though authored by Anne Byrne, the work is a product of the collaboration between Anne Byrne and Colm Byrne, sister and brother. We wish to thank the following: Caoimh Ó Broin, Nuala Ó Broin, Brendan Barry, Paul Gosling, Mary Clancy, Mary McAuliffe, Tony Varley, Sinéad McCoole, Dáibhí Ó Cróinín, Aoife Torpey, Cian Marnell, Mark McCarthy, Niall Murray.

The Sheehy Skeffington legacy and its influence on me today

MICHELINE SHEEHY SKEFFINGTON

> History does not begin at 1916 as some to-day would have it: there were many fights before it. Early years count a lot, and, as one gets older, they loom larger. Mine were spent in an old mill in Loughmore, Co. Tipperary … Ours was a rebel household – father had been out in '67 … We played Boycott and Evictions as children now play war games. We sang and recited rebel ballads, topical ones such as … the 'Land League Upheld' or Fanny Parnell's 'Hold the Harvest'.[1]

From early in my childhood I was aware that my grandparents were well-known and in some ways exceptional. I learned that I had inherited my left-handedness from my grandmother and that she was proud of having it free to smash more windows when the police grabbed her right arm before she was arrested for suffragette activities. As a child this seemed normal to me, but later stories of my grandparents became somewhat intimidating as I realized quite how remarkable they were as people. How could I ever live up to that. In recent years, however, I have sought to 'reclaim' knowledge of my grandparents and to try to understand their motivations and how they came to stand out as different from most of their contemporaries. This has been helped by the 2016 commemorations, through which I learned more information about my grandmother's family. So in this chapter I find, as my grandmother Hanna suggests in the quote above, that I must dig deeper into my grandparents' backgrounds to understand what influenced them to become who they were and to stand for what they did.

The Sheehy Skeffington's

Hanna Sheehy Skeffington grew up in a very politically active family. Born in Kanturk, Co. Cork, in 1877, her parents (David Sheehy and Bessie McCoy) soon moved to Loughmore, Co. Tipperary, where they lived in the millhouse and where her five siblings were born. As children, they had already acquired an acute

1 Hanna Sheehy Skeffington, 'Looking backwards', *Distributive Worker,* December 1941, cited in Margaret Ward (ed.), *Hanna Sheehy Skeffington, suffragette and Sinn Féiner: her memoirs and political writings* (Dublin, 2017), p. 381.

The eight-year-old Hanna Sheehy's stitch-work piece. It had been framed and was in the Sheehy Skeffington household and is now in the National Museum of Ireland. Photo by kind permission of the National Museum of Ireland.

sense of injustice from both their parents' families and, when playing at 'Evictions', none ever wanted to play the bailiffs! So it is little surprise that a framed stitch-work piece by the eight-year-old Hanna was among the family memorabilia. Entitled 'My Land League Hut' (now in the National Museum), it shows a three-storey large building with capacity enough to house many evicted families.

Hanna's father, David Sheehy, and her uncle Fr Eugene Sheehy had been to jail not once but six times each for Fenian activities. Born in Broadford, Co. Limerick in the early 1840s, they were acutely aware of rural poverty and landlord greed. Fr Eugene stood out among the clergy in opposing evictions, which earned him the names 'rebel priest' and 'Land League priest'. Hanna's aunt Kate Barry (née McCoy, Bessie's sister) was also strong in the Ladies' Land League. It was she who brought young Hanna, aged four, to see her uncle in Kilmainham Gaol. Here is Hanna's recollection:

> My earliest memory politically is of the 'Suspects' in Kilmainham, where I visited my uncle, Father Eugene Sheehy, gate-crashing into the place when the Ladies' Land League contingent came into the big hall to serve the mid-day dinners.[2]

2 *Distributive Worker,* December 1941, cited in Ward (ed.), *Hanna Sheehy Skeffington: suffragette and Sinn Féiner*, p. 381.

The McCoy family is from Loughill near Ballyhahill, Co. Limerick, where McCoys still live in the family home. I learned from them that Bessie and Kate had two brothers, Pat and Dan, who were rounded up and sent to Mountjoy as Fenians in the early 1860s and that Bessie, as a teenager, defied the priest and led the rosary in Ballyhahill church for their safeguard. Such activities as those of her parents, uncles and aunts on both sides must have been key to the formation of my grandmother's ideas. She grew up with a strong sense of justice and of tenant rights and the need for Irish independence – where women would play an equal role.

After her father became MP for the Irish Party, the family moved in 1887 to Dublin and Hanna, the eldest daughter, was the first to be enrolled in the Dominican school in Eccles Street. Her mother was keen that her daughters all got the same education as her sons – including later at university, which was then only recently available to women. After entering university in 1896, Hanna was 'amazed and disgusted' to discover that as a woman she hadn't even got the vote, that fundamental political power of the individual. She soon joined the Irish Women's Suffrage & Local Government Association, as did her three sisters and one of her two brothers, Richard.[3] Hanna's main political activity during the following ten years or so was to fight for women's right to vote. As women attended lectures separately from the men, they all would meet in the National Library – where they studied – and at any social gathering available, including at the homes of the Sheehy family, later made famous in his writings of a boisterous student colleague of theirs, James Joyce. Hanna soon was to meet and find much in common with fellow student Francis Skeffington.

My grandfather, Francis (or Frank), was every bit a troublemaker, a 'militant pacifist', a nationalist and himself a jailbird. However, no records have been found of any jailings of his relatives in the Skeffington or Magorian families (from Downpatrick and Ballykinlar respectively). He did get a good foundation in Irish nationalism, history and culture, albeit an unconventional one, for he had a very different upbringing to Hanna's. An only child, born in Bailieborough, Co. Cavan, in 1878, his schools' inspector father, Joseph Bartholomew Skeffington ('JB'), chose to educate him entirely at home in Downpatrick, where they had moved soon after his birth.[4] Frank said that JB was 'the best teacher I ever had', but must have missed the comradeship of fellow pupils, for when his only child, Owen (my father), was not yet four, Frank brought him to a small local Quaker school[5] for such companionship,

3 Margaret Ward, *Hanna Sheehy Skeffington: a life* (Cork, 1997). Richard Sheehy was a lawyer and taught Law in University College Galway until his death from TB in 1923. 4 Leah Levenson, *With wooden sword: a portrait of Francis Sheehy Skeffington, militant pacifist* (Dublin, 1983).

saying, 'If I see any sign of this child learning anything, I shall take him away at once'.[6]

Frank was not short of access to books and reading material and, by his own account, first became interested in feminism aged eleven when reading an article by W.T. Stead on Gladstone (Stead had stated that Gladstone had 'done nothing for women'). He learned stories of the Land League and of evictions from his father and soon developed a keen awareness of the injustices of the time, as well as the need for independence from Britain. Such ideas were to lead him to see Michael Davitt as his principal hero and whose biography he wrote within eighteen months of Davitt's untimely death.[7] JB was a very precise and dogmatic man and must have been quite domineering towards his only son, though he was very fond of him. But that son inherited his tough argumentativeness and, when someone calling themselves 'Shamrock' took him on in a local paper on the subject of the need for the Irish language, JB never suspected that the contributor was none other than his own son![8] Frank's free thinking and great integrity stem from those early days.

It may have been with a sense of relief that the young Frank left Downpatrick for Dublin to study in the then Royal University. He returned regularly especially to visit his mother and her family – he had several Magorian cousins – but took to university life with gusto. He stood out in his unconventional dress, for he always wore a baggy tweed jacket and plus fours – to get about more easily on a bicycle, but also because he abhorred conventionality. He later turned down a small university job as he would have had to have dressed more formally. By then he was not only an ardent feminist, convinced nationalist, militant pacifist and a socialist, but also a vegetarian, teetotaler and anti-vivisectionist. His isolated upbringing may have lead to an *insouciance* regarding what people thought of him and when, inevitably, he was taunted with the label 'crank', he used to retort 'a crank is a small instrument that causes revolutions'.[9]

W.T. Stead was a strong influence on Frank and, when in 1899 the Russian Czar called for an international court of arbitration and for universal peace, Stead had encouraged readers to supportive action. Skeffington set up a table in the hallway of Newman House on St Stephen's Green (where lectures were held in those days) and harangued all who came by to sign a petition.[10] He had

5 Rathgar Kindergarten and Training College. 6 Andrée Sheehy Skeffington, *Skeff: a biography of Owen Sheehy Skeffington* (Dublin, 1991). 7 Francis Sheehy-Skeffington, *Michael Davitt: revolutionary, agitator and labour leader* (London, 1908; republished as 'The Fitzroy Edition', London, 1967). 8 Eugene Sheehy, *May it please the court* (Dublin, 1951). The teenage Frank said Esperanto was far more useful than Irish, in his view a dying language. 9 Owen Sheehy Skeffington, 'Francis Sheehy-Skeffington' in O. Dudley Edwards and F. Pyle (eds), *1916: the Easter Rising* (London, 1968). 10 Levenson, *With wooden sword*, p. 27.

some success, but James Joyce, as usual aloof to politics and activism, refused.[11] Hanna, receiving lectures with her female colleagues in St Mary's University College, Merrion Square, graduated with a BA in languages and later an MA; Frank also obtained a BA and MA in languages and was then appointed first lay Registrar to the university. The university turned a blind eye to his eccentric dress code, but when he continued to campaign for equal rights for female students, he was asked to stop and, unwilling do that, he promptly resigned. This demonstrated his characteristic fixity of purpose, despite potential hardship to himself; financial in this case. Despite his annoying obsessions, he was the life and soul of a party and a good foil to Hanna's more steady and thoughtful demeanor. In 1903, the couple married and they took the unprecedented step of each taking each other's name, thus becoming the Sheehy Skeffingtons. The Sheehys took this in their stride, but the Skeffingtons were reputedly very put out by this highly unusual step – even today – taken by the groom. But it was a measure of how strong the couple's commitment was to having women play an equal role in shaping twentieth-century Ireland.

The Ireland of the new century was filled with a renewed enthusiasm for Irish culture, as well as nationalism. Frank is said to have met his friend Thomas MacDonagh while they were both teachers in St Kieran's College, Kilkenny, in 1901 and they were firm friends until their deaths in 1916. MacDonagh was also a strong believer in women's equality. Both Frank and Hanna, keen to make a difference, joined the Young Ireland Branch of the United Irish League on its foundation in 1904. The women had to storm the League's offices to ensure they were admitted and it was a very vibrant movement that included not just Hanna and Frank, but two of her sisters, her brothers and her three future brothers-in-law. Both her parents came to the presidential speech of their daughter Mary's fiancé, Tom Kettle.[12]

My grandparents, like their early twentieth-century contemporaries, espoused a range of ideas. They were strong nationalists and feminists, while others such as members of Inghinigh na hÉireann and Constance Marckievicz sought to gain independence first and believed that women would then achieve equality in the new state. Knowing what happened to women in the emerging Free State, we see how right Hanna was to retain her nationalist spirit, but not drop the suffrage cause. In 1908, impatient with the lack of progress on the women's vote, Hanna founded the Irish Women's Franchise League with Margaret Cousins. Its members were young, energetic women impatient to achieve equal power to that of their male colleagues. Inspired by the British

11 The episode, with Frank as McCann, is described in both James Joyce's *Stephen Hero* and *Portrait of the artist as a young man.* 12 Ward, *Hanna Sheehy Skeffington: a life.* For a discussion of Tom Kettle see Chapter 4 in this volume Niamh Reilly, 'The many sides of Tom Kettle'.

Francis and Hanna Sheehy Skeffington. My mother, Andrée, told me it was their wedding photograph, taken in a studio after the event. Women often posed for photos in graduation gowns – a feminist statement of independence. Frank, never wearing anything more formal than his baggy tweed suit, may have worn his graduation outfit in solidarity with Hanna. Photo by kind permission of the National Museum of Ireland.

The Irish Women's Franchise League banner, with English on one side and Irish on the other. Made by the Dun Emer Guild and using the Irish suffrage colours of green and orange. Photo courtesy of the National Museum of Ireland.

suffrage movement, they were keen to show difference – green and orange were the colours, not the (different) green and purple of the WSPU. A large green and orange banner had the IWFL name embroidered by the Dun Emer Guild in Irish on one side and English on the other. [13] It was carefully stored at home and I remember it as a child, as well as a large foldable platform with 'Votes for Women' on a brass plate that they brought out to address crowds wherever they could – Phoenix Park was a favourite venue.[14]

Hanna's father was an Irish Party MP, but never showed signs of supporting her or the suffrage movement. Too many of them were afraid that adding the perceived complication of women's suffrage would jeopardize the passing of the Home Rule Bill.[15] Her uncle Eugene was much more supportive, greeting her on her emergence from prison, after her first hunger strike. This was in 1912 when the IWFL, tired of not making progress despite drawing crowds at public meetings, decided to break windows in key public buildings to get noticed and arrested.[16] It was her uncle Eugene who gave her the desk I now have, to encourage her to study as a young girl.

13 Hanna Sheehy Skeffington 'The Countess: some memories', *Irish Press,* 4 Feb. 1936, cited in Ward, *Hanna Sheehy Skeffington,* p. 304. **14** Both banner and platform (one of three) are now housed in the National Museum of Ireland, Collins Barracks, Dublin. **15** Ward, *Hanna Sheehy Skeffington: a life,*, pp 74–6. **16** Ibid., p. 83 et seq.

Hanna on her release from Mountjoy Jail after her hunger strike, August 1912; Frank is to her left and her Uncle Eugene (in top hat) to her right. Photo kindly supplied by the National Library of Ireland.

Frank's sole earnings were now what he could get as a journalist. A keen believer in dialogue and the spreading of ideas, he was frustrated in not finding outlets for his articles, especially about suffrage activities. So he and James Cousins founded the suffrage newspaper *The Irish Citizen* in May 1912. Its name was a statement of Irish independence (for they were then still subjects of the crown) and it covered suffrage events in detail, especially key actions such as arrests and trials as well as advertising meetings. I myself have learned the vagaries of press coverage during my own activism, so this specifically focused paper must have been a real boon. The banner heading of the paper was – to my mind – pure Frank: 'For Men and Women Equally the Rights of Citizenship. From Men and Women Equally the Duties of Citizenship'. Frank believed that everyone had a duty to do right by their fellow citizens; thus the vote was but one way of contributing to an equal society. The IWFL grew in numbers and arrests were made time and again. Hanna was arrested again in 1913, before she could make a disturbance during a visit to Ireland by the leader of the Tory Party, Bonar Law; she swore she would 'deserve' her next imprisonment. She was released in poor health after five days' hunger strike. When not in prison herself, she led rallies outside Mountjoy Prison in support of imprisoned suffragettes. Such was the commotion that the authorities moved several of them to Tullamore to divert attention away from the jailbirds. But then in 1914, the First World War broke out and Frank, the pacifist, went into action. The *Citizen* put out a poster reading 'VOTES FOR WOMEN NOW! DAMN YOUR WAR!'

He made forty speeches around Dublin, campaigning against British recruitment in Ireland until he was arrested and sentenced to six months hard labour. Defending himself in court (he could not afford lawyers and saw it as a further opportunity to make his views public), he vowed to be out of prison long before that 'dead or alive' and promptly went on hunger strike, soon to be followed by a thirst strike, whereupon he was released. Thus the militant pacifist. He was anything but passive and was not afraid to put his own life in danger; he was just not prepared to kill for his objectives. This was eloquently explained in his Open Letter to his old friend Thomas MacDonagh, where, fervently nationalist as Frank was, he explained that he could not condone a group of people who held the killing of their fellow men as central to their objectives.[17] This view marked him out as highly unpopular with the British forces and he was recognized and arrested in Rathmines on Easter Tuesday while walking home from the city centre. None of the subsequent events that lead to his murder the following morning, along with two other journalists, Thomas Dickson and Patrick McIntyre, was either sanctioned or legal. Those events are amply described elsewhere (e.g., Levenson, *With wooden sword*, Ward, *Hanna Sheehy Skeffington*, 1997). But what his widow did afterwards is often forgotten. She embarked on a journey with her seven-year-old son Owen that was to greatly enhance the potential for an independent Irish state.

Hanna had demanded the full truth about the circumstances of Frank's murder, even travelling to see Prime Minister Asquith in London and from whom she refused £10,000 'hush money'.[18] The Simon Inquiry into the murder was wholly unsatisfactory so she vowed to 'tell the truth' herself about what had happened to Frank. She gave the slip to the British authorities and travelled in December 1916 to New York from Glasgow with Owen, using false passports under the names of Mrs Mary and Master Eugene Gribben. Soon after her arrival in the US, on 6 January 1917, she filled Carnegie Hall. Largely hosted by Friends of Irish Freedom, she subsequently toured twenty-one US states over

17 Reprinted in *Irish Times*, 21 March 2016: http://www.irishtimes.com/opinion/francis-sheehy-skeffington-open-letter-to-thomas-macdonagh–1.2580899 accessed 25 May 2017. **18** About €750,000 today.

eighteen months, filling even bigger venues. She was a polished orator, while keeping a wry sense of humour. Her entire speech was regularly printed on the front pages of broadsheets in host cities across the US. John Devoy, leader of Friends of Irish Freedom, said she had 'done more real good to the cause of Ireland ... than all the Irish orators and writers ...[over] the past twenty-five years'.[19] She was the only Irish representative of the time to meet with President Wilson, presenting him with a petition from Cumann na mBan and asking that Ireland be considered among small nations during peace negotiations.

Returning to Dublin in July 1918, she welcomed women finally getting the vote. She joined Sinn Féin, was appointed to the Executive and continued to be active in political struggles for independence, peace and justice. But when she was allocated a North Antrim seat to contest at the next election, she turned it down in disgust as unwinnable (she had no connection with that constituency). She was a candidate with a number of other women as Women Independents in the 1943 general election, but this 'bold enough challenge to masculine monopoly' did not win seats, partly as they had no party machine to support them.[20] Hanna had been elected to Dublin Corporation and then to Dublin County Council, chairing commitees aiming to change local government policies on many issues. She was also active in the Irish White Cross, the Spanish Aid Society (which she chaired) and she and her feminist colleagues were prominent in fighting the wording of de Valera's 1937 Constitution, while she continued to earn a precarious livelihood as a teacher in various technical colleges and as a journalist.[21]

Owen and Andrée Sheehy Skeffington

Hanna had only one child, Owen, my father. Having survived the turbulent times of his childhood, Owen never lost sight of what his mother strove for and achieved in her life, nor of what his father did and might have done in his own life, had he been allowed to live on to old age. He admired their integrity and indefatigable struggles for justice. Their lives were to guide him in his own battles for justice. As a student, he developed and encouraged freedom of speech and stimulating discussions – something his father had championed. He joined the Labour Party and later set up the Pearse Street Council of Action which fought against profiteering and to alleviate poverty in Dublin's slums – both my parents were involved in this. He won an independent seat in the Seanad from Trinity College Dublin where he was a lecturer and used his independent

19 Ward, *Hanna Sheehy Skeffington, a life,* p. 212. **20** Hanna Sheehy Skeffington, 'Women in politics', *The Bell,* 7 November 1943, cited in Ward, *Hanna Sheehy Skeffingotn,* p. 385. **21** M. Ward, *Hanna Sheehy Skeffington: a life* (Cork, 1997).

position to challenge hypocrisy and oppose dogma and oppression in many ways. He was not afraid to take on the Catholic clergy where he saw their pretense and abuse of power. He championed the battle to stop corporal punishment in schools, though failed to get Seanad support for a bill ostensibly because the schools were largely Catholic and managed by priests, whom no one dared oppose in the 1940s and 50s. Even through the 1960s he was a lone voice speaking the truth in any issues such as those dominated by the Church.

Many people sought my father's advice, support and guidance and as a child, I remember him always on the phone, patiently listening and talking through issues with countless people. He befriended and supported many 'misfits' and gave courage to the less fortunate, among them Peter Tyrrell, whom he encouraged to write his memoir of life in the Letterfrack Reformatory. This was recently published from the typescript that was with our family papers in the National Library of Ireland. Despite always battling for justice, my father was always upbeat, very witty and loved nothing better than family life or long discussions with friends over endless cups of tea during my parents' 'Friday nights' at home to all and sundry.[22] He chose to marry a Frenchwoman, Andrée, who was also strong and independent, herself from a left-wing free-thinking family. Seeing the difficulties of struggling Dublin families during her Council of Action days, she readily agreed to co-found the radical Irish Housewives Association with Hilda Tweedy. It fought governmental policy to bring down basic food prices and was the first consumer protection organization in Ireland. It was Andrée who spearheaded their campaign research and held to the mantra 'educate, investigate, agitate'.[23] She spoke out where she saw injustice and never let authorities get the better of her. She was also grateful to her potentially formidable mother-in-law who was supportive of the IHA and was a true friend in times of difficulty. She had a strong sense of history and it was largely she who ensured that family papers and memorabilia went to the National Library and to the National Museum. She was centrally involved in setting up a suffrage exhibition in 1975 that included many of those family possessions.[24] Her interest and knowledge of my grandparents' activism supported three biographies[25] and was in turn passed on to me as we sorted through family photos and papers. She then wrote an incisive and detailed biography of my father.[26]

22 A. Sheehy Skeffington, *Skeff.* **23** Rosemary Cullen Owens, 'Remembering Hilda and Andrée and their work' in Alan Hayes (ed.), *Hilda Tweedy and the Irish Housewives Association: links in the chain…* (Dublin, 2011). **24** Ibid. Working with Rosemary Cullen Owens, Andrée put the exhibition together and produced an accompanying booklet: Andrée Sheehy Skeffington and Rosemary Cullen-Owens (eds), *Votes for women. Irish women's struggle for the vote* (Dublin, 1975). **25** Levenson, *With wooden sword;* Leah Levenson and J.H. Natterstad, *Hanna Sheehy-Skeffington: Irish feminist* (Syracuse, 1986); Ward, *Hanna Sheehy Skeffington: a life.* **26** A. Sheehy Skeffington, *Skeff.*

Micheline Sheehy Skeffington

My life is therefore interwoven with this thread of history and a strong family sense of justice and support for the less fortunate. My parents taught me and my brothers their set of values regarding justice; about the need to speak out or act no matter how small the action might be. My father used to quote Herbert Spencer saying 'No matter how infinitesimal it is the thing you can do, it is infinitely important that you should do it'. This sustained him in his many battles that were at best won slowly and with great difficulty. My parents, like my grandparents, sought to raise us free of the influence of the Catholic Church and with no sense that girls were any less able than boys. We all went to a very egalitarian Montessori-style (Froebel) kindergarten Quaker school.[27] So at school and at home we never questioned the fact that women were equal and should have equal expectations in their careers and lives to men. So I found it a shock, like Hanna, when I had to deal with inequality in adult life.

Though I'm proud to come from a long line of troublemakers and jailbirds, I never knew any of them. Yet I feel a deep connection especially with my grandmother Hanna as a determined, strongly independent woman who never wavered from her principles and who, from early childhood, had a strong sense of politics and a need to right injustice. The family sense of duty, encapsulated in the banner heading of the *Irish Citizen*, carries on. I learned to speak out when I saw injustice and regularly fought for women's equality on committees and at conferences where too often I saw men taking the lead and women's views and research being overlooked. I also feel bound by the sense of integrity I inherited – particually from my grandfather – and in fighting injustice and discimination I am determined to always recognize the humanity of those I oppose. So, when the opportunity arose for me to strike a blow for women's equality, I knew I had my grandparents' and parents' support. In fact I felt I owed it to them to take action. In 2009, when I had applied four times for promotion to Senior Lecturer in my university, NUI Galway, and was told for the second time that I was deemed suitable, but not ranked high enough to be promoted, I learned that of the seventeen successful Senior Lecturer candidates that year, only one was a woman. I knew that this was not for want of suitable female candidates. So I felt I had no choice but to challenge it, even though at the time I felt I had very little chance of success.

It is fear that prevents most of us from speaking out or acting; fear of getting it wrong, of being criticized, or simply being noticed in public. In some cases, there is the very real fear of retribution in the workplace. But the case I

27 Rathgar Junior School, the successor to the Rathgar Kindergarten and Training College, which Owen had attended.

took was not public and I was motivated, win or lose, to expose the injustice, using my grandmother's reputation as leverage for publicity. As the case and its repercussions continue to this day, I have seen parallels, albeit of lesser impact, with Hanna's experience where the existing powers colluded to prevent an investigation, obstructed her freedom of speech and did everything to prevent the truth from being told. My focus was to do what I could to expose the reasons why women were consistently promoted at a slower rate than men. I had very good union (SIPTU) advice encouraging me not only to exhaust the NUI Galway appeals processes (which lead to nothing), but also to lodge a complaint with the Equality Tribunal. My requests under FOI showed scant material regarding the actual process of the promotion, but documents revealed that the sixteen successful men comprised 50 per cent of the male candidates, whereas the one woman comprised just 6.7 per cent of the female candidates. I was to be sustained by my ancestors through what ended up as more than a five-year battle.

Details of the case are elsewhere, but suffice it to say I had to prove that I was better than or equal to any one of the successful male candidates.[28] In the event, the Equality Tribunal ruling mentioned seven men against whom I compared more favourably. The resultant inequality of that round of promotions had a lot to do with the aim to increase the university's standing in international rankings that focus almost entirely on research criteria.[29] This had the resultant effect of discriminating against women, as pointed out in my Equality Tribunal ruling.[30] My case had implications for the other women, like me deemed suitable but not promoted to Senior Lecturer and their cases are currently in the judicial system, as NUI Galway management was unwilling to promote them or even investigate that promotion round. A campaign has formed to support them which in turn has put pressure on NUI Galway to initiate changes with regard to the status of women in the university.[31] These have yet to translate into meaningful improvements for female staff. But the actions have demonstrated two things; first, that an institution is very slow to make any radical progress, even under public pressure; second, that, with persistent pressure, just a few individuals can bring about changes beyond that of their own personal grievance.

I took my case because it was the right thing to do and I continue to campaign for the other five women on the same basis. It is they, as much as I,

28 Micheline Sheehy Skeffington, 'Sheehy Skeffington v NUI Galway' in Ivana Bacik and Mary Rogan (eds), *Women changing law, changing society: legal cases that changed Ireland* (Dublin, 2016). **29** B. Bekhradnia, *International university rankings: for good or ill?*, Report 89 (Oxford, 2016). **30** https://www.workplacerelations.ie/en/Cases/2014/November/DEC-E2014-078.html accessed 2 June 2017. **31** See the campaign web site www.michelinesthreeconditions.wordpress.com

who have helped inspire other recent actions such as the setting up of 'Waking the Feminists' at the Abbey Theatre and the introduction of gender quotas in politics and now in sport.[32] But to bring about a cultural change in third-level education, as in the nation, is a far greater process that will take a greater struggle. This struggle must be an active one; we cannot wait for things to change of themselves. If my grandparents are to influence change in modern society, I'd hope it would be through inspiring people to act and speak against injustice:

Two quotes below from Hanna are still strikingly relevant for us today:

> For until the women of Ireland are free, the men will not achieve emancipation[33]

> 'Eternal vigilance is the price of liberty.' Man is like the lepracaun: if you take your eyes off for a moment he slips away, and takes your hard-won liberties along with him. So, women should hold fast to all that pioneers and martyrs have won – and conquer fresh fields in addition. The old world, man-run for so long, and not over well at that, needs their enthusiasm, their hitherto untapped resources of power and energy, their co-operation in human evolution. That is the meaning of true feminism.[34]

In Irish academia, recent exposed scandals show to what extent any organization whose management has become too powerful not only gets away with increasingly inappropriate actions, but uses all its might to bully those who challenge these actions.[35] Too often these are women challenging the system, as they predominate among those excluded from the positions of power. As Hanna says in the quotes above, we need to give women full equality for a more just, a more evolved, society, one where power is not abused in this way. To ensure that this happens, women need the courage Hanna showed, to stand up against the unfairness and the discrimination, despite the inevitable abuse we are going to receive. And we need to be vigilant, so as not to lose the gains so long fought for.

32 See http://www.wakingthefeminists.org; http://www.irishtimes.com/sport/sports-bodies-face-funding-cuts-if-they-fail-to-hit-30-gender-quota-1.2902465. **33** Hanna Sheehy Skeffington, 'Sinn Féin and Irishwomen', *Bean na hÉireann*, 13, November 1909. Cited in M. Ward, *Hanna Sheehy Skeffington*, p. 54. **34** Hanna Sheehy Skeffington, 'How does she stand? Woman in 1933: A review and a stocktaking', *The Distributive Worker*, January 1934, cited in Ward (ed.), *Hanna Sheehy Skeffington*, p. 330. **35** RTÉ Investigates, 'Universities unchallenged', http://www.rte.ie/player/ie/show/rte-investigates-30003696/10730932/. Accessed 7 June 2017.

Acknowledgments

I am indebted to my cousin, Mary McCoy, for filling me in on family lore on Hanna's ancestors and to Margaret Ward for giving me the manuscript of her forthcoming book publishing Hanna's political writings. Thank you to my partner, Nick Scott, for comments on an earlier draft of the chapter.

The many sides of Tom Kettle

NIAMH REILLY

Tom Kettle (1880–1916) is not very well known in Ireland today beyond limited academic, political and media circles. Yet, historian Senia Pašeta notes he 'was associated with almost every major political and cultural development' during his lifetime.[1] In the first decade of the twentieth century competing visions of the future independent Ireland vied for space, from 'Irish-Irelander' to cosmopolitan. Protagonists were variously influenced by liberal, socialist, feminist, militant, pacifist, anti-imperialist, secular and religious ideas and methods. In this milieu, Kettle stood resolutely for constitutional democracy and an inclusive, non-sectarian, independent Irish nation. He was a critic of 'physical force' separatist nationalism. Kettle also cautioned against the insular tendencies of cultural nationalism, arguing that 'while a strong people has its own self for centre, it has the universe for circumference' and 'to become deeply Irish, [Ireland] must become European'.[2]

My interest in Tom Kettle is familial and academic. As a great-grand-niece of Kettle's, I grew up hearing my mother, Pat Kettle (1924–90), refer to him often with immense pride, as well as to his father A.J. Kettle who had close associations with Parnell. (In our home was 'Parnell's chair', supposedly the chair that Parnell would sit in when he visited my great, great-grandfather to discuss Land League business.) As a child I gathered that Tom Kettle was 'someone important' – I was told that he had been a Member of Parliament, a poet, a writer and a barrister. The presence of the bust of Tom Kettle in St Stephen's Green was a particular source of pride to my mother. The fact that he had died in the First World War was not emphasized. When my mother talked about Kettle no connection was made between him and the events surrounding the Easter Rising of 1916 and the lives and actions of its key protagonists. In my young mind Tom Kettle was a figure 'before' and 'separate' from these events and the conflicts that ensued in the pursuit of Irish independence. Later, I realized, on the contrary, he was deeply and prominently involved in public life and in the political debates that were the very backdrop against which the Easter Rising unfolded. More recently, I discovered that my own academic interests over the last two decades – traversing political theory, political economy, political sociology, women's rights and issues of war

1 Senia Pašeta, *Thomas Kettle* (Dublin, 2008), p. 1. 2 Thomas M. Kettle, 'Apology' (1910), in *The day's burden: studies, literary & political and miscellaneous essays* (Dublin, 1937), p. xii.

and peace – were all domains (among many others) that Tom Kettle had engaged with substantially as a writer, speaker, politician, academic and, finally, as a soldier.

As part of Ireland's Decade of Centenaries commemorations (1912–22), the complex legacy of Tom Kettle is receiving more sustained attention than at any time since his death. This renewed interest mainly revolves around Kettle's symbolic significance as one of the most high-profile Irish nationalists to die in action in the First World War. Tom Kettle devoted most of his relatively short life and copious talents to thinking, writing, arguing, planning and working for an independent Ireland, through peaceful political and cultural means. The story of how he came to spend the final weeks of his life in 1916 in France, leading a battalion of the Dublin Fusiliers in the Allied war effort, is laden with poignancy and paradoxes. Kettle's seemingly incongruous participation and death in the Great War and the oft-quoted poem he wrote a few days before his death, 'To My Daughter Betty, the Gift of God' (1916), are perhaps the best-known fragments of his biography.

In the context of ongoing centenary commemorations, the public reclaiming of Tom Kettle has emanated from quite different points along the contemporary Irish political spectrum, North and South. President Michael D. Higgins highlighted Kettle in his historic speech at Westminster in 2014 as an 'Irish patriot, a British soldier and a true European'; Charlie Flanagan in his capacity as Republic of Ireland Minister for Foreign Affairs and Trade oversaw the first state commemoration of Kettle in Dublin on the centenary of his death on 9 September 2016; and Northern Ireland MP Jeffrey Donaldson (DUP) co-hosted a commemorative event on the same day at Westminster, with the Irish Ambassador to the UK, Dan Mulhall, recalling in particular Kettle's death in the Battle of the Somme, fighting on the same side as Ulster unionists.

In this chapter, I want to step back somewhat from the narrative of Tom Kettle as the fallen First World War soldier, 'constitutional nationalist' and 'good European', on the wrong side of post-1916 Irish history. While each element of this account is well-founded, those who have examined Kettle's life closely have persuasively conveyed that he was a man greater than the sum of his parts, whose life and works invite further exploration and (re)interpretation.[3] Here, I wish to highlight aspects of Tom Kettle's wider perspective and

3 Pašeta, *Thomas Kettle;* Margaret O'Callaghan, 'Political formations in pre-First World War Ireland: the politics of the lost generation and the cult of Tom Kettle' in Caoimhe Nic Dháibhéid and Colin Reid (eds), *From Parnell to Paisley: constitutional and revolutionary politics in modern Ireland* (Dublin, 2010), pp 56–77; Gerald Barry (ed.), *Remembering Tom Kettle, 1880–1916* (Dublin, 2006); J.B. Lyons, *The enigma of Tom Kettle: Irish patriot, essayist, poet, British soldier, 1880–1916* (Dublin, 1983).

contributions before 1916 – as a distinctive voice in early-twentieth-century Irish political and social thought and as a tireless champion for the modern, progressive, democratic Ireland that he imagined. In particular, I focus on some of his less discussed ideas and areas of work, especially in support of social and economic justice and women's rights.

At the heart of all Kettle's writings is a deep commitment to classic Enlightenment values of reason, freedom and toleration, and the constitutional democratic politics that these values require. On this basis, he argued for both the freedom of the Irish nation and the imperative of Ireland supporting the Allied war effort. He was wholly committed to achieving independence for the island of Ireland and to doing so via constitutional methods, which for him meant 'home rule' to begin with. At the same time, in Kettle's writings the imperatives of addressing social and economic inequalities and achieving prosperity and development across the island of Ireland are inseparable from achieving independence. Undoubtedly, Kettle's approach to social and economic justice was also underpinned by deep intellectual roots in Catholic social teaching, which he endeavoured to integrate into his highly progressive worldview.

Life and death

Tom Kettle was the seventh of twelve children, seven girls and five boys, born into a north Dublin farming family. His parents were Andrew J. Kettle (1833–1916) and Margaret McCourt (1851–1927). My great grandfather, Andrew J. Kettle Jr (1874–1917), was Tom's oldest brother. In addition to being a farmer, their father had been prominent in the Land League, a staunch supporter of Parnell, and a lifelong champion of the Irish Party and home rule movement. In the first decade of the twentieth century Tom Kettle was viewed by many as a bright star of a new, expectant generation of educated middle-class Catholics, including 'young Irelanders' Hanna and Frank Sheehy Skeffington and aspiring writer, James Joyce.[4] While still in his twenties, Kettle earned a reputation as a gifted orator, essayist, journalist, parliamentarian and campaigner for an independent Ireland. He was an advocate for women's rights and a liberal Catholic intellectual. Encouraged into politics by his father, Kettle was elected Irish Party MP for East Tyrone in 1906 and re-elected in 1910. He was also a poet, a translator, a reluctant barrister and, from 1910, a professor at University College Dublin. In 1909, Kettle married nationalist, suffragist and university

4 See chapter 3 in this volume: Micheline Sheehy Skeffington, 'The Sheehy Skeffington legacy and how it influences me today'.

graduate, Mary Sheehy (1874–1967), Hanna's sister. Betty (1913–96) was their only child. For health reasons, as a young man, Kettle had spent substantial blocks of time in Europe during which time he became proficient in French and German.[5] He read widely and eclectically – especially in political philosophy, literature, sociology, economics and science, as well as theology. His personal connections to Europe and his attachment to classic Enlightenment thinking shaped his understanding of his own nested political identity as an Irish nationalist and a European.

After Kettle died in the Battle of the Somme in September 1916, Irish writer Robert Lynd remembered him as 'the most brilliant Irishman of his generation'.[6] Arthur Clery, a fellow University College Dublin (UCD) graduate and professor, said he had 'a quality of brilliance ... that no one else of his time quite possessed'.[7] Veteran nationalist MP Stephen Gwynn wrote that Kettle was the 'most brilliant speaker that ... I have ever heard ... [A]s talker or as speaker he had few equals'.[8] Contemporaries compared his eloquent 'sardonic enthusiasm' to that of Jonathan Swift and the 'hard, sparkling, polished brilliance' and wit of his prose to that of Oscar Wilde.[9] He was remembered by many for his kindness and humanitarian disposition. His wife, Mary Sheehy Kettle, underlined that her husband was 'a man of peace, who had nothing of the soldier in him except courage', while George Russell (AE), in his poem 'Salutation' (1916), memorialized 'Dear Kettle, of the generous heart'.[10] Robert Bingham, a young private who served in Kettle's division in France, wrote to Mary Kettle:

> He was a brave officer and like a father to me as I am myself an orphan boy at the age of 18 ... I was awfully sorry when God called such a brave man away. He refused a staff situation, he wanted to be with his comrades. He told me just before his death that I was going home and he was staying where he was. With that he gave me his watch.[11]

Kettle had been in Belgium at the request of the Irish Party buying arms for the Irish Volunteers when German forces invaded and the First World War commenced. He opted to remain there for several weeks as a war correspondent for the *Daily News*. By all accounts, he was profoundly affected by what

5 Lyons, *The enigma of Tom Kettle*, p. 38. **6** Robert Lynd, 'T.M. Kettle' in *If the Germans conquered England, and other essays* (Dublin, 1917), p. 137. **7** Arthur Cleary, 'Thomas Kettle' in *Dublin essays* (Dublin, 1919), p. 1. **8** Stephen Gwynn, *John Redmond's last years* (London, 1919), p. 185. **9** Cleary, 'Thomas Kettle', p. 13; William Dawson, 'Tom Kettle: the essayist', *Studies: An Irish Quarterly Review*, 20:89 (1931), p. 601. **10** Mary S. Kettle, 'Memoir' in *The ways of war*, by T.M. Kettle (Dublin, 1917), p. 2. **11** Tom Burke, 'In memory of Lieutenant Tom Kettle, "B" Company, 9th Royal Dublin Fusiliers', *Dublin Historical Record*, 57:2 (2004), p. 168.

he witnessed of the German military's calculated and systematic aggression against civilians, civilian life and cultural landmarks, especially churches, in a small, neutral nation, just as Ireland aspired to be. From Brussels on 8 August 1916, he reported: 'In every direction there opens a vista of waste and suffering. Already a long trail of wounded began to wind its sorrowful way back to the capital'.[12] He wrote how he 'assisted for many overwhelming weeks at the agony of the valiant Belgium nation'.[13] He described the impact of 'the material apparatus of butchery and destruction', which ensured that: 'the fabric of settled life has disappeared not by single houses but by whole towns'.[14] Kettle's first-hand experience convinced him of the imperative of Ireland supporting the Allies in the war effort against German aggression, which for him represented a fundamental threat to freedom, democracy and the existence of 'small nations'. As his wife described: 'it was as an Irish soldier in the army of Europe and civilization that he entered the war'.[15] He also hoped that the experience of nationalists and unionists fighting together would bridge the divide between the two sides and help efforts to achieve a united Ireland.[16] On his return from Belgium, Kettle joined the army. As a high-profile recruiter, he became a target of scathing criticism from separatist nationalists.[17] Kettle's letters to the Chief Staff Office of the Irish division of the army during 1914–16 indicate that he was dealing with bouts of alcoholism and related personal difficulties at this time. He repeatedly requested to be sent to the front but was refused, primarily on account of poor health, until July 1916.[18]

A few months before Kettle left for France, amid waning hopes that home rule for Ireland would be secured, a minority within the Irish Volunteers orchestrated the Easter Rising and proclaimed an Irish Republic. According to Pašeta, Kettle was based in the barracks at Newbridge, Co. Kildare, when the Rising erupted.[19] Along with a majority in Ireland at the time, he did not support the rebellion. Mary Sheehy Kettle gave this account of Kettle's point of view on the Rising and the events that followed:

> Easter week … had been for him a harrowing and terrible experience. MacDonagh who was shot was a fellow professor at the College as was also MacNeill, in whose favour he gave evidence at the court-martial. Pearse the leader was a friend of many years. With the rebellion he had

12 T.M. Kettle, 'Under the heel of the Hun: II. "Europe against the barbarians"' in *The ways of war* (Dublin, 1917), p. 112. **13** T.M. Kettle, 'Why Ireland fought: I. Prelude' in *The ways of war* (Dublin, 1917), p. 59. **14** Ibid. **15** Kettle, 'Memoir', p. 3. **16** William Redmond, letter to Arthur Conan Doyle, 18 Dec. 1916, published in *The Times* (London), 14 June 1917. **17** Senia Pašeta, 'Thomas Kettle: "An Irish soldier in the army of Europe"?' in Adrian Gregory and Senia Pašeta (eds), *Ireland and the Great War: a war to unite us all?* (Manchester, 2002), p. 19. **18** Pašeta, *Thomas Kettle,* pp 84–5. **19** Ibid., p. 88.

> no sympathy – indeed it made him furious. He used to say bitterly that they had spoiled it all – spoiled his dream of a free united Ireland in a free Europe. But what really seared his heart was the fearful retribution that fell on the leaders of the rebellion.[20]

Mary Kettle also described how the murder of Tom's brother-in-law, Francis Sheehy Skeffington, 'cast a deep gloom on his spirit'.[21] The execution of the rebel leaders ensured a decisive shift in popular attitudes in Ireland in favour of separatist nationalism. After 1916, the parliamentary nationalist tradition was eclipsed along with Kettle and the distinctive, progressive, liberal worldview he had striven to define and articulate and hoped to advance through Ireland's home rule parliament.

Tom Kettle and social progress: labour and women's suffrage

Kettle's progressive agenda viewed struggles against social inequalities and for democracy and home rule as interrelated. This is captured well in a speech he gave in support of the nationalist candidate for South County Dublin in December 1910. Lambasting the veto of the House of Lords, he declared:

> There has never been any act for widening franchise, there has never been any Bill for tenant farmers of Ireland, there has never been any Bill for the relief of workers in factories, there has been no Bill for wiping out the slums, and [giving] to working men houses fit for human habitation to live, there has been no Bill in the *whole record of progress,* which the House of Lords have not opposed.[22] [Emphasis added].

He finished by asking the crowd not to vote for a 'particular candidate' but to: 'Vote for democracy and vote for Ireland. Vote for the cause of labour, vote for government by the people for the people'.[23]

Kettle regularly addresses Ireland's pressing social inequalities and the plight of labour in his essays, including three written specifically in response to the 1913 Lockout. In 'Labour: war or peace' (1913) he satirizes 'the exaggerations of our modern fear' of 'unspeakable … agitators, hideously devoted to the hideous cult of Syndicalism', which he discerns in the 'transcripts of the railway train, the club smoking room, and the golf-links, that is to say of the three foci of middle-class civilization'.[24] He comments:

20 Kettle, 'Memoir', p. 32. **21** Ibid., p. 30. **22** T.M. Kettle, 'Professor Kettle's speech', *Wicklow People,* 10 Dec. 1910, p. 4. **23** Ibid. **24** Thomas M. Kettle, 'Labour: war or peace' (1913), in *The*

> People ask indignantly: Why is Labour discontented? But how could it be anything else? The condition of the workers of these islands is not such as either to command or deserve permanence. Thirty per cent of them, more than twelve million human beings, count themselves fortunate if they are able to hold their places in the dim borderland where destitution merges into mere poverty.[25]

In 'Labour and civilization' (1913) Kettle asserts: 'The function of the economic system is to feed, clothe, and shelter, in a human way its human units. Since ours does not accomplish this, we must amend it that it shall do so'.[26] He does not underestimate the challenge involved in 'amending' the system of distribution, noting: 'The business world as we have inherited it … was not framed on any high ethical model.'[27] At the same time, Kettle's dispute with radical socialism is clear. He rejects calls for the abolition of private property but urges that: 'Every voluntary and every State proposal that tends to broaden the basis of property – co-operation, co-partnership, prosperity sharing, manufacturing guilds, taxation of unproductive surpluses – ought to be welcomed by us'.[28] Kettle rejected Syndicalism in particular for its 'revolt against Parliamentary government', reasoned debate and the specification of 'definite programmes', which for him were the essential ingredients of democratic government.[29] In the context of the 1913 Lockout, Kettle's sympathies were overwhelmingly on the side of the workers who 'fought with admirable courage … and a great deal of idealism and soldierly sacrifice'.[30] He was sceptical, however, about the tactics of Jim Larkin, 'picturesque, eloquent, prophetic, at once dictatorial and intimate', who 'organized not so much a trade union as an army'.[31] When the dispute had ended, Kettle lamented: 'Not a single member of the submerged fourth [living in poverty] seems to be any nearer a living or … an economic wage'.[32]

Against the confrontational methods of revolutionary socialism, Kettle was adamant that informed debate and good-faith negotiation were the only viable mechanisms for resolving conflicts and achieving social progress. For him, 'class-war … preached in whirling superlatives' was not only counterproductive but anti-democratic.[33] He dismissed the demonization of Dublin's down-to-earth workers in the dispute, quipping they are 'the most unpromising material for a chapter in demonology' and, on the other side,

day's burden: studies, literary & political and miscellaneous essays (Dublin, 1937), p. 149. **25** Ibid., p. 152. **26** Thomas M. Kettle, 'Labour and civilization' (1913), in *The day's burden: studies, literary & political and miscellaneous essays* (Dublin, 1937), p. 125. **27** Ibid. **28** Ibid., p. 127. **29** Kettle, 'Labour: war or peace', p. 160. **30** Kettle, 'Labour and civilization', p. 119. **31** Ibid., p. 117. **32** Ibid., p. 120. **33** Ibid., p. 119.

insisting that the 'ordinary Dublin employer is neither so big nor so bad as he appears in AE's stormy vision'.[34] Kettle was never an armchair commentator. At the time a Professor of National Economics at UCD, he established the Industrial Peace Committee in October 1913 to campaign for 'an immediate truce between the conflicting parties' to enable negotiations to take place and to 'consider and propose measures tending toward permanent peace between employers and employed in Dublin and toward economic prosperity of the city and the country'.[35] Members and participants in the work of the Committee included an array of academics, professionals, writers and artists, as well as religious leaders.[36]

Although the Committee did not succeed in achieving its aims, its efforts during autumn 1913 offer a window on Kettle's ideas about and practical commitment to deliberative, democratic citizenship. Over several weeks, the Committee coordinated deputations to and from the leading employer and trade union bodies; public engagement via meetings, dissemination of circulars and gathering of signatures of support; and preparations for a hoped-for peace conference.[37] For Kettle, the mobilization of 'public opinion' in support of the call for a 'truce' was a pivotal part of the Peace Committee's strategy of fostering informed civic participation. The Official Report of the Committee (most likely written by Kettle as its Chairman) states:

> The Committee bring forward these facts [about the industrial dispute] trusting the public to give them their just weight, and believing that the present deadlock will be ended when *public opinion* unmistakably declares itself against further war, waste and ruin, and in *favour of reason, humanity* and *civic patriotism.* The Committee would urge upon *citizens* of Dublin the *duty* of exerting every *legitimate influence* they possess to bring about immediate negotiations between the two parties.[38] [Emphasis added].

The above passage captures many of the tenets of Kettle's political philosophy – the prioritization of reason, deliberation and the rule of law, an accent on humanity and care suggestive of Catholic social teaching, and a notion of situated political identity and attachment to place, contained in his interpretation of 'civic patriotism'. In his essay 'The agony of Dublin' (1913), Kettle

34 Ibid., p. 114; T.M. Kettle, 'The agony of Dublin', *Irish Review*, 3:33 (Nov. 1913), p. 444. **35** [T.M. Kettle], 'Dublin Industrial Peace Committee Official Report', *Daily Express*, 21 Oct. 1913. **36** Padraig Yeates, 'Lockout chronology, 1913–1914', SIPTU website, n.d. http://www.siptu.ie/media/media_17016_en.pdf; Lyons, *The enigma of Tom Kettle.* **37** [Kettle], 'Dublin Industrial Peace Committee Official Report'. **38** Ibid.

attributes to workers (but not to employers) 'a sincere warmth of civic patriotism, a *pride in* and *a care for* Dublin the city, Dublin the capital'[39] [emphasis added].

In the end, the workers' side declared itself 'ready to attend such a conference should [the Committee's] efforts meet with success' while the employers refused to participate, ultimately ensuring the failure of the initiative.[40] Kettle sums up the debacle that had unfolded as he saw it: 'The workers have talked wildly and acted calmly; the employers have talked calmly but acted wildly'.[41] He castigated employers who attempted to outlaw trade unionism and concluded that 'the prospect for industrial peace is bound up not with the suppression, but with the extension of trade unions' and 'the employer who fights against recognition is always wrong'.[42] In stark contrast to contemporary neoliberal understandings, Kettle envisioned a distributive, humanitarian and developmental state, which he described as 'the name by which we call the great human conspiracy against hunger and cold, against loneliness and ignorance'.[43] Furthermore, although Kettle doubted the feasibility of global labour laws, he believed that 'an internationalization of labour laws for Western Europe is desirable and perhaps possible'.[44]

Similarly, Kettle's support of women's rights and equality is often ignored or downplayed in mainstream accounts of his significance. On this issue, however, Pašeta considers Kettle to have been 'one of the leading advocates in the UK more generally' and not only in Ireland.[45] She notes that Kettle and his future brother-in-law, Francis Sheehy Skeffington, were two of a small number of allies of female student campaigners in their efforts to achieve equality with UCD's male students.[46] Later as an MP, according to Mary Sheehy Kettle, her husband played a pivotal role in ensuring that the Irish Universities Act (1908) permitted women to hold professorships on the same salaries as men.[47] In 1905, Kettle and Sheehy Skeffington co-edited *The Nationist,* which served as the unofficial journal of the Young Ireland Branch (YIB) of the United Ireland League. According to Pašeta, John Redmond and the Irish Party establishment did not approve of the editorial slant of the journal, which 'supported women's suffrage and sympathized with the poor'.[48]

During Kettle's career as an MP (1906–10) he became a prominent and articulate advocate on behalf of women's suffrage, speaking at dozens of events

39 Kettle, 'The agony of Dublin', p. 447. **40** [Kettle], 'Dublin Industrial Peace Committee Official Report'. **41** Kettle, 'The agony of Dublin', p. 446. **42** Kettle, 'Labour: war or peace', p. 166. **43** Thomas M. Kettle, 'Philosophy of politics' (1905), in *The day's burden: studies, literary & political and miscellaneous essays* (Dublin, 1937), p. 16. **44** LA34/250, Thomas M. Kettle Papers (LA34), UCD Archives, University College Dublin. **45** Senia Pašeta, personal communication with the author, 26 Sept. 2016. **46** Pašeta, *Thomas Kettle,* p. 50. **47** Ibid., p. 48. **48** Ibid., p. 43.

over the course of his parliamentary career and later as an Irish Party activist. In his speech 'Why bully women?' (1907), Kettle condemns the British Liberal Party for refusing to meet a deputation of suffragists, declaring that:

> It means one thing, and one thing only, namely that women are regarded not as partners in state, but as a 'lesser tribe without law'. It seems they are treated as a species of alien, inferior animal. The thing is a spiritual outrage. Women knock on the doors of 'the People's House' only to be batoned away, and told it is the other people's house. The state has a welcome for women in the jail, in the hospital, in the factory, but it has none in the Council room … Our political society allows women every burden and no respect.[49]

Concern about the conditions of women workers and the economic hardship they experience is a recurring theme in Kettle's writing about women. In an essay on the International Socialist Congress in Stuttgart in 1907, some of which Kettle attended, he notices the women working in the hotel hosting the socialist gathering. He observes: '[One] has fallen asleep, her head leaned back against a beech trunk. In the lines of her face, there comes out, as often in sleep, a certain forlornness, a sense of defeated dreams. It is a commentary.'[50] The waitress' demeanour is contrasted to the single-minded, energetic intensity of the conference delegates. Kettle asks: 'But in which of all the Utopias, smouldering in certain fierce eyes that met yours today in Stuttgart, will there be no stain of the burden and sorrow of women?'[51]

A report of a speech by Kettle in 1909 to the Irish Women's Franchise League recounts how he urged the gathering to 'brush aside everything posing as an argument which was advanced against women's suffrage', noting that 'In the last analysis [women] found themselves up against the blank wall of prejudice'. The report continues that Kettle recognized there were working women among the 'captains and leaders' of the suffrage movement who knew that:

> [To] be without a vote was to be handicapped, and the economic complement of the deprivation of the franchise was the miserable seamstress … who was working 13 hours a day for 5*s.* 6*d.* a week … Undoubtedly there was a strong economic current. It was taken as commonplace that where a woman was doing precisely the same work as a man, whether manual or intellectual, she was as a matter of course,

49 T.M. Kettle, *Why bully women? An argument for the Conciliation Bill* (Dublin, 1907), p. 5.
50 Thomas M. Kettle, 'International socialists' (1907), in *The day's burden*, p. 88. **51** Ibid., p. 89.

> to be employed at a lower wage. She was to be deprived of economic independence and economic equality.[52]

In November 1910, six members of the Irish Women's Franchise League were given jail sentences for attempting to petition the parliament. Margaret Ward notes that Tom Kettle 'was one of the few MPs to come to the women's support'.[53] While the majority of Irish Party MPs remained indifferent to their situation, Kettle telegrammed the Home Secretary Winston Churchill on behalf of the jailed suffragists demanding that they should be treated as political prisoners.[54]

In 1912, when Kettle was no longer an MP, a growing rift between him and his sister and brother-in-law, Hanna and Frank Sheehy Skeffington, deepened. A third women's suffrage Bill had been defeated with the help of Irish Party MPs.[55] Understandably bitterly disappointed, the Irish Women's Franchise League (IWFL), led by Hanna Sheehy Skeffington, began to use increasingly militant tactics to advance the cause – a departure that did not enjoy unanimous support across the women's suffrage movement.[56] Around this time, a long-awaited third home rule bill had also been introduced; it was expected to pass and was greeted at the time with enthusiasm by most nationalists across Ireland. In this context, Irish Party leader John Redmond's implacable opposition to women's suffrage hardened as he and the Party elders viewed the suffrage movement as a potential threat to the passage of the home rule bill. In keeping with his own primary commitment to achieving Ireland's independence via parliamentary and constitutional means, Kettle disagreed with the IWFL's insistence on seeking a suffrage amendment to the bill at that juncture. Kettle was clearly convinced that votes for women would be achieved without difficulty in post-home rule Ireland. He explained his position as follows:

> The effect of [the home rule bill] has been to produce in Ireland a sense of unity and solidarity such as we have not had hitherto in my time … From the very first day upon which this Parliament is established it will … grow by its own inherent vitality; and looking into the future, I see it … *worked intelligently for the benefit of all. I see minorities respected, I see every subordinate class coming to its own after national freedom has been attained.* At the end of it *I see Ireland completely controlling her own political life …* [Moreover] anybody with the least Parliamentary experience knows that any amendment, however

52 [T.M. Kettle], 'Votes for women, meeting of Irish Franchise League. Speech of Mr T.M. Kettle, MP', *Freeman's Journal*, 16 Feb. 1909, p. 10. **53** Margaret Ward, *Hanna Sheehy Skeffington: a life* (Cork, 1997), p. 72. **54** Ibid. **55** Ibid., p. 71. **56** Ibid., pp 76–7.

> innocent in itself, however desirable in itself, might create at any moment a dangerous Parliamentary situation. A cloud – no larger than a man's hand – might overshadow the whole horizon[57] [emphasis added].

Hanna and Frank Sheehy Skeffington, whose belief in parliamentary methods had been dwindling for some time, had a very different view. They were highly critical of Kettle for failing to go against Redmond and the Irish Party elders to press the party to support women's suffrage.[58] This disagreement over tactics was a source of tension and bitter exchanges among the three, as family members and as erstwhile political allies.

Kettle's decision to prioritize securing home rule over taking a necessarily confrontational and unwinnable stand on women's suffrage within the Irish Party at this time was understandable given his unwavering commitment to achieving constitutional democracy for Ireland. It was also understandable that the IWFL, the most radical Irish women's suffrage organization, would condemn Kettle's failure to prioritize women's suffrage at this key juncture, even if it meant Kettle going against the Party leadership and/or disrupting agreed Party strategy. Kettle, however, never concealed his political priorities and principled adherence to moderate political methods. His agenda for political, social and economic development was highly progressive and egalitarian, far beyond the imagination of the typical Irish Party MP of his day. It would be shortsighted not to appreciate the significance of Tom Kettle's long-standing and well-documented efforts on behalf of women's rights and equality. Few male parliamentarians since, in the Republic of Ireland or Northern Ireland, have come close to engaging with questions of women's rights and equality to a comparable degree and depth as Kettle.

Conclusion

As with all founding narratives, the story of the origins of independent Ireland has tended to amplify and valourize the most 'revolutionary' actors, events and turning points. In Ireland's case, the events of the Easter Rising, the elevation and iconography of its leaders, the various associated symbols of the Irish nation, and a sharp distinction between 'Irish-Ireland' on one side and 'Anglo-Ireland' and Britain on the other, have been predominant motifs in the country's founding narrative. Within the hegemonic Irish-Ireland paradigm

57 T.M. Kettle, 'Speech of Professor Kettle', *Freeman's Journal*, 24 April 1912, p. 8. **58** Pašeta, *Thomas Kettle*, pp 56–9.

that emerged post-1916, there was little space available to recall Tom Kettle's ideas and role in pre-1916 political struggles to achieve democracy and social progress in Ireland. His long association with the obliterated Irish Parliamentary Party and his firm support for the Allied war effort placed him outside if not against the new Ireland in the either/or thinking that took root. When Kettle was remembered, understandably, the principal focus was on his anomalous identity as a constitutional nationalist and a 'British solider' who died in the First World War.

My research for this chapter has helped to contextualize my childhood recollections of how my mother spoke about Tom Kettle, what was said and what was left unsaid. The contrast of the deep personal pride she expressed in being a grand-niece of a man of such talents and her silence on his public and political roles vis-à-vis the Easter Rising and the trajectory it set for independent Ireland is telling. Arguably it reflects not only the limitations of an individual or family point of view but also the effect of wider political discourse, operating to elide some political biographies and identities and affirm others.

In recent decades, Ireland's membership of the EU, the success of the Good Friday Agreement, and patterns of globalization, migration and economic development have all contributed to a reweaving of the fabric of Irish national identity. In this context, the current phase of commemoration appears to be enabling more nuanced engagement with the established founding narrative as well as the possibility of rediscovering forgotten threads of history before 1916 and reflecting on their relevance today. From this perspective, the present chapter has focused on some of the less discussed areas of Tom Kettle's work, specifically in relation labour and women's rights issues. Clearly, much remains to be fully documented and assessed in the context of further retellings of his legacy and place in the wider struggle for an independent and more equal Ireland.

From family history to history: my grandfather and I

RÓISÍN HEALY

Both of my grandfathers were stripped of their weapons at the end of Easter week 1916. My maternal grandfather, Patrick Mills, a national schoolteacher from Mayo, was obliged to hand over his legally held rifle to a member of the Royal Irish Constabulary. Living on the remote island of Inishkea, Mills knew nothing of the Rising and had used the rifle for the sole purpose of shooting rabbits. While he was sympathetic to the cultural revival – he later taught Irish for Conradh na Gaeilge – and a keen observer of political events, he took no active part in the Irish revolution. By contrast, my paternal grandfather, Richard Healy, was in the thick of the action. Armed with a Martini-Henry rifle he had bought from an Irish soldier home on leave from the front, he spent Easter week fighting as a Volunteer in the GPO and the O'Connell Street area. After the surrender, he was brought to Richmond Barracks and subsequently to Knutsford Prison and Frongoch Internment Camp in Wales. Upon release, he resumed his revolutionary activities, taking an active part in the War of Independence.

Richard Healy fit the profile of contemporary revolutionaries. Born in 1894, he was twenty-two by early 1916 and thus part of the 'revolutionary generation' identified by R.F. Foster and others. In common with most Volunteers, he was Roman Catholic. Although from a rural background – he grew up on a farm in Kilcollen, Conahy, Co. Kilkenny – and was just one of two men from Kilkenny in the GPO in Easter week, he reflected the predominantly urban composition of activists in that he had been living in Dublin since 1910. He had been sent to the capital to become an apprentice to his uncle, John Healy, who owned a public house at the corner of Parnell and Marlboro' Streets. Richard's family belonged neither to the richest nor poorest sections of Irish society, but could be characterized as comfortable. His father owned a farm of 40–50 acres and employed one male servant. His uncle had done well since moving to Dublin, paying the highest rates of all property-owners on Parnell Street, according to the electoral rolls of Dublin City Council.[1]

1 Voter No. 289, Mountjoy Ward, Division 2: Dublin Harbour, Electoral Rolls, 1912, Dublin City Council, http://databases.dublincity.ie/burgesses/advanced_new.php

His political formation also echoed that of other revolutionaries. At the Christian Brothers secondary school in Kilkenny, which he attended until he was sixteen, he was exposed to a strong nationalist reading of Irish history, which has been shown to have encouraged pupils to engage in revolutionary activity.[2] Other former pupils of the Christian Brothers included Todd Andrews, Terence MacSwiney and Ernie O'Malley.[3] Republican ballads, which he himself liked to sing, provided another source of hostility towards the British presence in Ireland. Healy also came under the influence of the cultural revival. A keen hurler, he joined the GAA not long after it passed a series of rules from 1901 to 1905 against members playing so-called foreign games. Healy enjoyed his county's considerable success in these years. Kilkenny appeared in eleven all-Ireland finals from 1894 to 1916, seven of which it won, including three in a row from 1911 to 1913. He regularly went to the Phoenix Park to play hurling on Sunday mornings before the public house opened for business.

Moreover, he had close contacts with advanced nationalists through his work. His uncle supported the Fenians and his premises became known locally as the 'war office', so popular was it with revolutionaries. It was located just to the east of what R.F. Foster has described as a 'hotbed of radicalism', the area around Sackville Street and Rutland Square, now O'Connell Street and Parnell Square respectively.[4] The chair of the IRB Military Council and later signatory of the Proclamation, Thomas Clarke, who owned a newsagent's down the street, was a regular visitor to the pub. So too was Sinn Féin leader Arthur Griffith. The building had doors on both Parnell Street and Marlboro' Street and, once alerted by the lookout that a RIC man was on his way down one street, revolutionaries could slip out on to the other. As a barman, or 'grocer's assistant' as it was then known, Healy became a member of the Irish National Union of Vintners, Grocers and Allied Trades Assistants and it was at their headquarters, Banba Hall on Parnell Square, in a telephone booth, that he took his oath to the IRB in early 1913. Many of his fellow-barmen joined the Volunteers upon its establishment in November 1913. Healy joined a few months later and was assigned to 'D' Company, 2nd Battalion, known colloquially as 'the grocers' company'. The grocers often worked twelve-hour shifts, finishing up late at night, and had to train separately from the rest of the Volunteers, often on Sunday mornings. Their work allowed them to help in other ways, however, such as monitoring the activities of British forces, passing

2 On the profile of activists in this period, see Joost Augusteijn, 'Accounting for the emergence of violent activism among Irish revolutionaries, 1916–1921', *Irish Historical Studies* 35 (2007), pp 333–4 and G. White and B. O'Shea, *Irish volunteer soldier, 1913–23* (Oxford, 2003). 3 R.F. Foster, *Vivid faces: the revolutionary generation in Ireland, 1890–1923* (London, 2015), pp 39–40. 4 Foster, *Vivid faces*, 8.

messages between revolutionaries and hiding weapons.[5] Healy and his company also took part in the Howth gun-running of July 1914.

Upon the outbreak of the First World War, 'D' Company split into those who supported Redmond's call to support the British war effort and those who resisted it. Healy was one of just 45 of the original 200–300 members who decided to undermine rather than support the British state in time of war. This was somewhat higher than the average 7 per cent of the Volunteers generally who remained in the Irish Volunteers rather than join Redmond's National Volunteers. Although not privy to the plans for a rising at Easter, he mobilized on Easter Monday, going first to his battalion's assembly point at St Stephen's Green, before being deployed to O'Connell Bridge and then to the General Post Office.[6] It was an intense experience. On Tuesday, Thomas Clarke ordered him 'to wipe out a sniper'. Whether he was successful or not is not clear. Seven soldiers of the British army, at least two of whom were born in Ireland, died that day and many more subsequently from injuries sustained in the Rising.

On Thursday, he entered the rebel-held Hibernian Bank on the corner of O'Connell Street and Lower Abbey Street. In an interview with the *Banba Review,* he recounted what happened next: 'In the house, I made my way up the stairs and as I reached the top, Tom Weafer, a volunteer from Wexford, a captain in the 2nd Battalion, was shot in the back and died in the arms of a Cumann na mBan.'[7] The woman in question was Leslie Price, who went on to marry Tom Barry in 1921 and to serve as Chairman of the Irish Red Cross from 1950 to 1973. He and another Volunteer, Paddy McGrath, also from Kilkenny, helped to pull Weafer away from the window. Upon his return to the GPO, a dangerous dash across Sackville Street, much of which was in flames, Clarke promoted him, largely because he was the only Volunteer present in uniform – only one-third of Volunteers involved in the Rising wore a uniform. Clarke then placed him in charge of the uppermost section of the building. Healy later confessed to having been terrified by the artillery fire, eighteen pounders fired from Trinity College, directed at the roof. He also recalled passing by the body of The O'Rahilly as they evacuated the GPO the following day and Pearse and Connolly giving orders, including the eventual decision to surrender on Saturday.[8]

5 On the role of barmen in the Rising, see Eddie Bohan, 'The 1916 Rising and the barman', blogpost, http://1916easterrisingcoachtour.blogspot.ie/2015/05/the–1916-rising-and-barman.html, posted 20 May 2015. 6 Pension Application of Richard Healy, MSP34 REF805, Military Service Pension Collection, Department of Defence. 7 Healy mistakenly recalled Weafer's death as taking place on Tuesday rather than Thursday, 'How Dublin's 1916 Easter Rising spurred Ireland on freedom trail', *Chicago Daily News*, 9 April 1966. 8 For an account of fighting in the O'Connell Street area, see 'Impressions of the street fighting by a civilian eyewitness', originally published in *The Record of the Irish Rebellion* (June 1916), reproduced in Mick O'Farrell, *1916: what the people saw* (Dublin, 2013), pp

Ironically, British forces stationed in Healy's home on Parnell Street were directing fire on the GPO. They commandeered his uncle's house, which was five storeys high and thus offered a view of the GPO and surrounding area. From there, they reported on the success of the shelling from the *Helga* and sent instructions to dispatch riders on how to improve their aim. His uncle, like all the men of the area, were rounded up and brought to Parnell Square, while his uncle's wife and children were confined to one room. British officers also used the premises as a mess. John Healy was horrified when, at the end of the week, the commanding officer, Captain Taylor, promised his wife to put in a good word for the family in Dublin Castle. John contacted some clerks in the Castle to have the file removed, lest he later be seen as a collaborator.

Upon the surrender, Richard Healy was marched to the Rotunda Hospital where he spent the night of Saturday, 29 April, described by another Volunteer, as a 'night of horror' with men piled up on top of one another.[9] Healy noted the antipathy of many Dubliners, especially the wives of soldiers serving in the British army, towards them, saying, 'When we were marched off to Richmond Barracks on Sunday, 30 April, people spat on us.'[10] After prolonged questioning there, they were brought to North Wall, full of trepidation about their future. Healy recalled the response given one of his fellow-prisoners who wondered what might happen them: 'They're going to bring us out into Dublin Bay and then torpedo us. They'll blame it on the Germans.'[11] Such fears turned out to be unfounded. Rather they were brought to Knutsford Gaol near Manchester on 1 May and then in June to Frongoch Internment Camp in Wales. He spent four months there, alongside many future leaders, before availing of the general amnesty and returning home in August. Despite the harsh regime endured by the internees, Healy spoke little of this time, apart from remembering that he played football with Michael Collins.[12]

As with many other rebels, imprisonment inflamed rather than suppressed his revolutionary ardour. He returned to active duty in 'D' Company upon his release and helped to train the company in rifle practice and drill. Parades took place on the grounds of All Hallows' College initially, but, when the authorities got suspicious, were moved to Phoenix Park, where the Volunteers gathered under the ruse of playing a football match.[13] Healy rose through the ranks of the Volunteers, becoming a second lieutenant in 1917, a first lieutenant in 1919

223–49. For other first-hand accounts of the Rising drawn from the Bureau of Military History, see Fearghal McGarry, *Rebels: voices from the Easter Rising* (Dublin, 2011). **9** Hopkinson (ed.), *Henderson's Easter Rising*, p. 67. **10** 'How Dublin's 1916 Easter Rising spurred Ireland on freedom trail'. **11** *Banba Review*, Jan. 1963. **12** Seán O'Mahony, *Frongoch: university of revolution* (Dublin: FDR Teoranta, 1987) and Lyn Ebenezer, *Fron-Goch and the birth of the IRA* (Llanrwst, 2006). **13** Witness statement 774, James Foley, Bureau of Military History, 28 Nov. 1952.

and a captain in 1920. Given his long working hours as a barman, he played a limited role in the War of Independence, moving guns around the city and going on armed patrols. The latter could prove dangerous, however. On one occasion, on 17 October 1920, he and eleven other barmen were gathered in Banba Hall on Parnell Square armed with weapons in preparation to go out on patrol when the Black and Tans raided the premises. Healy escaped, but the last man out, Henry Kelly, was captured and shot dead. His former commanding officer, another barman, Patrick Moran from Roscommon, was executed in 1921 for his alleged involvement in the murder of a suspected intelligence officer by the Cairo Gang. A commemorative plaque on Banba Hall lists, in all, nine members of the Vintners' Union who were killed in the War of Independence.

The War of Independence drew in a much larger group of people than those who were out in 1916 and Healy's ardour appears to have rubbed off on those around him. According to the Military Service Medal series database, all four of his brothers in Kilkenny were awarded medals for their service in I Company, 3rd Battalion, in the years from 1917 to 1921. Like many other veterans of these years, Healy did not wish to engage in battle with his former comrades and took no part in the Civil War. That is not to say that he was unaffected by it. Anti-Treaty forces occupied and damaged the house in Parnell Street, where he was still working. He focused in these years rather on his professional and personal life, in time progressing to own his own public house and to marry and start a family. He experienced tragedy in the death of a son and his first wife, but remarried soon afterwards. The continued importance of nationalism was evident in the Irish names he and his two wives chose for nearly all their children, born between 1926 and 1936 – Valentine, Éamonn, Donal, Seán, Brian, Kevin and Úna. His own siblings' names – Nicholas, Michael, Anne, Edward and John – bore no mark of the cultural revival.

It has been suggested that, for veterans of the Rising, 'Participation in the Rising was to be their major reference-point for the rest of their lives – a guarantee of membership of a nationalist elite, a badge of social and political respectability.'[14] Certainly, the events of 1916 to 1921 continued to play a central role in Healy's life in subsequent years. He socialized with veterans from the revolution. Indeed, at one point in the 1930s, he sold a public house he had acquired in Inchicore to move back into the city centre, in the hope of attracting custom from other veterans. He applied and was awarded a military pension in 1935, a process that required him to recount his service in the revolu-

14 Michael Hopkinson (ed.), *Frank Henderson's Easter Rising: recollections of a Dublin volunteer* (Cork, 1998), p. 6.

tionary years and have it verified by other veterans.[15] He stood in the middle of the back row of the photograph of the survivors of the GPO garrison taken at Croke Park in 1936. For reasons that are not known, he did not provide a statement to the Bureau of Military History, which was collecting witness statements from 1947 to 1957, but he continued to talk in private and in public about his experiences in those years. He took part in the commemorations in 1966 and gave interviews about his experiences in the revolutionary years to the *Banba Review* and the *Chicago Daily News* and received an award from the Vintners' Union as the only member involved in the Rising still alive in 1966.[16]

Richard's past impressed those who married into the family, such as my mother, a schoolteacher who had grown up on Achill Island. She discovered that her father-in-law had aided in death the uncle of the Weafer children who used to holiday regularly in her village. My grandfather's past also impressed me. As a child I made regular visits, usually on a Sunday, with my father to see him, who by that time was a widower and living with his daughter in Drumcondra. While it was hard to reconcile the elderly man in a three-piece suit smoking a pipe and drinking the occasional glass of whiskey with the man of action of earlier years, his funeral in 1982 (he died at the age of 88) identified him clearly as a veteran of the Irish revolution. He was buried in Glasnevin Cemetery alongside many leading nationalists and revolutionaries. A tricolour flag was draped over his coffin and a gun salute made over his grave.

My grandfather provided me with a personal connection to a national story – the achievement of independence. His record of revolutionary activity also offered a stimulating contrast to the stories told by my maternal family, which had moved to Dublin and lived close to us. These were stories of a very different Ireland shaped by geographical remoteness, economic deprivation and a harsh environment. These included the drowning of ten fishermen off Inishkea in 1927, seasonal migration from Achill to Scotland and the Kirkintilloch disaster of 1937 and the washing up of mines and corpses onto the seashore during the Second World War, along with the lighter diversions of deliveries of library books, country dances and local eccentrics. The combined family memories of revolutionary activity in the heart of the capital and stoic lives on the western seaboard helped to weave my siblings and me into the national historical narrative that prevailed well into our childhoods. They also compensated for the lack of historical connection to where we lived, a new suburb five miles from the centre of Dublin.

15 On pensions, see Marie Coleman, 'Military Service pensions for veterans of the Irish Revolution, 1916–1923', *War in History,* 20:2 (2013), pp 201–21. **16** *Banba Review,* Jan. 1963; *Chicago Daily News,* 9 April 1966; the *Irish Press* contained an illustration of the event, 25 April 1966, and excerpts from the *Banba Review* article, 1 May 1966.

When searching for a special topic to write about for my Leaving Certificate examination in history, my grandfather's life was an obvious choice. Although he was dead by this time, the interviews he had given and family memories allowed me to build up a picture of his early life. The essay gave me my first experience of primary source research and of visiting an archive. My father brought me to the Military Archive in the Phoenix Park, where the officer on duty explained that my grandfather had regrettably not contributed a statement to the Bureau of Military History. I wrote a 2,000 word account, but ended up not using it on the day of the exam. Unusually, the Department had changed the format of the question and I wrote an essay about nationalist revolutions at the other end of Europe, in the Balkans, instead. My account of my grandfather continued to influence my intellectual formation, however. It became my first publication, in a student journal at UCD, where, inspired by my first taste of research and by the example of a maternal aunt and uncle who had studied history, I did a BA in history and German.

My connection to a participant in the Easter Rising made me sceptical of the revisionism that was the source of so much debate among scholars at the time, the late 1980s and early 1990s. Even tutorial discussions on the French Revolution focused on the legitimacy of violence as a force of political change. I knew my grandfather not to have any natural inclination to violence or reckless self-sacrifice and understood his decision to take up arms as the result of a firm conviction, shared by many others, that British rule was unjust and oppressive and that military action was the best means available to overcome it. I was frustrated by the narrow national framework of the debate and, fascinated by the much greater challenge of coming to terms with the past in post-war Germany, decided to divert my attention to German history and to do my postgraduate studies in the United States. Yet debates about Irish history continued to influence my research. Working in a field dominated by German, British and American historians, I realized that Irish history gave me a familiarity with sectarianism, which was foreign to scholars from elsewhere, and wrote my first book on Catholic-Protestant relations in Imperial Germany, as revealed in attitudes towards the Jesuits. I subsequently returned to Irish history, but from a transnational perspective, writing a monograph on nationalist assertions of an affinity with Poland, another country whose national aspirations were frustrated by foreign occupiers.

The centenary of the Easter Rising has given me the opportunity to reassess my grandfather's experience from the vantage point of nearly thirty years of studying German, Irish and Polish history. I am now more aware of the extent to which his political formation fits into a general pattern across the

Continent. As he was learning to appreciate traditional national games and acquire the physical training for military action in the GAA, nationalists throughout central and eastern Europe were doing the same in the Sokol movement. While the Christian Brothers educated him to reject foreign rule, the Jesuits were doing the same to young Poles in the German, Austrian and Russian empires. Moreover, he had plenty of counterparts in Russia and the Balkans who joined secret societies to prepare for armed revolution. I am also conscious, however, of how exceptional my grandfather and the other Easter rebels were in launching an insurrection so soon into the First World War. While there had been anti-imperial revolts in European overseas colonies before April 1916, the Easter Rising was the first major revolt against a belligerent power within Europe during the war. It took place before the Basmachi revolt against conscription among Moslems in Russia, the Arab Revolt against the British Empire and the Bolshevik Revolution and appears to have spurred anti-imperialist forces well beyond Ireland.[17]

I am also struck by the relatively low death rate by comparison with other nationalist conflicts on the Continent in the same decade. While local community conflicts and traditions of casual violence did much to raise the death toll in places like Silesia and the Balkans, ideology appears to have played a greater role in the political conflict in Ireland in the revolutionary decade. I am still disturbed by the matter-of-factness with which my grandfather describes being asked to 'wipe out a sniper' and his failure to record whether he met his target. I am not, however, as preoccupied with this question as German writer Uwe Timm, upon finding an entry in the diary of his brother, then a Wehrmacht soldier on the eastern front in the Second World War, describing a Russian smoking a cigarette as 'fodder for my MG'.[18] The principles laid down in the Proclamation, for which the rebels fought, were noble ones and already enjoyed much support nationally and internationally – national freedom, religious and civil liberty, equal rights and equal opportunities. Having become an activist for gender equality, I am especially encouraged by the early commitment of the rebels to a cause that still has to be achieved one hundred years later. While the rebels did not ask or receive permission to launch their military attack, no conspirators do, and it is not at all clear what a popular mandate might have looked like at a time when not all men, let alone any woman, had the right to vote in national elections in Ireland. I am relieved, however, that my grandfather did not take part in the internecine conflict that followed the War of Independence and that he did not live in a context that presented more

17 Enrico Dal Lago, Róisín Healy and Gearóid Barry (eds), *1916 in global context: an anti-Imperial moment* (London, 2018). **18** Uwe Timm, *In my brother's shadow: a life and death in the SS* (London, 2005).

difficult moral choices, such as that between collaboration and death which faced many of his central and eastern European contemporaries in the decades from 1914 to 1945.

While the only professional historian among Richard Healy's descendants, who number 110 at latest count, I am just one of many who have used the centenary as an opportunity to reflect on his legacy. My grandfather's four surviving children attended a ceremony at Dublin Castle to mark his contribution. I sat alongside my two brothers, two uncles, an aunt and cousin on O'Connell Street at the official commemorations on Easter Sunday 2016. In June, a cousin organized a wreath-laying ceremony at my grandfather's grave, followed by a personalized tour of sites associated with his role in the Rising. About fifty members of the extended family turned up, many meeting one another for the first time. In August, the Kilkenny branch of the family organized a plaque in memory of my grandfather in the graveyard of his parish church, attended by army officers and local TDs as well as family members.[19] As I reflect on the burden of history experienced by those whose ancestors' actions are cause for shame, I am grateful that my grandfather's actions have allowed this exercise in mining the family past to be a source of pride and even inspiration.

19 'A 1916 hero from Connahy remembered', *Kilkenny People*, 26 Aug. 2016.

Martin Savage: Sligo's working-class hero

ANGELA SAVAGE

The two Sligo names most closely associated with the Easter Rising of 1916 are those of Constance Markievicz (nee Gore-Booth) and Martin Savage.[1] The former grew up in a mansion, built of Ballisodare limestone, on a 32,000 acre estate at Lissadell, north of Sligo town, while the latter, my grand-uncle, was raised in a two-roomed thatched cottage on about sixteen acres at Streamstown, Ballisodare, between the Ox Mountains and the sea.[2] Although from very different social backgrounds, each played a significant role in the fight for Irish freedom. In this chapter, I will first give an overview of his short but eventful life which included action in the Easter Rising and the War of Independence, culminating in his death. I will then discuss how his heroic life impacted my life as I chose to use the pen, rather than the gun, to elicit change in Ireland.

I have very clear memories of Easter Sunday 1966 when my father, Martin, brought me to the commemoration ceremony for his uncle Martin Savage in the old graveyard in Ballisodare, Co. Sligo. I was wearing a beautiful Aran jumper that my mother had knit for my thirteenth birthday, and which I was happy to wear the following week as I sat the County Council Scholarship examinations. Martin, the youngest boy of thirteen children, was born on 12 October 1897 and went to school locally, leaving in his early teens following national school, as would have been the norm. He worked as a grocer's apprentice in Sligo town and in 1915 moved to Dublin to continue that work, initially in Dun Laoghaire and in 1916 as a barman at Keogh's licensed premises, 21 Bachelor's Walk.[3]

Coming from a nationalist background he soon became a member of the Irish Volunteers.[4] He was a member of the IRB centre in 41 Parnell Square, then the Foresters' Hall and was a friend of Frank Henderson and Paddy Moran. He was also a member of the Keating branch of the Gaelic League and joined Irish-language classes under Brid Ni hEigeartaigh.[5] He was one of the

1 Michael Farry, *Sligo, 1914–1921: a chronicle of conflict* (Trim, 1992), pp 79–80. 2 Rita Savage, Streamstown, personal communication, 20 June 2016. 3 John C. McTernan, *Here's to their memory: profiles of distinguished sligonians of bygone days* (Cork, 1977), pp 209–12; John C. McTernan, *Patriot sons and daughters: worthies of Sligo, profiles of eminent sligonians of other days.* (Sligo, 1994), pp 209–12. 4 BMH WS 1152 (Michael O'Dea), p. 2, http://www.bureauofmilitaryhistory.ie/reels/bmh/BMH. WS1152.pdf, accessed 14 July 2016. 5 BMH WS 336 (Garry Holohan), p. 36, http://www.bureauofmilitaryhistory.ie/reels/bmh/BMH.WS0336.pdf, accessed 14 July 2016.

Martin Savage as a teenager.

first officers of D Company, 2nd Battalion of the Dublin Brigade, which was set up for those men who were on night work and men such as grocers' assistants and barmen who would be working late.[6] These men went on parade on their half-holiday and on Sunday mornings. Before 1916, the company had about twelve members, while at its peak in the early 1920s there were about 140. The company was restricted to the area between Parnell Square and Phibsborough to the Royal Canal.[7]

6 Michael Hopkinson (ed.), *Frank Henderson's Easter Rising: recollection of a Dublin Volunteer* (Cork, 1998), p. 37. **7** BMH WS 774 (James Foley), pp 1–2, http://www.bureauofmilitaryhistory.ie/reels/bmh/BMH.WS0774.pdf, accessed 14 July 2016; Padraic O'Farrell, *Who's who in the Irish War of Independence, 1916–1921* (Dublin, 1980), p. 142.

Martin Savage, as an eighteen-year-old, fought in the GPO during Easter week according to the rigorous documentation admitted in the pension application by his family in 1922.[8] However, he is included in the Roll of Honour of the Four Courts Garrison which was compiled in 1936.[9] This anomaly may be due to his being moved to the Four Courts later in the week where the fighting continued for longer.[10] After the surrender, he was one of more than 3,000 prisoners who passed through Richmond Barracks.[11] During his incarceration there, he gave his hard-backed notebook containing the names and addresses of all the Volunteers in his Company to Fr Columbus Murphy OFM Cap who tore out and burned the incriminating information.[12] The notebook also contained thirteen black-and-white portrait photographs, two of which can be positively identified as Martin Savage and they show him to be a very dapper and good-looking teenager. On 1 May, he was part of the first group of 200 deported to Knutsford Detention Barracks in Cheshire[13] and was later moved to Frongoch Internment Camp in north Wales.[14] There, he was in the company of Michael Collins, Dick Mulcahy, Paddy Moran and Garry Holohan, the latter commenting 'we had plenty of talent in the way of singers and actors'.[15]

The prisoners at Frongoch Camp were released on 22 December 1916, and Martin Savage arrived home to Streamstown in time for Christmas with his family. According to his nephew Mick Savage, 'He came home from England a fairly shook man'.[16] In the new year, he returned to Dublin, initially to work in Merrion Row as a grocer's assistant and later as sub-manager at the newly opened Spirit, Grocery and Provisions store of Mr William Kirk, a Presbyterian, at 137 North Strand Road, where he lived over the premises. He was well-known in republican circles and was 1st Lieutenant of D Company and later Assistant Battalion Quartermaster of the 2nd Battalion of the Dublin Brigade.[17] He was described as being a 'very cheery young boy, good-looking in an almost girlish way, with a big shock of dark hair brushed back from his very mobile face. I never had seen him that he was not smiling and everybody, who met him and knew him, loved him'.[18]

8 Military Service Pension Collection, File 1D107, www.militaryarchives.ie/collections/online-collections/military-service-pensions-collection, accessed 15 July 2016. **9** The Roll of Honour of 1916, http://microsites.museum.ie/rollofhonour1916/map/allpages.aspx, accessed 15 July 2016. **10** Paul O'Brien, *Crossfire: the battle of the Four Courts, 1916* (Dublin, 2012), p. 85. **11** *1916 Rebellion handbook* (Dublin, 1998) p. 69. **12** Capuchin Archives, Ireland. CA/IR/1/2/5 1916. **13** *1916 Rebellion handbook*, p. 69. **14** W.J. Brennan-Whitmore, *With the Irish in Frongoch* (Dublin, 2013). **15** BMH WS 328 (Garry Holohan), p. 74, http://www.bureauofmilitaryhistory.ie/reels/bmh/BMH.WS0336.pdf, accessed 14 July 2016. **16** Mick Savage, Streamstown, personal communication, 20 June 2016. **17** BMH WS 1687 (Harry Colley), p. 41, http://www.bureauofmilitaryhistory.ie/reels/bmh/BMH.WS1687.pdf, accessed 14 July 2016. **18** BMH WS 511 (Michael Lynch), p. 79, http://www.bureauofmilitaryhistory.ie/reels/bmh/BMH.WS0511.pdf, accessed 14 July 2016.

Lieutenant Martin Savage in his twenties.

In 1918, the Lord Lieutenant lived in the Viceregal Lodge in the Phoenix Park (now Áras an Uachtaráin). At this time the role was entrusted to Sir John Denton Pinkstone, or Lord French, a veteran of the Boer War and Commander-in-Chief of the British Expeditionary Force that set sail for France in August 1914 until his forced resignation at the end of 1915. The new

Lord Lieutenant, as commander of all crown forces on the island, advocated a draconian, security-oriented approach to the growth of the Irish separatist movement and had been receiving death threats since January 1919.[19] French, who regarded himself as Irish, intended to retire to Ireland and in 1917 bought Drumdoe House, Co. Roscommon.[20]

Following overwhelming support for Sinn Féin in the 1918 general election, on 21 January 1919, coinciding with the first meeting of Dáil Éireann, the first shots were fired in the Anglo-Irish War with the Soloheadbeg ambush. The Irish copied and developed the guerrilla tactics adopted by the Boers in South Africa – the tactics of ambush and the exploitation of the Flying Columns. The British replied with a terror campaign of night raids, widespread searches, random arrests and shootings. In mid-1919, Michael Collins was Minster for Finance, Director of Intelligence, Director of Organization, and President of the Supreme Council of the IRB. In the autumn of 1919, shortly after Volunteers took an Oath of Allegiance to the Republic, Brigadier Dick McGee was arrested during a raid by the British forces on 76 Harcourt Street and Michael Lynch was appointed Acting O/C of the Dublin Brigade. About this time, it was decided by GHQ Staff to hold conventions in every brigade area in Ireland with a view to tightening up organization and co-ordinating efforts.

Following the Dublin Brigade convention, Michael Lynch realized the amount of sensitive information he had to hand so he sent for Martin Savage and handed him all the papers belonging to the convention and, in addition, Brigadier McGee's private papers, which were most important, containing among other matters the names of all the Squad, Michael Collins' assassination unit. Martin was warned not to appear at any parades, drills or functions of any sort while he had those papers in his possession.[21] Although he wasn't happy to be shut off from his friends in his company, the importance of the papers was impressed upon him and he agreed.

Late on the evening of 18 December, Michael Collins received intelligence that Lord French was to return by train from a private party that he had hosted at his country residence, Drumdoe in Frenchpark, Co. Roscommon, on the following morning and would alight at Ashtown railway station, about two miles from the Viceregal Lodge in the Phoenix Park, Dublin.[22] On the Friday

19 Marc Duncan, 'Ireland's Lord Lieutenant: 'a fount of all that is slimy in our national life', www.rte.ie/centuryireland/index.php/articles/irelands-lord-lieutenant-a-fount-of-all-that-slimy-in-our-national-life, accessed 21 July 2016. **20** Patrick Maume, 'French, Sir John Denton Pinkstone, 1st earl of Ypres, Viscount French of Ypres and High Park' in James McGuire and James Quinn (eds), *Dictionary of Irish biography* (Cambridge, 2009), http://dib.cambridge.org/viewReadPage.do?articleId=a3364, accessed 14 July 2016. **21** BMH WS 511 (Michael Lynch), p. 79, http://www.bureauofmilitaryhistory.ie/reels/bmh/BMH.WS0511.pdf, accessed 14 July 2016. **22** Dan Breen, *My fight for Irish freedom* (Dublin, 1964), pp 81–95.

morning, Paddy Daly, leader of the Squad, along with Michael McDonnell, led an ambush with Volunteers Dan Breen, Tom Keogh, Sean Tracey, Seamus Robinson, Sean Hogan, Vincent Byrne, Tom Kilkoyne, Jim Slattery, Ben Barrett and Joe Leonard.[23] On the fateful day Martin Savage left his place of work to bank money for his employer and then, following a chance encounter with Breen, Hogan and Leonard, and despite efforts to dissuade him, he joined the group to cycle to Ashtown.[24] The group met at Kelly's public house, situated about 500 yards from the railway station at the intersection of the Ashtown to Phoenix Park (Pelletstown) road with the Navan Road, and ordered minerals, pretending to be rival handball players. Daly then divided the unit into two sections, one under himself to lay in wait behind the hedge with handgrenades; the other men, including Martin Savage and under McDonnell, were to block the road leading into the Phoenix Park with a full dung-cart that lay in a hollow in the yard of Kelly's public house. Having heard the train-whistle, the men proceeded to their posts.

Lord French's entourage was met by a guard of fifty soldiers to drive the half mile to enter the Park at the Ashtown gate and then on to the Lodge. What had not been foreseen was that Constable O'Loughlin had come along to do point duty in the middle of the road.[25] Savage, Keogh and Breen were interrupted as they attempted to push the cart across the road to block the path of French's car. The policeman was dragged off the road after one of them lobbed a grenade at him, which did not go off but knocked him unconscious. When the convoy appeared more quickly than anticipated, and with the road not blocked, the grenade throwers concentrated their attack on the second car on the basis of incorrect intelligence. This car was bombed to a halt but French was actually in the first car, along with Detective Sergeant Halley, a lady friend and the driver. When the attack started, the driver immediately sped off and in through the gates of the Phoenix Park, with only Halley sustaining a wound to his hand. Number three car containing French's military escort came by, blazing gunfire. Sergeant Rumbold, in charge of the escort car, killed Martin Savage with a bullet to the right cheek, which passed out through the back of his head, as he was in the act of pulling the pin from a grenade.[26] He had turned twenty-two the previous month. His last words to Dan Breen, who was shot in the leg, was 'I'm done, Dan! Carry on!'. The entire ambush of 19 December 1919 was over inside a minute.

23 BMH WS 225 (Michael McDonnell), pp 5–6, http://www.bureauofmilitaryhistory.ie/reels/bmh/BMH.WS0225.pdf, accessed 14 July 2016. **24** BMH WS 423 (Vincent Byrne), p. 19, http://www.bureauofmilitaryhistory.ie/reels/bmh/BMH.WS0423.pdf, accessed 14 July 2016. **25** BMH WS 547 (Joe Leonard), pp 5–6, http://www.bureauofmilitaryhistory.ie/reels/bmh/BMH.WS0547.pdf, accessed 14 July 2016. **26** *Irish Times*, 20 Dec. 1919.

As the Volunteers had arrived on bicycles, they had no vehicle to remove Martin Savage's body and, on finding Kelly's door closed, they had no alternative but to leave the body in the yard. Lorry loads of Dublin Metropolitan Police and Royal Irish Constabulary arrived in rapid succession, while parties of soldiers came from the various barracks in Dublin and its neighbourhood. The body of the dead man was placed in a military lorry and driven to the Phoenix Park where it was placed in one of the buildings inside the gate near the Phoenix monument. When Michael Lynch heard the news of Martin's death, he immediately realized the implications for the Dublin Brigade and sent Tom Ennis to Martin's room to clear it of all papers. He did so in the nick of time; he was fired on by the military as he crossed the road on leaving the house. The whole Dublin Brigade was thereby saved from extinction.[27]

The inquest was opened on Saturday afternoon at 5 p.m. in the disused police barracks at Bessborough inside the Phoenix Park gate. Mr Christopher Friery, solicitor, and Coroner for North Co. Dublin, presided. Only formal evidence of identification was given. The identity of Martin Savage was in doubt for a considerable time, but eventually it was traced via a deposit receipt for a sum of £70, lodged in the name of Kirk in a Dublin bank on the Friday morning, which was found in his possession. The receipt led to his employer, Mr William Kirk, who when interviewed stated that 'Mr Martin Savage entered his employment two years ago, and a more industrious and gentlemanly young man it would be impossible to meet, while he was most attentive to his religious duties'.[28]

Details of the ambush were reported at the resumed inquest on Monday: 'On searching the body they found the ring of what is known as a Mills bomb round one of the fingers of the right hand.' These bombs are such as are used by the military, and by manipulating the ring upon a pin, a spring flies off and the bomb explodes within a time dictated by the length of fuse wire.[29] It is assumed, therefore, that the dead man had thrown at least one bomb before he was shot, and there were two marks where bombs had torn up the surface of the roadway near the cart. On further searching the body, the police found a German automatic pistol and a Smith and Weston revolver. Both these weapons were fully loaded, no shot having been discharged from either of them.[30]

27 BMH WS 511 (Michael Lynch), p. 82, http://www.bureauofmilitaryhistory.ie/reels/bmh/BMH.WS0511.pdf, accessed 14 July 2016. **28** *Irish Independent,* 20 Dec. 1919. **29** The grenades were fitted with five-second delay fuses, to be used in open fighting, rather than the one- to two-second fuses which would have been more appropriate for this ambush of moving vehicles. BMH WS 511 (Michael Lynch), p. 83, http://www.bureauofmilitaryhistory.ie/reels/bmh/BMH.WS0511.pdf accessed 14 July 2016. **30** *Irish Examiner*, 23 Dec. 1919.

The coroner suggested the following verdict: 'That the deceased ... died from the effects of a bullet wound inflicted by a soldier under circumstances which constituted an act of justifiable homicide, in that he inflicted the wound in self-defence and in the course of preventing a deliberately planned crime, namely, the murder of Lord French and his escort'. The jury, after an hour's consideration, returned the following verdict: 'That the deceased, Martin Savage, met his death as a result of a bullet fired by the military escort at Ashtown Cross on the 19 December, 1919. The jury beg to tender their sympathy to the relatives of the deceased'.[31]

The inquest was attended by Martin's two brothers; Michael from Streamstown and Patrick who wore the uniform of the Australian Naval Force, and the body was claimed by them.[33] They wished it to be placed in a Dublin church for the night before taking it for burial in his native Sligo the next morning. Representations were made at the Pro-Cathedral and at his parish church, St Laurence O'Toole's, Seville Place, but these were refused. Instead, his coffin was taken to Broadstone Station where he was left overnight in a mortuary van, attended by his brothers and friends.[34]

Many members of Martin Savage's battalion were unhappy that GHQ did not organize a public funeral in Dublin. Chief-of-Staff of the IRA, Richard Mulcahy, held firmly that IRA members should not unnecessarily leave themselves open to detection or arrest. Frank Henderson, Commandant of the 2nd Battalion, addressed the Companies of the Battalion, including D company, on the Monday night before the removal of the remains. The following morning, about thrity or forty young men, including members of D Company, were present at Broadstone Station when his remains were entrained. They stood to attention and saluted as the train moved out.[35]

There was a large attendance of relatives and friends at Collooney railway station to meet the body. The coffin, covered with the republican colours, was carried to the graveyard in Ballisodare, a distance of two miles, on the shoulders of mourners. For an hour or so before the arrival of the funeral, the graveyard was occupied by an armed force of police. They remained there during the burial service and did not retire for some time after the people had left. The proceedings passed off without incident.[36]

On the day immediately after the death of Martin Savage, the *Irish Independent* published an editorial in which it referred to him and other IRA

31 Ibid. **33** *Freeman's Journal*, 23 Dec. 1919. **34** BMH WS 575 (Michael McDonnell), p. 6, http://www.bureauofmilitaryhistory.ie/reels/bmh/BMH.WS0225.pdf, accessed 14 July 2016. **35** BMH WS 821 (Frank Henderson), pp 69–72, http://www.bureauofmilitaryhistory.ie/reels/bmh/BMH.WS0821.pdf, accessed 14 July 2016. **36** *Irish Independent*, 24 Dec. 1919.

soldiers who took part in the attack on Lord French as 'would-be assassins'. GHQ considered that the article reflected poorly on the men engaged in the national struggle and was an invitation to the British to treat them as criminals. Action, which took the form of a raid on the printing works of the *Independent* newspaper and the smashing of vital machines, took place on the Sunday evening. It was ordered as a warning to the proprietors, and the proprietors of all newspapers, that such unpatriotic comment at the height of the fight for freedom would not be tolerated.[37] Michael Lynch and Peadar Clancy organized this action and up to thirty men, over half an hour, with sledge hammers and crow bars and heavy wrenches, left the machine room in a shambles. However, the *Irish Independent* appeared on the streets of Dublin the following morning, having been printed by one of the other Dublin newspapers: the leading article which was critical of the ambush was reproduced.[38]

Martin Savage was the second Volunteer officer to be killed in the War of Independence (the first was Robert Byrne, Mid-Limerick Brigade, in April 1919).[39] However, the attempt on the life of Lord French ensured that Martin Savage's death received extensive media coverage, both in Ireland and internationally, including a major report in the *New York Times*.[40] The Vatican, according to a Rome message, was 'gravely concerned over the incident, which it regrets, as it does also the failure to effect an Irish settlement, which would have averted such a calamity'.[41]

Two disturbing issues arose for the authorities in the aftermath of the attempted assassination of Lord French. With the exception of the staff at the Viceregal Lodge, no one was supposed to know that he had been on a private visit to a friend in Roscommon, but the raiders evidently had very accurate information. The other issue was how the dozen other assailants were able to make good their escape in broad daylight: despite extensive investigations, none was ever captured.

In an application to the Compensation (Personal Injuries) Committee, Martin Savage's father Michael stated that Martin, prior to his death, was in receipt of a salary £91 p.a. plus board and upkeep.[42] From this, he gave about £50 p.a. to his family in Streamstown. The compensation applied for amounted to £2,000: £100 p.a. for at least 20 years. In April 1924, under Section 8 of the Army Pensions Act, 1923, a gratuity of £50 was awarded. A

37 BMH WS 781 (Patrick J. Kelly). p. 57, http://www.bureauofmilitaryhistory.ie/reels/bmh/BMH.WS0781.pdf, accessed 14 July 2016. **38** BMH WS 569 (John Anthony Caffrey), p. 3, http://www.bureauofmilitaryhistory.ie/reels/bmh/BMH.WS0569.pdf, accessed 14 July 2016. **39** *Irish Press*, 1 Jan. 1980. **40** *New York Times*, 23 Dec. 1919. **41** *Irish Independent*, 22 Dec. 1919. **42** Military Service Pensions Collection File 1D107, http://mspcsearch.militaryarchives.ie/docs/files//PDF_Pensions/R1/1D107MartinSavage/W1D107MartinSavage.pdf, accessed 15 July 2016.

subsequent letter[43] from Michael Savage dated 15 August 1924 to the Army Finance Officer read

> Dear Sir, I was anxiously waiting to hear from you about my case, or am I to receive only the £50 gratuity paid me on May 4th 1924. I was led to believe that I would be entitled to a quarterly pension for life. If £50 is all I am to get for the loss of my son ye might as well have kept it.

His family applied again under the 1932 Act and was unsuccessful, but finally in 1946 received a 1917–21 service medal with bar.

Martin Savage was commemorated in 1948 with a memorial erected by the National Graves Association at Ashtown Cross near the Halfway House (formerly Kelly's) pub. It was rededicated following construction work for the new roundabout in 1991. Each December, on the Sunday closest to 19 December, following Mass at the nearby church on the Navan Road, a procession of relatives, friends, veterans of the Dublin Brigade and politicians has marched to the memorial where an oration is given, followed by the trumpeting of the *Last Post* and *Reveille,* before lunch in the Halfway House pub.

My parents attended in 1955 as evidenced by a photo published in the *Irish Press,* a copy of which was displayed prominently in our home.[44] The Savage family from Streamstown and Martin's sister Agnes' family in Dublin have been more active participants through the years and the Streamstown family has provided a new headstone and has been involved in the upkeep of his grave in Ballisodare where a commemoration is held each Easter Sunday at noon. My brother Martin, having recently retired, is involved in the regeneration of the disused graveyard under the Leader Rural Development Programme. I don't remember any discussion, either within my family or in the community, of my grand-uncle, apart from that 1966 commemoration. In 2016, however, a plaque was erected on his Streamstown home, where Mick and Rita Savage live. The bridge in Ballisodare will be named the Martin Savage Bridge in 2018. Many housing estates, including one in Sligo town and another in Ashtown, have been named after him. GAA and soccer clubs are both located at Martin Savage Park in Ashtown, and Feis Shligigh awards the Corn Martin Savage in his memory each year for aithriseoireacht d'iomaitheoirí (6–8 mbliana d'aois).

My grand-uncle was one of the many working-class, not formally educated, but highly motivated young men and women who fought for Ireland's

43 Ibid. **44** *Irish Press,* 19 Dec. 1955.

independence. I hung a large photograph of him in my home for years, without really knowing much about him. I too came from a working-class family, the second eldest of seven, born into a cottage without running water. I feel I inherited some of his desire to escape poverty but also his altruism and bravery. I, however, had the good fortune to benefit from an essentially free education, up to fourth level: I am the only member of my family to have attended university.

Martin Savage showed immense bravery in giving up his life at twenty-two. At that age, I had just finished a science degree at University College Galway, thanks to a County Council Grant, and, prior to that, the aforementioned County Council Scholarship from 1966 to attend a boarding school. So, in September 1975, I headed off to Vancouver, Canada, to pursue a PhD in chemistry and afterwards enjoyed research fellowships there and in Germany, as an Alexander von Humboldt fellow.

Looking back now, I can see that I chose to use the pen as my weapon to elicit change, rather than the sword or the gun. Five years of boarding school started me on my letter-writing road. My mother Eileen, although having left school at fourteen, had lovely handwriting and we corresponded regularly. This continued through my university days in Galway and later as a student in Vancouver, where I joined Amnesty International (AI) and was involved in many letter-writing campaigns. During my time in Germany I continued my membership of AI, sending handwritten letters all over the world, some of which yielded success, with prisoners of conscience being released.

Perhaps it was this success, combined with my training in scientific writing, where results and conclusions based only on the *facts* are presented, that led me to put pen to paper over what I saw were clear injustices. And those eight years abroad, particularly the six years in Canada, provided me with a life of freedom where I could make my own decisions and have my own value judgements. My two years in Germany, while scientifically very beneficial, brought to light the racism, sexism and xenophobia that were part and parcel of life there. And so I was happy to return in 1983 to a junior lectureship at University College Galway.

As a volunteer with the Samaritans I took many phone calls from lonely and suicidal people, and began to recognize some of the hidden secrets of life in Ireland. A common theme was the escape to cities abroad, either for holidays or for longer spells, of young gay men. In 1986, when the reality of the AIDS epidemic was being recognized internationally, my fellow Samaritan and colleague Dr Evelyn Stevens and I could see that the Irish government and statutory agencies were essentially ignoring the crisis and that action needed to be taken. Evelyn and I, after attending a training course in Dublin, called a public meeting in Galway, and AIDS West was set up. Our mandate was twofold: to give support to those affected by HIV/AIDS and their families, and to provide clear, unbiased information about the disease.

As both of us were scientists – Evelyn lectured in microbiology – we were able to review the latest international literature on the disease and, in a series of six articles for the widely-read *Galway Advertiser*, we clearly spelled out the methods of transmission of the HIV virus, and attempted to counter the hysteria growing in many quarters, not helped by some uninformed and sometimes homophobic members of the medical profession. We ran a weekly telephone information line, produced information leaflets (in both English and Irish), hosted an international 'Visual AIDS' exhibition of posters and ran 'safer sex' clinics in the university, despite the protestations of some staff.

As the west of Ireland representative for the national 'Condom Sense' campaign, which campaigned for the sale of condoms from vending machines, I was a member of a delegation which met with the Minister for Health, Brendan Howlin. I also met with the UCG President, Dr Colm O'hEocha, on World AIDS Day in 1992 and asked for his help in having condom vending machines installed in the university, pointing out that someone from Galway, who had died from AIDS, was being buried that day – he was aware that a former student had died of AIDS some time previously. His support ensured that Buildings Office staff withstood the barrage of criticism from those who were opposed to the installation of condom vending machines in ladies' and gents' toilets in the Library building.

On Valentine's Day 1992, I made the front page of the *Galway Advertiser*, in a report on the illegal installation of condom vending machines in a night club in Salthill: later that month I was 'read from the pulpit' during the annual Novena in Galway. I also made the RTÉ evening news when I asked Taoiseach Albert Reynolds, who was on a walkabout on Shop Street, when legislation would be introduced to allow for the sale of condoms from vending machines. Eventually, on Easter Sunday 1993, on a flight home from a conference abroad, I was delighted to read in a newspaper that Minister Brendan Howlin was to introduce the necessary legislation. It was now time to hang up my AIDS activist boots.

I oversaw first-year chemistry labs for up to 800 students for twenty-five years, and a simple experiment that all undertook was the test for nitrate, which could identify a nitro group from any source, be it nitroglycerin in explosives or nitrocellulose from playing cards. It was abundantly clear that the forensic evidence used to convict the Birmingham Six was deeply flawed and so I served as scientific advisor to a Dublin-based, non-party political group set up to campaign for the men's release – one of many formed in Britain, Ireland, Europe and the US following the rejection of their 1988 appeal.

I also undertook a letter-writing campaign to *inter alia* the Royal Society of Chemistry (letter ignored) and to the British government (letter acknowledged) and copied all correspondence to the six inmates. Eventually, their convictions were declared unjust and unsatisfactory and quashed by the Court of Appeal on 14 March 1991. Later that year I was invited to a function in Dublin to mark their release and it was wonderful to speak with some of the men and hear that they indeed remembered my letters and were grateful that I and so many others believed them and were working for their release.

Like many of my colleagues, I was very involved in both the setting up of the Women's Studies Centre in the late 1980s and in the presidential election campaign of Mary Robinson in 1990. Just after she took office, Dr Jane Conroy, Dr Tadhg Foley and I wrote to President Robinson and invited her to officially open the Women's Studies Centre. She replied that she would be happy to so do and we forwarded her letter to the Quadrangle inviting the Buildings Officer to provide us with the long-promised premises. After initial consternation, the WSC was provided with a space in Corrib Village and President Robinson made her first visit of many to the university: I was delighted to act as host for the event.

When President O'hEocha retired in 1996, there was an open competition for his successor, with staff having a vote. As an active member of the SIPTU trade union, I was aware that one issue that needed rectifying was the need for an on-campus crèche, as in all other Irish universities. Although being in my forties and with no conscious interest in motherhood, I wrote to each applicant and received only one reply – from Prof. Pat Fottrell, who agreed that if elected he would have a crèche built. In the autumn of 1997 I wrote one of the most significant letters of my life, as part of the application process to adopt a girl from China. I met Li Lu during the first week of January 2000, on the day the university's wonderful, modern, crèche opened its doors. What amazing synchronicity and karma.

I enjoyed a very happy, fulfilling, and busy life in academia for many years, publishing and lecturing internationally in the field of glycoscience, winning millions of euro in research grants, designing and teaching new courses and being awarded a Personal Professorship. In 2008, I suffered burnout and so took another brave step – to escape academic life through early retirement and focus on nurturing myself and my beautiful daughter.

I like to picture my grand-uncle, who lived close to the GPO, standing proudly when Padraig Pearse read the Proclamation of the Irish Republic, which included the lines 'The Republic guarantees religious and civil liberty, equal rights and equal opportunities to all its citizens, and declares its resolve to pursue the happiness and prosperity of the whole nation and of all its parts, cherishing all the children of the nation equally'. My hope for Li Lu is that she will see that ideal realized.

Acknowledgment

I would like to thank my brother Martin for his encouragement and support in writing this chapter, and Rita and Mick Savage for helpful discussion. I would like to dedicate this work to my recently-found eldest brother William Blakford, born Patrick Healy in 1949 in London.

'He did everything, he was the most reliable man we had': Commandant Pat Fallon (1885–1958), South Mayo Brigade

ENDA FALLON JR, DAITHÍ FALLON & CIAN Ó NÉILL

Commandant Pat Fallon was laid to rest in July 1958 in the presence of J.E. MacEllin, Chairman of the Irish Press; Mr M. O'Morain, Fianna Fáil (FF), Minister for the Gaeltacht; Mr P.A. Calleary (FF), TD; Senator T. Ruane (FF); the most senior surviving members of the anti-Treaty IRA in the west including Maj. Gen. Michael Kilroy, Brig. Paddy Maye, Brig. Tom Maguire; and many Mayo IRA Volunteers including P. Keville, J. O'Reilly and L.J. Sheridan. The oration at his graveside was given by Paddy Mullaney, one of the last anti-Treaty IRA prisoners to be released from the 'Glasshouse' in the Curragh after the Civil War.

Commandant Pat Fallon was a committed republican. He was mobilized during Easter week, took part in an action in Balla, Co. Mayo, and was imprisoned in Richmond Barracks in the aftermath. He participated in the majority of actions carried out by the South Mayo Brigade Flying Column and was involved in gun-running activities in England, accompanying Dick Walsh, the organizer of the IRA in Co. Mayo. Unfortunately, the guns procured by them were confiscated by 'Collins' Crowd' in General Headquarters (GHQ) and diverted to other parts of the country. From then on, there was a lack of trust between the organizers of the Mayo Brigades and GHQ. He took the republican side during the Civil War, and was captured and held initially in Athlone where he witnessed the aftermath of the January 1923 executions. He then spent the remainder of 1923 in Tintown 2 at the Curragh Camp and was released on 23 December 1923. Following his release, he joined Fianna Fáil upon its foundation, but continued his friendships with former comrades of all shades of green. He adopted an intermediary or conciliatory role in local events to ensure that tensions and political differences did not spill over into violence. He was a committed Balla and Mayo man.

Pat Fallon, like many other veterans of the revolutionary period, chose not to speak about his military involvement to his family and others. Most of what we know about our grandfather/great-grandfather comes from oral sources within the family. There are a number of witness statements and pension files available which more-or-less corroborate the oral history, but inevitably there are contradictions within sources which in some cases require forensic examination to fully resolve. Pat Fallon's story was quite straightforward, certainly as told to us. For us as children the narrative was fairly clear and the conclusions we arrived at almost by a process of osmosis were that we were the good guys (Fianna Fáil and the 'Old IRA') and the others (Fine Gael, the Free State and Michael Collins) 'sold us out'. This wasn't a state of affairs emphasized or explicitly enunciated by anyone in the family, it was just the natural scheme of things and was implicitly accepted.

We cannot recollect any great desire to delve into our grandfather's IRA past during that time. We had never met him, there was little written about him, and there were no letters, diaries or communications in existence from that period, due to the constant weekly raids by the British military on his family's home place in Ballymackeogh, Balla, Co. Mayo. Life takes over and like all young people growing up we looked to the future and not to the past. Our motivation for writing this chapter is to formally and publicly recognize our grandfather's contribution to the Irish republican fight for freedom from British rule. We want to highlight the sacrifices and the difficult decisions he made to dedicate himself to armed resistance to British rule in Ireland. We are also attempting to explore what impact it had on his family, whether it shaped and influenced the outlook of our own families and whether there is any legacy for the generation following us.

Revolutionary activity, 1914–23

1914	Joined the Volunteers in Balla, Co. Mayo, and subsequently the Irish Volunteers.
May 1916	Arrested by British military on the 16 May with five others as a result of the arms seizure in Balla and imprisoned in Castlebar and subsequently Richmond Barracks, Dublin.
1918	Helped to organize an operation for landing arms from Germany in Mayo under the command of Fintan Murphy from General Headquarters (GHQ).
Jan. 1920	Participated in an operation to attack a munitions train from Castlebar to Dublin.
May/July 1920	Involved in raiding trains at Balla and Manulla for military supplies and mail respectively. Went on the run after the first raid and didn't return to his home and business until Dec. 1923.
July 1920	Four Mayo Brigades of Óglaigh na hÉireann (IRA) formed.
Nov. 1920	On the reorganization of the Mayo Brigades Pat Fallon was appointed Quartermaster of the Balla Battalion Óglaigh na hÉireann (IRA). He was subsequently appointed Quartermaster South Mayo Brigade Óglaigh na hÉireann (IRA) after the arrest of Joe Brennan.
Dec. 1920	Transferred arms obtained by Dick Walsh to the various Mayo Brigades.

7 Mar. 1921	Ambush of British military at Kilfaul, Partry, Co. Mayo. At least two British soldiers were killed and the senior serving British officer in the south Mayo area was seriously wounded.
Apr. 1921	Gun-running in London with Dick Walsh. A shipment of guns transported through Liverpool docks, but intercepted by GHQ for their own use. A significant number of arms paid for by money obtained directly from the people of Mayo or through bank and post office raids in Mayo were diverted ostensibly to the Cork brigades.
3 May 1921	Ambush at Tourmakeady, Co. Mayo. Involvement unclear. Oral history and obituary in *Irish Press*, 8 July 1958, says Pat Fallon was involved; however, no documentary evidence exists to support this. Pension files seem to indicate he was in England obtaining arms at the time.
Truce Period	Rearming and training in Moore Hall and the Glen of Imall.
Dec. 1921	Takes over command of Ballinrobe Infantry Barracks on its evacuation by the British.
Summer – Dec. 1922	Member of Flying Column South Mayo Brigade, 2nd Western Division IRA; took part in raids on Free State forces in Mountbellew, Co. Galway, and Mount Talbot, Co. Roscommon.
6 Dec. 1922	Arrested by Free State forces near Mayo Abbey visiting Winifred Gilligan, his future wife. Initially imprisoned at Castlebar and then transferred to Athlone on the 20 January, the day of the executions in the ball alley at Custume Barracks. Subsequently served time in Tintown 2 in the Curragh Camp, where he participated in escape attempts and hunger strikes
23 Dec. 1923	Released from the Curragh and returned to civilian life.

Table 1: Synopsis of major IRA activities of Pat Fallon.

Easter Rising 1916 and the aftermath

Pat Fallon was one of the verifying officers for the South Mayo Brigade during the 1934 round of pensions. In his military pension file there is a handwritten letter from Pat Fallon to the Minister of Defence dated 7 April 1941 in which he states 'I beg to apply for a 1916 (Easter Week) medal'.[1] A similar application can be found in the pension file of Richard 'Dick' Walsh, then a Fianna Fáil TD for Mayo and a member of the Irish Volunteer National Executive. While there is no response recorded in Pat Fallon's file there is one in Walsh's. The reply is a formulaic one from the Department of Defence to state that 'this medal is issuable only to persons who were awarded a certificate under the Military Services Pensions Acts of 1924 and 1934 entitling the person to a pension in respect of the Easter Week Period'.[2]

One of the online sources on the 1916 Rising is the 'Easter 1916 applicants at action sites map'. Balla, Co. Mayo, is marked as an action site with one name listed, James Ruane. Ruane received the only 1916 service medal awarded in Co. Mayo. The only first-hand accounts that we have so far found of this event

1 Patrick Fallon pension application, MSP, M34C178, p. 11. 2 Richard Walsh pension application, MSP, W34A13, p. 22.

are the witness statement of Dick Walsh and Pat Fallon's interview with Ernie O'Malley.[3] While Fallon's statement identifies the protagonists involved on the crown side, Walsh's account of Easter week in Balla and its aftermath is much more comprehensive.[4] It is useful to note that there was little or no information in Mayo as to what exactly was happening in Dublin during Easter week.

To summarize Walsh's statement, the local Volunteers in Balla were mobilized during Easter week awaiting orders under Walsh's command. On Sunday 30 April 1916, an opportunity arose to intercept a cache of arms being transported from Kiltimagh to Castlebar with a National Volunteers escort.[5] Members of the escort had been sworn in as special constables after news broke about the Rising. The convoy stopped at McEllin's hotel, Balla. While the escort was in the hotel, a group of six Balla Volunteers (including O/C Dick Walsh) captured the guns and ammunition:

> Murphy came hurriedly into my house stating that the motor car containing Moclair and his pals were after pulling up at McEllin's Hotel. The occupants of the car went into the hotel and Murphy stated he saw the rifles in the motor car outside. I decided to go down immediately and sent Murphy to collect all the men he could. We could only mobilize five or six men – Tom Murphy, Pat Fallon, Pat Keville, Michael Golden and Jim Reilly, who also co-operated. We took the rifles away with us out of the motor car. Moclair and his crowd saw us through the hotel window taking them, but did not make any move to prevent us. We heard later that Moclair and Tom Quinn at least were armed with revolvers.[6]

A second-hand account of the action is in the statement of Thomas Howley.[7] The Volunteers hid the guns, were subsequently arrested and brought to Castlebar Jail and later transferred to Richmond Barracks. The surrender in Dublin had happened on Friday 28 April, unbeknownst to them. After protracted negotiations in Richmond Barracks they were released, having arranged for the guns to be returned.

James Ruane appears to have been involved in this event, at the least

3 Richard Walsh, BMH, WS 400; Patrick Fallon pension application, MSP, MSP34REF3097; Pat Fallon interview, University College Dublin Archives (UCDA), Ernie O'Malley notebooks, P17b/109; Richard Walsh pension application, MSP, MSP34REF18536. 4 Richard Walsh, BMH, WS 400, pp 11–21. 5 The National Volunteers was the name taken by the members of the Irish Volunteers who sided with John Redmond and the Irish Parliamentary Party when the organization split regarding whether the Irish Volunteers should take an active part in the First World War. 6 Richard Walsh, BMH, WS 200, pp 11–21. 7 Thomas Howley, BMH, WS 1122, p. 2.

bringing intelligence from Kiltimagh about the movement of the guns, but he is not named by Dick Walsh as one of the six involved in the actual operation. However, the statement of his brother Senator Sean T. Ruane differs from Walsh's:

> They found out the contents were rifles … so the two cycled to Balla, five miles distant …They notified Dick Walsh, who, with another and themselves, arranged to act if the opportunity presented itself. It did. The occupants of the car drove up to McEllin's Hotel. On their way out they were held up. Some days later, when the Rising finished, D. Walsh and a few other boys, one named Murphy, were arrested and lodged in Castlebar Jail.[8]

In 1924, James Ruane, who was pro-Treaty, received a military service pension for the Easter week period. Anti-Treaty Irregulars were ineligible for this pension, including both Pat Fallon and Dick Walsh. In 1934, those who were anti-Treaty became eligible for service pensions for the first time. Pat Fallon applied for a pension for all of the period, including Easter week. He received a substantial Grade C pension of £96 per year for the period commencing 1 April 1917 to the end of the Civil War but none for Easter week, apparently because the action had happened after the surrender in Dublin. As his application letter for a 1916 medal states:

> We mentioned this in our applications for military service pensions, but the referee maintained that the operation was one day late and we did not press the claim. We now maintain we are entitled to a 1916 medal as recognition for this operation. I am in receipt of a military service pension from 1916 to 1923.[9]

At the time of receiving and accepting his pension in 1936, Pat Fallon was not aware of the consequences of not receiving pension recognition for Easter week. Despite this, he still stated his reluctance to appeal this on the basis that 'I will be bringing every other fellow appealing after me.'[10] While the family had previously been aware of the 1916 action, it is only in the year of commemorations that we have understood the implications of the decisions made in both the 1924 and 1934 Pension Acts. Pat Fallon himself clearly felt that the action warranted inclusion in the Roll of Honour of 1916.

8 Sean Ruane, BMH, WS 1588, p. 10. **9** Patrick Fallon pension application, MSP, M34C178, p. 11. **10** Patrick Fallon pension application, MSP, MSP34REF3097, p. 17.

Tourmakeady

The Tourmakeady ambush was the second major armed confrontation between the South Mayo Brigade and crown forces and took place on the 3 May 1921. After the initial ambush, part of the IRA column retreated across the Partry Mountains. They were subsequently surrounded by British reinforcements from nearby barracks and pinned down by consistent machine-gun fire for most of the day. Later in the evening the IRA managed to retreat through the British lines under cover of darkness. Conflicting accounts from Tom Maguire, the IRA column commander, and Lt Ibberson, a British army officer, have emerged with respect to the extent of the battle and the number of British troops involved. Whatever the truth, it is clear that the 'victory' was with the IRA. Crown forces had an opportunity to capture or eliminate an entire IRA column, which was surrounded in open country by a vastly superior force, but yet they were unable to do so.

Pat Fallon's obituary in the *Irish Press* and other notifications in the aftermath of his death in 1958 all stated that he took part in the ambush.[11] Family oral history also placed him at the event. However, Pat Fallon's pension file and his statement to Ernie O'Malley do not support this.[12] This was surprising to us given the detail of the events of Tourmakeady described by our father Enda and the evidence of Pat Fallon's daughter Peg and niece Nora Fallon. Surprisingly, a friend from Ballyglass near Balla having become involved in a discussion of the topic remarked that 'everyone knows Pat Fallon was at Tourmakeady'. It is difficult to arrive at a rational explanation for the differences in these two versions of events. One possible reason could be that family members heard the story from someone else in Balla and that Pat Fallon, maintaining his vow of silence, neither confirmed nor denied it. It may simply be that his children never asked him and the event was never discussed at home.

Impact on the family

Pat Fallon's republican activities and his attitude to them had a significant influence on subsequent generations of his family and their lives. The extent of that influence differed depending on whether their physical or mental well-being or their attitudes to the national question and politics in general are under consideration. Pat Fallon was a self-employed carpenter and joiner before the War of Independence and so he had a particular set of skills that

11 *Irish Press,* 8 July 1958; *Mayo News*, 19 July 1958; *Connaught Telegraph,* 12 July 1958; *Western People,* 30 Aug. 1958; *Western People,* 19 July 1958. **12** Patrick Fallon pension application, MSP, MSP34REF3097; Pat Fallon interview (UCDA), Ernie O'Malley notebooks, P17b/109.

would have been in demand in the post-Civil War era when the newly formed Free State was been nurtured. However, government jobs and contracts would not have been available to him, as 'Irregulars' were banned from being employed by the state. Nevertheless, his ability to take up where he left off in 1919 was probably significantly influenced by the fact that the South Mayo Brigade areas were predominantly anti-Treaty during the Civil War. He was viewed positively as both a local republican leader and an important member of the community, and it is in this context that people would have supported his business at that time. Unfortunately, many of his anti-Treaty comrades would not have been so lucky. The general lack of opportunities available to them allied with the embargo on working for the new Free State meant that many were forced to emigrate.

Pat managed to build up a successful contracting, carpentry and joinery business and a shop and petrol pumps in Balla during the decades after the Civil War. He married Winifred Gilligan in 1924 and they had seven children: Peg, Tom, Una, Pat Joe, Kevin, Enda and Bernie. Kevin died shortly after birth, Patrick Joseph died in 1936 aged seven, and his wife Winifred died shortly afterwards in 1937. At the time of Winifred's death his eldest child was twelve and the youngest was four. It was unusual at that time for a single man to bring up six children alone. He was motivated by the well-being of his family and the equal treatment of his daughters and sons. At this time, he was also supporting his niece Nora whose father Tom was a conscripted Somme veteran and IRA activist in the Manchester area. Tom survived the First World War but died in 1925 as a result of his overall health failing due to his experiences on the Western Front and having contracted TB during the war. Circumstances meant that Nora's mother was unable to look after her, and as a result she was brought home to her grandparents' home in Ballymakeogh, and subsequently to Balla, and was raised there. Our own father Enda even thought that she was his sister until around the time he went to secondary school. Pat Fallon paid for the education of his five children and his niece. They all attended boarding school either in St Jarlath's College, Tuam, Co. Galway, or Gortnor Abbey in Co. Mayo. Four of the six went to university, one trained as a nurse and his oldest son Tom worked in and eventually took over the family business. There is an interesting story that one of his neighbours suggested that he should put up a good dowry on his daughters so that they could be married off. Pat Fallon's response was that he would rather use the money to educate them and enable them to make a life for themselves, an enlightened position to take at the time.

Outwardly his involvement with the Irish Revolution did not have any impact on Pat Fallon's mental well-being, though his physical health undoubtedly suffered as a result of being on the run and spending time in jail, which included at least one period on hunger strike. He was a pragmatic man and got on with his life on his return to Balla in 1924. Nevertheless, in a recent conversation with his eldest daughter Peg (1925–2016), she remarked that he may have had some regrets regarding what he had done and that this influenced his relationship with the Catholic Church in the last few years of his life. It's not clear what she meant by this though we do know that anti-Treaty fighters ignored the orders of the Church during the Civil War even under threat of excommunication. Despite this there were sympathetic clergy who he refers to as 'good' in his witness statement to Ernie O'Malley; others who didn't support the republican movement were referred to as 'bad'. The tone of that statement is quite matter-of-fact and makes little reference to how he felt, what motivated him or what his fears and concerns were.

There are only two short passages in his witness statement to Ernie O'Malley which reveal more of him. In one he refers to the uncertainty around who would be selected for execution when imprisoned in Custume Barracks during the Civil War. We presume that at the time no one really knew who was going to be executed and as it turns out McKeon's men avoided shooting senior officers held in Athlone. This period obviously played on his mind as he also referred to one of the execution squad later that day who was drunk and indiscriminately firing his weapon in the barracks yard. On another occasion when in General Headquarters in Dublin after the weapons he and Dick Walsh had procured in England were confiscated by Collins' men, he refers to them as a 'dark' crowd. Presumably this is a reference to Collins' squad. But, of course, the event was not contemporaneous with the O'Malley interviews, which were carried out in the 1940s. Consequently, it could have been influenced by the events of the Civil War and his and Dick Walsh's antipathy towards Michael Collins. It is then ironic that he was to become a lifelong friend of Toddy Andrews, the Fianna Fáil TD and former member of Collins' Squad. He also maintained friendships with Tom Maguire, his former senior officer who remained a physical force republican, and Michael McHugh, who was imprisoned with him in Richmond Barracks after 1916 but took the pro-Treaty side during the Civil War.

Clearly Pat Fallon was prepared to fight and die for the republican cause as evidenced by his participation in the Partry ambush in March 1921. He was active and on the run for long periods where capture could have meant torture and execution. On at least one occasion he was stopped by British forces but he managed to avoid arrest through the goodwill of a member of the RIC who took his weapon off him and concealed it before the British military could identify him as an armed rebel. He risked his life smuggling guns from

England through Liverpool docks to Dublin. He took part in the Civil War presumably because of the oath he took and out of loyalty to his comrades. Incidentally, his brother Jim, who was a member of the Balla Battalion of the South Mayo Brigade, emigrated to the US and didn't participate in this conflict. Pat endured prison and hunger strike. In short, he was prepared to do what it took.

One of the questions that arises is what was Pat Fallon not prepared to do for the republican cause? We wonder whether he would have been willing to participate in the execution of an informer or the assassination of a member of the crown forces or loyalist sympathizers. After the Tourmakeady ambush, Thomas Hopkins, a member of the RIC who was home on leave from Co. Tyrone, was killed by the IRA near Ballindine, Co. Mayo. We do not know who carried out the operation or who gave the order for it, whether it was sanctioned locally or by Brigade Staff. At the time, Pat Fallon was one of the most senior active Brigade officers – Tom Maguire was seriously wounded and Michael O'Brien had been killed by the British on the Partry Mountains. However, we cannot be sure whether he was still in England procuring arms or whether he had returned to Mayo. We suspect that he would have been prepared to carry out all 'lawful' orders, which included executing informers and shooting members of the crown forces. In his Ernie O'Malley statement, he talks about informers and says that they (his comrades in the South Mayo Brigade) had 'their suspicions but no evidence'.[13]

We do not know whether Pat Fallon engaged intellectually with republican ideology, but he had a great desire for self-determination as a right and not something to be conferred by a foreign parliament. The scope and extent of British domination at that time should not be underestimated. It is clear that civic life was dominated by the British and their culture and symbolism. After Pat Fallon's release from the Curragh in December 1923, we know nothing of his republican involvement until the foundation of Fianna Fáil in 1926. Clearly when he gave his allegiance to Fianna Fáil he was making a statement that he would not return to physical force republicanism. One family narrative is that he was visited in turn by election agents of both Fianna Fáil and Fine Gael with planned schedules of election rallies, some to take place outside Sunday masses. The story goes that he was sufficiently trusted by both sides so that he could 'negotiate' changes to schedules to ensure that both parties did not descend on the same churchyard at the same time. Thus, he made an explicit but understated contribution to keeping the peace. He assiduously refused to discuss his role in the War of Independence and the Civil War and even advised former

13 Pat Fallon interview (UCDA), Ernie O'Malley notebooks, P17b/109.

comrades to do the same. Enda Fallon, his son, told one of his children that when he was a child he overheard his father telling his neighbour Pat Keville, a member of the Balla Battalion, not to say anything to his children about the events of the period.

It would be reasonable to ask whether the 'republican flame' was extinguished on Pat Fallon's death. The answer is probably no. Perhaps surprisingly, the Fianna Fáil republican label wasn't always apparent among subsequent generations; nevertheless, it was only necessary to scratch beneath the surface for it to reveal itself.

The next generation – Francis 'Enda' Fallon (1932–2007)

Our own father Enda Fallon was a mid-ranking civil servant in the Irish Land Commission in Castlerea, Co. Roscommon, and as a result he was careful not to be seen to be politically aligned and therefore we would have had little involvement in the local Fianna Fáil organization. He was wary of the potential for his children to get involved after the 'Troubles' broke out in 1968/9 given his own father's background. From time to time Enda Sr would have strongly expressed the view that the Provisional IRA and the 'old IRA' were different and that nothing could legitimize the atrocities carried out by the Provisional IRA. There are a number of interesting anecdotes on how Pat Fallon's past influenced, albeit in a minor way, Enda Fallon's family. One related to the fact that he had enquired from Deputy P. Calleary TD from Ballina, an old IRA comrade, regarding the political affiliations of our mother Josephine Curry's family. This we believe wasn't unusual at the time, but was probably more prevalent than we now realize. Many weddings and family events were boycotted by one side or the other in the post-Civil War period. Pat Fallon's eldest daughter Peg married Gerry O'Connor, the son of an RIC man. It might have made it easier that Gerry's father had been posted to the Channel Islands at the time, however Peg has stated that on telling her father of her love for Gerry, Pat Fallon's response was, 'it's alright there were some good and some bad'. In another incident in 1963, on one of his first days in the Irish Land Commission office in Castlerea, Enda Fallon was approached by a Mr Frawley who informed him that the last time the two families encountered each other was on the Partry Mountains in 1921 when Pat Fallon was shooting at his father, Head Constable Martin Frawley RIC, in the aftermath of Tourmakeady. While they both may have accepted this as fact at the time, we now know that it was unlikely that this happened.

The next generation – Tom Fallon (1926–2001)

Pat Fallon's reluctance to talk about his extensive participation between 1916 and 1923 was passed on to his son Tom, who also lived in Balla. Tom's daughter Jacqueline recalls that while her father would tell stories of his own childhood in the 1930s and 1940s, including accounts of political disputes he witnessed, he was loath to discuss his father's revolutionary past, perhaps keeping with Pat's silence. This resulted in little knowledge among his grandchildren regarding Pat's past. It is also interesting to note that during the 50th anniversary of the Easter Rising in 1966, his granddaughter Jacqueline recalls no discussion within the classroom in primary school regarding family experiences of the period. This is completely at odds with the current centenary celebrations suggesting a collective unwillingness to discuss family involvement; a feeling that the past was still too close, divisions still too raw. However, this is not to say that his grandchildren knew nothing of their grandfather. Instead of a narrative of military actions, they heard of his kind personality, willingness to assist others, and his ultimate dedication to his family, an aspect of his life his daughter-in-law Bernie spoke of often. It was this side of his life which was most of interest to his grandchildren in Balla; his granddaughter Noreen recalling that Pat Fallon's wedding photograph in her family home was an object of fascination. It was his personality, rather than his military achievements, which created the picture of the man who, sadly, most of his grandchildren were never able to meet.

Given the current focus upon the revolutionary period, his great-grandchildren have the benefit of a broader knowledge of Pat Fallon's military involvement. The centenary celebrations, along with the wealth of archival material released in the last decades and the work within the family to uncover it, has overcome much of the silence of previous years, allowing a clearer picture to emerge. There is a great sense of pride among his grandchildren and great-grandchildren, that he was involved so heavily within this period and that he took such an active part in the Irish Revolution. What becomes clear talking to his grandchildren and great-grandchildren is an appetite to ascertain not only what he did, but more importantly, why he did it. Noreen and Jacqueline, his granddaughters, wonder what motivated him to leave his life behind to go on the run? What was his social context and the convictions that led him to become a revolutionary? While for many years the silence around Pat Fallon's revolutionary activities precluded a full picture of this part of the family's history, this has been reversed to some degree through new archival material. However, with this new wealth of information and the resultant focus upon his military past, it is important to ensure that it is not this aspect of his life alone that comes to define him in the eyes of future generations. In this regard, it is important to remember the personality which was so important to his children, grandchildren, and those who knew him; namely his kindness, generosity and dedication to his family. It is important that these aspects are not superseded by his revolutionary activity, but instead join together to tell the story of a man who was not only a soldier and revolutionary who risked his life for the cause of Irish freedom, but also rebuilt his business and life following the war and, despite personal loss and tragedy, remained an integral part of his community and dedicated himself completely to his family.

Conclusion

A number of quotes from historical sources sum up the kind of person Pat Fallon was and how we would like him to be remembered. Patrick May and Dr Powell, South Mayo Brigade, said of Pat Fallon:

> He did everything, he was the most reliable man we had and most active … his responsibility and position and all the rest of it was shouts beyond the others: he was out on his own. At any time when we had difficulty Maguire would always take him into consultation and any problems that I had I always took him as being the last word.[14]

Mayo County Council led a tribute to Pat Fallon after his death:

> Proposing a resolution of sympathy with his relatives, Mr Bernard Commons said that everyone mourned his loss. Pat Fallon was one of the most outstanding figures in his own area while throughout Mayo people knew a great deal about him and everything they knew was good. Although politically opposed to him he (Mr Commons) always found him a staunch friend and anything he could do for anybody irrespective of their political leanings, he would do it. As an officer in the IRA he gave his service for his country when it was needed. It was the efforts of men like Pat Fallon who made it possible for the Council to be assembled and hold a meeting. He opposed the Treaty and was a staunch supporter of Fianna Fáil. No matter who called at his door he was always there to greet them and do them a good turn. He was the essence of good nature and everyone from his neighbourhood mourned him.[15]

14 Patrick Fallon pension application, MSP, MSP34REF3097, pp 22–3. **15** *Connaught Telegraph,* 2 Aug. 1958; *Western People,* 2 Aug. 1958.

A life less ordinary: Barney 'the Miller' and the War of Independence

BERNADINE BRADY

Growing up in Cavan, my siblings and I took for granted that we lived in a free state. We enjoyed the luxury of state-funded education and experienced no conflicts over our identity or allegiance. With the exception of the turbulent and tragic backdrop of the Troubles in Northern Ireland, we had few concerns of a political nature and could, for the most part, focus on being young, figuring out what we wanted to do in life and wondering if Cavan would ever win the All-Ireland again. When we learned about the struggle for Irish independence at school, my understanding of it was that it was 'out there' and in the distant past; something that other people did. It was only in later years that I came to appreciate the role that my grandfather had played in these events and that the freedom we enjoyed was secured by the political struggles that he and others from his generation had engaged in at a young age.

My grandfather, Bernard Brady (known as Barney), died in 1965, long before I was born. My impression of him as a serious, strict man was influenced by two photos of him; in one he was stone-faced in a dark brooding photograph with his wife while in the second he is alone and wearing an army uniform, young and handsome, but again serious. As a child, I assumed that nobody every smiled or the sun never shone 'in the olden days' and the images of Barney certainly reinforced this view. Barney was born in 1893 in Coreagh, Virginia, where his father was a farmer and also ran a mill. He attended a local national school until he was fourteen years of age before leaving to work on his family farm. As was customary in Cavan at the time, Barney's family had a nickname, 'the millers' – one that endures to this day, long after the mill has closed. He played Gaelic football at county and club levels, winning an Ulster senior championship medal with Cavan in 1915 and a Cavan senior championship medal with the Virginia Blues team in 1916.

While some stories about Barney's political activities have been passed down through the generations, we are lucky to have access to a witness statement given by Barney in 1957 as part of the Bureau of Military History Collection, 1913–21. This collection includes 1,773 witness statements given between 1947 and 1957, in order to gather primary source material for the revolutionary period in Ireland from 1913 to 1921. In this six-page meticulously worded statement, Barney describes his political activities from 1913, aged

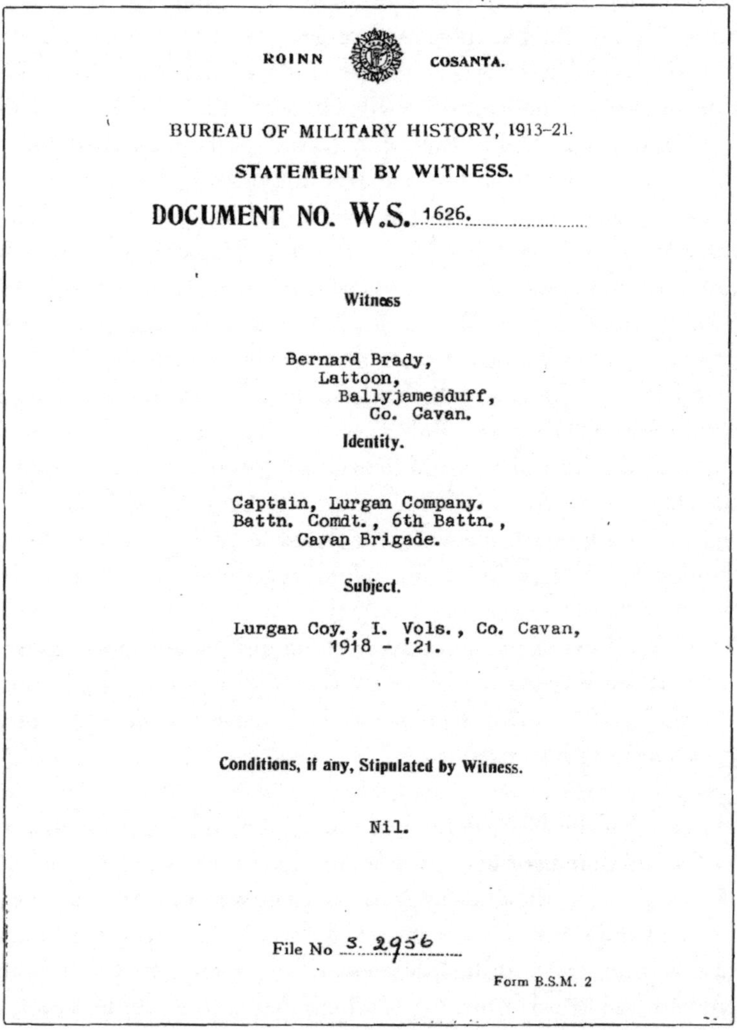
ROINN COSANTA.

BUREAU OF MILITARY HISTORY, 1913–21.

STATEMENT BY WITNESS.

DOCUMENT NO. W.S. 1626.

Witness

Bernard Brady,
Lattoon,
Ballyjamesduff,
Co. Cavan.

Identity.

Captain, Lurgan Company.
Battn. Comdt., 6th Battn.,
Cavan Brigade.

Subject.

Lurgan Coy., I. Vols., Co. Cavan,
1918 - '21.

Conditions, if any, Stipulated by Witness.

Nil.

File No S. 2956

Form B.S.M. 2

Cover page of Barney Brady's witness statement held in the Bureau of Military History

twenty, when he helped to organize a company of Irish National Volunteers and a Sinn Féin club in Virginia, up to the Truce in 1922. In this chapter, I describe the context of the struggle for independence in Cavan, referring to Barney's role as described by him in his statement. I then proceed to reflect on Barney's story and its implications for myself and my family.

The nature of the struggle for independence varied greatly throughout Ireland, due to the diverse dynamics of local politics and circumstances. In Cavan and other (now) border counties, the events were shaped by the presence of a relatively large Protestant/unionist community and responses to the British First World War effort. According to the 1911 census, just under one fifth of the population of Co. Cavan (91,173) was Church of Ireland, Presbyterian and Methodist, with Catholics accounting for the remainder of the population. The Home Rule movement, led by John Redmond, was gaining momentum at this time and was supported by the largely Catholic population, while there was also considerable unionist activity in Cavan, with Lord Farnham campaigning vigorously against Home Rule. While Reilly[1] describes the attitude of the local nationalist newspaper *The Anglo-Celt* to the unionist activities as 'derisory' (p. 180), the unionist movement grew in strength, and had an estimated 3,042 members by November 1913. However, the nationalist movement was also strong in the county, with reports of 40,000 men having attended a Home Rule meeting in Cavan in 1913.[2] Following the formation of the Irish National Volunteers in November 1913, tensions grew considerably in the county, with increased drilling on both unionist and nationalist sides. It was at this time that Barney established a company of the Irish National Volunteers in Virginia. He was aged twenty at the time.

> I helped to organize a company of the Irish national volunteers in the town of Virginia in the year 1913. I was appointed chief officer or captain. An ex-British soldier named Reilly was our drill instructor. Our strength was about 100.[3]

The breakout of the First World War initially relieved the tensions between nationalist and unionist sides in Cavan and elsewhere, with all parties except Sinn Féin supporting the British war effort. There was considerable pressure on young men throughout Co. Cavan to volunteer for the British army and the response was positive initially. More than 1,100 men with Cavan addresses enlisted with the British army, 654 of whom died in the war. However, as the war progressed, support for the war declined and the recruitment of Volunteers slowed considerably. Interestingly, Reilly[4] notes that agriculture, which was the main economic activity of the county, prospered during the war years, which may have partially explained why farmers were particularly reluctant to join the army. Owing to heavy casualties sustained in the early years of the war, the British army was under additional pressure to recruit new members and the

1 Eileen Reilly, 'Cavan in the era of the Great War' in Raymond Gillespie (ed.), *Cavan: essays on the history of an Irish county* (Dublin, 2004), pp 177–95. 2 Ibid. 3 Bureau of Military History, Bernard Brady witness statement, ,http://www.bureauofmilitaryhistory.ie/reels/bmh/BMH.WS1626.pdf#page=2, accessed 14 May 2017. 4 Eileen Reilly, 'Cavan in the era of the Great War', pp 186–7.

Barney in his army uniform (year unknown).

conscription of Irish men was mooted as a possible solution. The possibility of conscription began to be discussed in earnest in the Cavan press by early 1916.[5]

Editorials in *The Anglo-Celt* with headlines such as 'why Ireland objects to conscription' became commonplace, setting out the records of service and support that the county had provided since the beginning of the war.[6] Feelings of resentment were expressed that the armed unionist forces in the county had not volunteered for the war effort to the same degree as nationalists, yet were prepared to fight against Home Rule. John Redmond and the Irish National Volunteers' stance in supporting the British war effort became unacceptable to many of its members, leading them to break away and form a group known as the Irish Volunteers.

Barney was among those opposed to Redmond's stance and he described how the Virginia branch of the Irish National Volunteers that he had formed

5 Ibid. **6** Ibid., p. 189.

was disbanded in 1915 in protest. Two Sinn Féin clubs and a company of Irish Volunteers were subsequently formed, with Barney leading the one in Lurgan. The company of the Irish Volunteers in Virginia numbered 12 initially but by 1918, the membership had increased to 100. The growth in membership was fuelled by fears over conscription. The main activities of the group included learning to foot drill and marching to surrounding areas to help in setting up Sinn Féin clubs and companies of Volunteers. Barney described the purpose of the clubs established in Virginia and Lurgan as follows:

> Those committees were responsible for the organization of anti-conscription meetings and the collection of funds for the purpose of opposing the measure. The very Revd Fr Gaffney, Parish Priest, was chairman of the Lurgan committee. At one of these meetings, a Mr Sheehy MP, father of the present Judge Sheehy, spoke for some time, after which Fr Gaffney addressed the audience. He said that if Mr Sheehy and his party were unable to prevent the enforcement of conscription in Ireland, Sinn Fein would do so with black-thorn sticks. The statement was received with great applause, after which the entire audience, with the exception of two people, proceeded to a nearby hall led by a Sinn Fein flag, where the meeting was continued without Mr Sheehy.[7]

The fears regarding enforced enlistment were realized when a conscription bill was passed in Westminster on 16 April 1918. An estimated 15,000 to 20,000 people attended an anti-conscription protest meeting in Virginia the following week, while large protests also took place in other parts of the county.[8] The efforts to introduce conscription to Ireland were eventually abandoned in the face of mass opposition. However, the movement against conscription provided a strong impetus to the movement for Irish independence, as Barney noted that 'When the scare had subsided, most of the new members remained with the company'. Thus the events of the Great War can be seen to have had a considerable influence on the movement for Irish nationalism in Cavan.

McMonagle[9] argues that the democratic foundations of the Irish state began to be laid from 1917 onwards as Sinn Fein, under the leadership of its founder Arthur Griffith, mobilized people to become democratically active. Because Ireland was under direct rule from Westminster, the population had become disengaged from formal political processes. This was exemplified in

7 Bureau of Military History, Bernard Brady witness statement, 8 Eileen Reilly, 'Cavan in the era of the Great War', p. 193. 9 Dermot McMonagle, *29 Main Street: living with partition* (Cavan, 2013).

East Cavan, where the then-MP was ninety-five-year-old Samuel Young, who was elected in 1892 and returned unopposed for five general elections, a period of 25 years.[10] Sinn Féin did not support Home Rule but advocated full independence, to be achieved through non-violent civil disobedience, passive resistance and non-co-operation.[11] Part of this strategy involved the establishment of Sinn Féin local civil courts, which encouraged people to boycott the British courts system and resolve their disputes using these local structures. The Sinn Féin civil courts were used widely, including by Protestant families, to settle complex land disputes. McMonagle believes that these courts, which started in Cavan and Clare in 1917, were 'a major act in dismantling British legal and political authority in Ireland, without firing a shot'.[12] He also argues that they 'enhanced the ability of our fledgling state to form the unarmed Garda Síochána in the middle of it' (McMonagle, p. 5).[13]

In 1918, a by-election was held in East Cavan and Arthur Griffith, the Sinn Féin candidate, was elected. Griffith was in an English jail at the time for the 'German Plot', reportedly trying to secure German money and arms for the Sinn Féin cause. Barney reports that all the Volunteers in Virginia and Lurgan worked hard for his success and that he was elected by a good majority. Barney's narrative reflects the accounts of McMonagle who highlighted that, because East Cavan had not had an election for 26 years, considerable efforts were required to mobilize the electorate to register and turn out to vote.[14] Passionate rallies were held throughout East Cavan and up to 4,000 Volunteers were mobilized. Sinn Féin's success with the by-election in East Cavan boosted the party's cause throughout the rest of Ireland, resulting in the election of 73 Sinn Féin candidates to Westminster in November 2018 on an abstentionist policy. Sinn Féin proceeded to establish the first Dáil in Dublin on 21 January 1919.

In his statement, Barney describes how he was appointed as a delegate to a Sinn Féin convention held in Dublin in October 1918 but contracted the flu while there, which he described as being 'of epidemic proportions in Ireland at this period'. He spent three months in Sir Patrick Dunn's Hospital before he was well enough to come home. It appears that the 'Spanish flu', which had hit mainland Europe, was widespread in Ireland, with approximately 80,000 people infected. Death rates are estimated at over 40 million in Europe and 23,000 in Ireland.[15] Dorney highlights that the outbreak of 'Spanish flu' in

10 Ibid. **11** Ibid. **12** Ibid., p. 77. **13** Dermot McMonagle, 'Cavan's forgotten contribution to the War of Independence', *History Ireland*, 15:6 (2007), http://www.historyireland.com/20th-century-contemporary-history, accessed 14 June 2017. **14** McMonagle, *29 Main Street*, p. 68. **15** John Dorney, 'Ireland and the great flu epidemic of 1918', http://www.theirishstory.com/2013/05/16/ireland-and-the-great-flu-epidemic-of-1918/#.WPeD2_nyvIU, accessed 28 April 2017.

Ireland was probably transmitted by soldiers returning from the war but the epidemic was accentuated by the intense political activism, and therefore movement of people, surrounding the general election of 1918. McMonagle states that the British government chose to ignore the seriousness of the disease in Ireland until early 1919 when it was declared a notifiable disease and the pandemic had peaked.[16]

On returning home after his lengthy stay in hospital, Barney notes that, while he and his fellow Sinn Féin members were 'elated' at the 1918 general election result which saw Sinn Féin winning 73 seats nationally, the Virginia Company was not in a good state:

> When I got home in January 1919, the Virginia company had ceased to exist. The captain had been arrested while I was in hospital and was serving a sentence in Belfast jail for drilling or a similar offence. It appears that Phil Wrett assumed command of the company after McDonnell's arrest. He was a heavy boozer and, while in a drunken bout, would give military orders such as 'halt' … with the result that the company ceased to meet or have anything to do with him. More often than not, Wrett gave the orders while the RIC were present.[17]

Barney outlines how he confined his activities to establishing the Sinn Féin club in Lurgan for most of 1919 before helping to reorganize the Virginia Company towards the end of the year. He became captain of the Lurgan Company, which had a membership of 32 at that time, and he describes how companies were also established in neighbouring towns and villages. By this time, the War of Independence had started, with many Sinn Féin leaders arrested and sent to English prisons and prohibitions on many political organizations and public events. While Sinn Féin was a political and civil organization, it began from 1917 to engage in acts of civil disobedience. McMonagle[18] describes activities undertaken by the Volunteers such as burning of RIC barracks, raiding houses for guns and hi-jacking of post trucks, which prompted antagonism from RIC officers and the 'Black and Tans'. Barney reported that a cluster of local Sinn Féin companies were brought together at this time to establish a battalion, which was known as the Virginia (or 3rd) Battalion, Co. Cavan. He describes the activities of the battalion as follows:

> After its formation, all shotguns in the area were collected. In certain cases we had to raid the houses of people opposed to us and Sinn Féin

16 Dermot McMonagle. *29 Main Street*, p. 86. **17** Bureau of Military History, Bernard Brady witness statement. **18** McMonagle. *29 Main Street*, p. 86.

> generally and seize their guns. In the Lurgan area, we got 50 shotguns. During the year an RIC barracks, which had been vacated in Mullagh, was burned down by members of Virginia and Newcastle companies … Throughout the year roads in the area were extensively blocked.

This piece of the narrative resonates with stories I had heard from my uncle about Barney having to go to neighbouring homes to seize guns. Many of these would have been neighbouring Protestant farmers well known to him and, not surprisingly, he had spoken of these actions as making him quite unpopular. His witness statement goes on to describe how the battalions in Co. Cavan and Co. Meath were re-organized several times, with Barney taking the role of O/C of the Lurgan (or 6th) Battalion. The following paragraph marks the end of Barney's witness statement:

> Road blocking continued right up to the Truce. After the Truce I attended a training camp set up by the divisional staff at Dunboyne and spent about a fortnight there. I later spent a period in a brigade training camp in the Bailieboro Company area. I later joined the National Army with the rank of Commandant.[19]

Following the Treaty, Michael Collins began to build a National Army from pro-treaty IRA units. Barney was obviously on the pro-Treaty side as his statement indicates that he became a Commandant in the National Army. Unfortunately, the details of Barney's activities end here, with no detail provided regarding his activities in the Army or during the Civil War. As with the rest of Ireland, IRA members split between pro- and anti-Treaty sides in Cavan and the conflict was often vicious and brutal. Dorney argues that, despite the relatively low body count, the Civil War was a time of bitterness and fear among civilians as well as soldiers and guerrillas in the border counties.[20] One of the more infamous incidents of the Civil War occurred in Ballyconnell, Co. Cavan, in January 1923 when an anti-Treaty IRA Volunteer from Roscommon, Michael Cull, was killed by a National Army officer while raiding a shop in the village. To seek revenge for Cull's death, the anti-Treaty column of 50 men based in the Arigna hills (of which Cull had been a member) visited a ferocious revenge on the small town, killing two civilians and ransacking the premises in the town. Dorney highlights that the conflict in Co. Cavan was frequently not a simple matter of pro- versus anti-Treaty fighters

19 Bureau of Military History, Bernard Brady witness statement. **20** John Dorney, 'The Irish War of Independence: a brief overview', http://www.theirishstory.com/2012/09/18/the-irish-war-of-independence-a-brief-overview/#.WUEkTOvyu72.

but also involved the use of violence to settle local agrarian disputes that were brought into sharp focus during the war.[21]

According to military census records from 12–13 November 1922, Barney is recorded at the Trim Barracks in Co. Meath as having the rank of Commandant, with his marital status recorded as 'single'. He did not remain single for long after this military census was taken as he married less than two weeks later, on 27 November 1922. Barney and his new bride lived in Mullingar, Co. Westmeath, for some time, where he was then stationed. Barney would then have been aged twenty-nine, having been active in political events since the age of twenty. His parents were anxious for him to give up his military activities and to settle down to a normal life and purchased a farm and house for him near Ballyjamesduff, Co. Cavan, in 1925. Barney is presumed to have left the army at this time and became a full-time farmer. There are no accounts of subsequent military involvement on his part but it appears that he remained loyal to the pro-Treaty party, Cumann na nGaedheal (later Fine Gael), throughout his life and played an active role in local politics. He died on 1 July 1965 at the age of seventy-two.

In terms of the impact of my grandfather's life on myself and my siblings, it would be misleading to suggest that stories of his endeavours featured prominently in our lives, possibly because he had died before we were born so we could never relate to him in the way we would have to a living relative. Because my siblings and I grew up during the Troubles, our parents would not have been keen to draw attention to or glorify our grandfather's IRA involvement. However, it is argued that every family has its own narrative that helps them to make sense of their experiences and to articulate what they stand for. Having a knowledge of family history, or a strong inter-generational self, can help children to develop a stronger sense of identity and belonging and to realize that they belong to something bigger than themselves.[22] While I did not explicitly think about my grandfather's activities very much, on reflection, I realize that his experiences had helped to shape our family narrative and sense of belonging, which in turn had given me a deeply rooted Irish identity and sense of civic responsibility.

Every so often we are reminded of our grandfather's legacy. In 2016, 100 years after the Rising, contractors employed by my mother to replace a roof on an outhouse found an army belt and other items that had belonged to Barney stored in the attic of the building. These items and others belonging to Barney have been donated to Cavan County Museum. Also, in 2016, my nephews,

21 Ibid. **22** Bruce Feiler. 'The stories that bind us', http://www.nytimes.com/2013/03/17/fashion-/the-family-stories-that-bind-us-this-life.html, accessed 28 April 2017.

Jack and James Brady, became the fourth generation of the family to win senior championship medals with Ramor United (previously Virginia Blues), a century after Barney, their great-grandfather, had won a medal in 1916. Hopefully, they will also emulate his achievement by winning an Ulster medal with Cavan and even attempt to out-do him by winning the All-Ireland.

It is difficult to tell someone else's story, particularly if you have never met them and must rely on the memories, recollections and anecdotes of others. While an invaluable source, the written narrative also leaves many unanswered questions, such as how it felt to take so many steps into the unknown. Barney recounted his witness statement with a sense of the ending, knowing how it turned out, but he had no idea as he went along, where his leaps of faith would take him. The single-mindedness and determination of Barney and others like him has given us the luxury of living in a democratic Irish republic, indeed with the luxury of taking our freedom for granted.

Acknowledgment

I would like to thank my mother, Mary Brady, for her invaluable assistance with much of the information in this chapter. Thanks also to the editors for their guidance in relation to the historical sources used in this account.

Jack Morrogh and 'Sinn Fein's foredoomed dreams'

ANTONY WHEATLEY

Included below is a famous photograph from the 1916 Rising that has appeared in several publications on the 1916 Rising over the years.[1] The photograph caption of the time tells it all: 'Irish Rebellion – May 1916. A group of officers with the captured rebel flag'. What is less well-known about the photograph is that the soldiers were all probably Irish. The man standing directly under the flag was my great-uncle Major John (Jack) Morrogh from Cork. I have known of the existence of the photograph for some time, but paid little attention to it until 2004, when an article was published by Senan Molony indicating that Jack probably took the last photograph of the *Titanic* in 1912 off the coast of Cork. In that article, the 1916 Rising photograph was included.[2] I believe that this photograph changed the course of Jack Morrogh's life resulting in him leaving Ireland in 1922 and never returning to live there. His children, all born in Ireland and raised in South America were likewise never to live in Ireland, nor indeed to consider themselves Irish. Jack died in 1954 and his widow Aileen spoke little of his involvement in the Easter Rising other than to say that he was sent to Dublin to put down the insurgency, but wasn't directly involved himself. If that were the case, then why was he in a photograph taken under the statue of Charles Stewart Parnell after the surrender of the Irish Volunteers and Irish Citizen Army forces in Easter week? I thought the issue worthy of further investigation.

Jack Morrogh

Jack Morrogh was born into a large and very wealthy Catholic family in Cork city. His father, John Morrogh, made a fortune in diamonds in South Africa before returning to establish business interests and become a Westminster MP.

1 Conor Kostick and Lorcan Collins, *The Easter Rising: a guide to Dublin in 1916* (Dublin, 2016); John Gibney, *A history of the Easter Rising in 50 objects* (Cork, 2016); Pádraig Óg Ó Ruairc, *Revolution: a photographic history of revolutionary Ireland, 1913–1923* (Cork, 2014); Shane Hegarty and Fintan O'Toole, *The* Irish Times *book of the 1916 Rising* (Dublin, 2006); Neil Richardson, *According to their own lights: stories of Irishmen in the British army, Easter 1916* (Cork, 2015). 2 Senan Molony, 'Titantic: the last photographs?' in *Encyclopedia Titanica* (2004), https://www.encyclopedia-titanica.org/titanic-the-last-photograph.html, accessed 12 July 2017.

Irish Rebellion – May 1916.
A group of Officers with the captured rebel flag.

Photograph of British army officers with the captured Sinn Fein flag, April 1916. Jack Morrogh is directly under the flag with a walking stick in his right hand.

Both John and his wife were married twice and had thirteen children between them. Jack graduated from Castleknock in 1899 and was accepted into the Royal Military Academy at Sandhurst in January 1902. He graduated in December of that year and his final grades reveal that academically he was probably just an average student, coming eighth out of the nine officer cadets. Handwritten on his Sandhurst record is that he received a commission from the Royal Irish Fusiliers in May 1903.

Jack's movements from 1903 to the beginning of the First World War are sketchy at best. He served with the Royal Irish Fusiliers in India, probably for most of the time. In 1908 and 1909, he is mentioned on a couple of occasions in *Faugh-A-Ballagh* ('Fág an Bealach' or 'Clear the way'), the regimental gazette of the Irish Fusiliers (also the battle cry of the Royal Irish Regiment, about whom we will hear a lot later on). On two occasions he was noted to have played cricket for the 2nd Royal Irish Fusiliers at Ferozepore (Firozpur) in the Punjab: Jack opened the batting and bowled a bit too! He also played polo for the battalion. It is believed that he resigned his commission in 1910, when he returned to Ireland to marry Aileen Egan from Cork. He remained associated with the army as an officer of the Special Reserve of Officers.

The couple settled in Crosshaven, Co. Cork, where his extended family had a long association with the Royal Munster Yacht Club. The couple had four children, three girls – Kate (1911), Patricia (1917), and Joan (1920) – and a boy, John (1915). Given the wealth of his father, one must assume that Jack's inheritance allowed him to live the life of a gentleman. In 1912, Jack and his brothers played in both the Past (Jack, Willie and Dom Morrogh and Paddy Collins [his half-brother]) and Present teams (Stephen Morrogh) in the annual Castleknock College Present vs Past cricket match. There were so many Morroghs in the Past side that they were called the Gentlemen of Crosshaven!

In April 1912, Jack Morrogh, assisted by his younger brothers Stephen and Vincent, took a photograph of the *Titanic* as it left Cork Harbour, where it stopped off on its maiden voyage from Southampton to New York. As we all know, the ship sank on 14/15 April 1912 when it hit an iceberg in the North Atlantic, with the loss of 1514 lives. Jack's photograph of the *Titanic* was subsequently published in the *Castleknock Chronicle* 1911/12. As noted, the story behind the photograph of the Titanic was published by Senan Molony in *Encylopedia Titanica,* in 2004.

The First World War and Easter week

At the outbreak of war in 1914, Jack Morrogh again enlisted in the British army and was assigned to the Royal Irish Regiment as a lieutenant but was soon promoted to captain. In addition, five of his brothers/stepbrothers also enlisted. An article on the six brothers appeared in the *Cork Examiner* in 1915, shortly before the eldest of them, Frank, was killed while serving with the Royal Munster Fusiliers at Gallipoli.

With the 2nd Battalion of the Royal Irish Regiment, Jack Morrogh was sent to France and was wounded at the Battle of Ypres at St Julien in May 1915. His wounds were severe, as the surgeon was unable to remove a bullet from his throat, where it remained lodged till the day he died. Jack was returned to Ireland to recuperate and when he was fit for light duties, he was posted to the 3rd Battalion of the Royal Irish Regiment which was garrisoned at Richmond Barracks, on the west side of Dublin city. The battalion was made up of 18 officers and 385 men. The battalion's function was primarily for training and comprised of raw recruits, training staff, men unfit for active service and battle-hardened soldiers who had serviced and been wounded in France, and who were awaiting medical clearance to return to the front. Jack Morrogh fell into the latter category. In November 1915, Jack was promoted to the rank of Major at the age of thirty-one.

The military actions of both the republican and British forces during Easter week 1916 have been well covered in two recent books by Molyneux and Kelly, and Richardson.[3] Much of what we know of the daily activities of the 3rd

3 Derek Molyneux and Darren Kelly, *When the clock struck 1916: close-quarter combat in the Easter Rising* (Cork, 2015); Neil Richardson, *According to their lights: stories of Irishmen in the British army,*

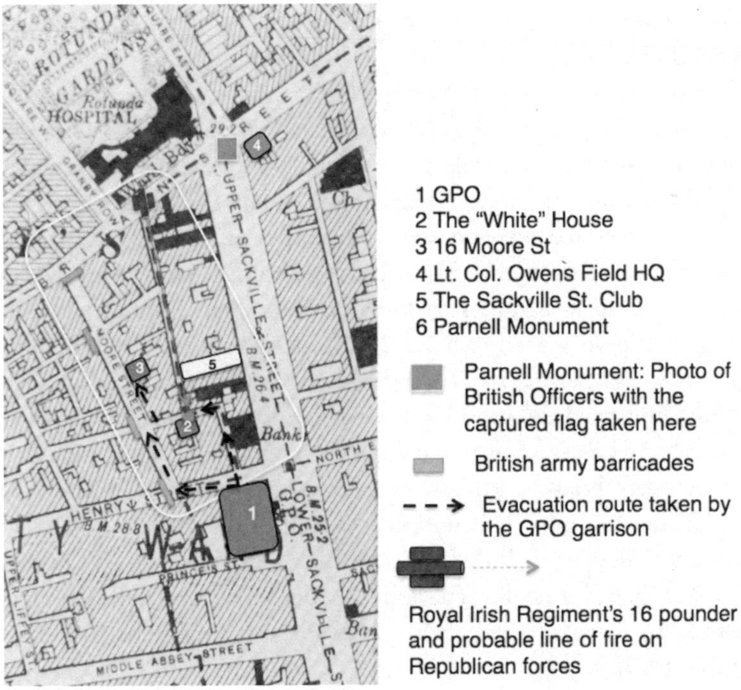

Map of military action around the GPO during Easter week, 1916

Battalion of the Royal Irish Regiment we have gathered from the witness statement made by Private Albert Desborough in 1957.[4] The Royal Irish Regiment soldiers saw significant action at the South Dublin Union (where 6 were killed and partook in the encirclement of the GPO, establishing their headquarters on Great Britain Street. Jack Morrogh is first mentioned on Thursday, when he led a group of sharpshooters on to the rooftops to fire at rebels both in the GPO and the surrounding streets. One of these snipers wounded the GPO commander, Commandant-General James Connolly, when he ventured out to oversee street defences. It is reported that Connolly when he was hit in the arm by the bullet did not flinch but calmly walked back into the GPO before reacting. The wound was not serious and following treatment, Connolly resumed his duties. Later in the day, Connolly was more seriously wounded in the leg and the only doctor in the GPO, a British army doctor (Lt George Mahony, an Irishman), did his best to treat him, but his leg had been fractured. He was left in excruciating pain until he surrendered, when he was treated by a surgeon in Dublin Castle. The individuals who shot Connolly on the second occasion are unknown, but they may well have been Jack Morrogh's group of

Easter 1916 (Cork, 2015). 4 BMH WS 1604 (Albert Desborough).

sharpshooters since they were perfectly positioned to shoot at anyone who ventured out of the GPO.

When the rebel forces evacuated the GPO, Major Jack Morrogh and his men advanced down Upper Sackville Street to about 70m north of the GPO, where they occupied the Sackville Street Club (No. 59 Sackville Street). From the back of this building, he could clearly see Moore Lane and Henry Place. By this stage, rebel forces were massed around what at the time was referred to as 'the White House' on Henry Place. From his vantage point, Jack Morrogh was right in the thick of things. He was no more than 30m from the rebel forces with a clear view of their activities. He alerted his commanding officer, Lt Col. Owens, of the situation. Armed with this information, Lt Col. Owens ordered the gunnery crew, probably positioned no more than 200m away at the top of Moore Lane on Great Britain Street, to blast the White House with five artillery shells. From pointblank range they could not miss. With so many exhausted Volunteers in such a confined space, the explosions must have been devastating. Its effect made Padraig Pearse realize that the whole GPO garrison would be slaughtered if he didn't surrender soon. In a letter hand-delivered by a messenger to General Lowe, late on Saturday morning, Lt Col. Owens summarized the situation:

> We have been engaged with Sinn Feiners in Moore Street and Moore Lane and from reliable information from Major Morrogh, Royal Irish Regiment, who observed from the back of the Sackville Street Club about 100 Sinn Feiners he located in a white house at the southern end of Moore Lane.
>
> On receipt of this information I ordered the Gunner Officer to put five shells into the house, the result being that a Red Cross Nurse [presumably Nurse Elisabeth O'Farrell] of the enemy has come in with a verbal message from the so-called Commandant Pearse, Republican force, to the effect that he wishes to treat (with) the Commandant of the Forces.[5]

Before Pearse decided to surrender, James Connolly also made an effort to surrender. Escorted by Nurse Elizabeth O'Farrell and carried on a stretcher by six of his men, he approached Lt Col. Owens' headquarters and told Owens

5 Typescript copy of message from Lt Col. R.L. Owen 3rd Battalion, Royal Irish Regiment, at the Parnell monument, Sackville Street, informing the recipient that a Red Cross nurse [Elizabeth O'Farrell] has brought a message from Patrick Pearse, with typescript copy of covering note to General Lowe from Major Thomas A. Salt, staff officer to Colonel Portal, DSO, Dublin Castle, 29 April 1916. http://catalogue.nli.ie/Record/vtls000652474/HierarchyTree, accessed 10 July 2017.

that he and his officers were prepared to surrender if the rank-and-file Volunteers could go free. When Owens responded he did so like General Melchett, in the BBC comedy *Blackadder Goes Forth*. As Private Desborough recounted:

> For a moment there was a tense silence. I saw the colonel getting red in the face, then spluttering he ejaculated – 'What!! ... you bloody rebel ... you ... dare ... If I had my way I'd shoot you. I am the one to make terms not you. Listen, if you and your men don't lay down their arms and surrender before nine tonight, and without conditions attached ... I'll order the bombardment of the entire city ... Take him away'. Without a word, the colonel turned on his heels and re-entered the orderly room ... The six men raised the stretcher to their shoulders again, and the nurse taking her place at their head, they marched off.[6]

Before hostilities had ceased, but after the GPO had been evacuated by republican forces, the Sinn Féin flag was still flying on the GPO. Jack Morrogh accompanied by his Company Sergeant-Major, Frederick Banks, climbed up and took down the flag. Clearly very proud of the trophy, the troops strapped it to a rifle later on for photographs. This is the flag that appears in the famous photograph taken of Jack Morrogh and his fellow officers when hostilities had ended. In addition, a second photograph taken at the same time is of two soldiers posing with the rifle and flag.

For the actual surrender, Pearse was again escorted by Nurse O'Farrell (although in the official photograph her legs were erased). Pearse surrendered to Brig. Gen. Lowe who was accompanied by his son Lt John Lowe, who later went on to a Hollywood acting career, under the name of John Loder. Following the surrender, the republican soldiers led by their field commander, Sean McLoughlin, marched to the top of Sackville Street where they laid down their arms. Brig. Gen. Lowe was apoplectic with rage when he saw the marching rebel troops still had their weapons at this stage. The Volunteers were then held in the open near the Rotunda until they were processed. Republican leaders were separated out and taken to Kilmainham Gaol, while ordinary prisoners were escorted to Richmond Barracks, about 1km away, where they were to be guarded by Jack Morrogh and his comrade soldiers.

There is no further mention of Jack Morrogh in official records, but I among others in his extended family have been told that he was involved in the events leading up to James Connolly's execution. Due to his medical condition,

6 BMH WS 1604 (Albert Desborough).

Connolly was imprisoned in Dublin Castle where he received medical treatment for his leg wounds. According to our family testimony Jack Morrogh was given the unenviable task of firstly informing him that he was to be executed, and second escorting him to Kilmainham Gaol, most probably from the Royal Hospital, where he had been taken by ambulance on the day of execution (15 May). I have not been able to find any information either to confirm or refute Jack Morrogh's role in Connolly's execution. Might it have happened? Well, several events would indicate that it was not outside the bounds of possibility. First, the trials of the leaders took place in Richmond Barracks where Jack was stationed. Second, Lt Col. Owens served on at least one court-martial, that of Eoin MacNeill, Chief-of-Staff of the Irish Volunteers, who not only was in no way involved in the Easter week fighting, but had tried to call the Rising off. MacNeill was spared the death penalty but was sentenced to life-in-prison.[7] He was released from prison in 1917. In addition, Private Desborough who was also at Richmond Barracks was used as a messenger in the arrangements for the marriage of Joseph Plunkett, one of the rebel leaders, to Grace Gifford, just hours before his execution.[8] Either way, would Connolly have held an involvement in his execution against Jack Morrogh? Most probably not. Connolly had expected to die even before the fighting began. On the Monday morning he was heard saying to Captain Seán Connolly, an officer in the Citizen Army, 'Good luck, Seán, for we won't meet again'.[9] In addition, when Connolly was asked to say a prayer for the members of his firing squad just before execution, he simply replied, 'I will say a prayer for all men who do their duty according to their lights'. Finally, it is highly unlikely that Jack Morrogh or the men of the Royal Irish Regiment were involved directly with any of the fourteen executions. The twelve firing squads used were drawn from the Sherwood Foresters, under the command of firstly Major Rhodes (Pearse, McDonagh and Clarke executions) and afterwards of Major C.H. Heathcote (the remaining eleven executions).[10] It is likely that the Sherwood Foresters were chosen because of the heavy casualties the regiment of about 2,000 men suffered (200 dead and wounded) at Mount Street Bridge at the hands of about eighteen members of C Company, 3rd Volunteer Battalion.

Back to the frontlines, POW and escape

After the Easter Rising, Jack Morrogh's movements are unknown until he appeared back on the Western Front with the 7th Battalion of the Royal Irish

7 Richardson, *According to their own lights.* **8** Ibid.; BMH WS 1604 (Albert Desborough). **9** Molyneux and Kelly, *When the clock struck 1916.* **10** Typescript copy of message from Lt Col. R.L. Owen … to General Lowe from Major Thomas A. Salt.

Regiment, in the spring of 1918.[11] Following ferocious fighting at the Battle of St Quentin, at which the regiment sustained heavy casualties, Jack was captured on 21 March and sent to a prisoner-of-war (POW) camp in Germany called Holzminden Camp in Lower Saxony. The regime at the camp was harsh. In a piece he later wrote entitled 'Holzminden' on his time in the camp, Jack related a story of an Australian officer who tried to crawl under the wire camp-fence and was caught by a German guard. The Australian got up and walked towards the guard, who without warning drew his gun and shot the Australian dead.[12]

While in the camp Jack was invited to join an escape team that was preparing a tunnel for an escape. So Jack became a tunneller, in what must have been claustrophobic and at times dangerous work. On the night of the 23/24 July 1918, twenty-nine officers broke out of the tunnel and made their escape. Eventually, six of the escapees made it to neutral territory. Jack Morrogh decided to walk to neutral Holland, 160 miles away and he almost made it. After his second week of hiking across Germany, he made it to the banks of the river Em, with Holland on the opposite bank. His luck, however, ran out and he was captured by German soldiers and returned to Holzminden Camp where he remained until the German surrender. On 15 December 1918, he was repatriated to the UK. After the war, Jack Morrogh was honoured with a 'Mentioned in Dispatches' for his escape from Holzminden. Apparently, repatriated First Workld War POWs were frequently court-martialled for having surrendered during battle, so Jack Morrogh's award could be regarded as exceptional treatment.[13]

War of Independence

Following release from the POW camp, Jack Morrogh was transferred to the Royal Irish Regiment, 1st Battalion, based in Tidworth, England. In May 1919 he was appointed senior Major. In January 1920, the whole battalion was moved to Germany to oversee post-war elections and were based at the town of Allenstein (the modern-day Polish city of Olsztyn). However, at some stage in 1920, Jack Morrogh returned to his home in Crosshaven and was assigned to the military base at Camden Fort. IRA activity in the area was minimal until January 1920 when the Carragaline Company was formed under the command of Edward Sisk, himself from Crosshaven.[14] In the early stages, the Carragaline Company restricted its activities to raiding the homes of people considered hostile or unfriendly looking for guns and ammunition. In early 1921, these

11 Seán Enright, *Easter Rising 1916: the trials* (Sallins, 2014). **12** 'Holzminden' – an account written by Major John Dominick Morrogh (unpublished). **13** This is according to a comment by Jonathan Maguire, Royal Irish Fusiliers Museum, Armagh. **14** BMH WS 1505 (Edward Sisk).

IRA men collected 'an arms levy from all the well-to-do people in the area. In this company we collected almost £20. The people were told the money was being collected in lieu of the Income Tax which they were advised by the IRA not to pay to the enemy'.[15]

The Morrogh family received the attention of the local IRA. One evening, when Jack was away from the house, a group of young IRA volunteers broke into their house. His wife, Aileen, recognized one of the gang and berated him when they approached the bedroom in which one of the children slept. Although family lore has it that the IRA lads obediently left the house without achieving their objective, it now transpires that a granddaughter, Veronica Morrogh, later heard that they found Jack's guns under a bed.

Later, a more serious incident occurred. Jack, Aileen and the four children were driving on a dirt road somewhere in the vicinity of Crosshaven when they were stopped by an IRA roadblock manned by three armed men. Jack's daughter, Kate, who was about ten at the time, vividly remembered the incident for the rest of her life and could describe the three men in detail many years later. Jack was forced to stop the car and as the men approached he said to his wife 'This is it, Aileen'. The ten-year-old Kate knew that this meant that her father expected to be shot. As the IRA man bent down and spotted the children in the back of the car, he said 'You may go on, today, Major Morrogh'. Kate was so terrified by the events that she had nightmares for years afterwards. Jack Morrogh now knew that he was a marked man and that he should either face up to the possibility of assassination at some stage or he had to get out of Crosshaven. He chose the latter option and immediately left for England and when safely there, he was joined by Aileen and the children.

Neither Aileen and Jack nor his children ever returned to live in Ireland. It would appear that he continued with his military career only until 1922 when the Royal Irish Regiment was disbanded. Within the family it is believed that when the regiment was being disbanded, officers of 'independent means' were asked by their superiors to resign their commissions, leaving positions for men for whom the army was their livelihood. Jack Morrogh took this advice and declined the army pension he was entitled to. A true army man, I feel 'the Major' regretted this decision to leave the army for the rest of his life.

South America here we come!

Still a wealthy man, Jack Morrogh decided to emigrate to Uruguay to take up the position of a ranch (estancia) manager. He may have chosen Uruguay so as

15 Ibid., p. 4

to join a friend. At the time, there were thriving British and Irish communities in both Uruguay and Argentina. Life in South America suited the Morroghs. As the son of a former British MP and very wealthy businessman, I presume it permitted the Morroghs to mix in the higher circle within the ex-pat community. Although the Morroghs settled in Uruguay, his girls went to school at the Michael Ham Memorial College in Buenos Aires, across the river Pate in Argentina. Things, however, changed in 1929 with the Wall Street Crash, which swallowed up all his money, although he may also have been subjected to embezzlement by unscrupulous business associates. Thereafter life was not easy for the Morroghs, although Aileen responded better to the changed financial circumstances. They moved to Buenos Aires where the family was kept going due to Aileen's industry. The Catholic school allowed the girls to attend without paying fees, because of the generosity the Morrogh family had shown to the Church back in Ireland. Following the loss of his money, Jack Morrogh was like a fish out of water. His daughter Joan told her family that Jack was really a Victorian gentleman used to money and position in life. He never got over losing his fortune and he was unable to deal with the real world outside of army life. He had been a wonderful man until his financial losses 'knocked the stuffing out of him'. Although he was of very pleasant disposition, he could be awkward to deal with on occasions. My mother, Ursula, remembers him fondly, as he used to write to her and send her stamps for her collection.

During the 1930s Jack returned to Ireland to visit. It would appear that he had accompanied a friend, probably as a paid companion, who was returning for medical treatment. My mother, who was a girl of about ten-years-old, remembers the 'Major' as being rather dashing! During the visit he met up with an acquaintance from his time in Ireland. After a few drinks, his 'friend' admitted that during the War of Independence he had been sent by his IRA superiors to the Morrogh's house in Crosshaven with orders to shoot Jack. Fortunately for Jack, he was not at home. While others have told this story in a humorous vein, I have always found it unsettling.

The Second World War and beyond

The outbreak of the Second World War in 1939 must have seemed like a godsend to Jack. He saw the war as an opportunity to resume his military career, despite his age. He initially made his way to Port Stanley in the Falkland Islands, and reported for duty. However, still wishing to see action, Jack Morrogh made his way alone to England in 1942. His efforts to re-enlist in the army were declined, most probably due to his age (fifty-eight). This must have

Life in Uruguay. Jack Morrogh and his four children (Kate, Patricia, John and Joan).

been a shattering blow to the once proud army officer and it served to add to his feeling of worthlessness. Jack did not return to his wife and family in Argentina (his marriage had effectively come to an end), nor did he return to Ireland to be with his extended family. Instead, Jack remained in London, living in humble circumstances. When he grew ill in the 1950s with cancer, his wife Aileen came and nursed him until his death on the 7 December 1954.

Impact on the family

Three granddaughters, one of whom lives in Argentina and the other two of whom are in the US and England respectively, are of the opinion that the move to South America was successful and that life there was happy. This they gathered from personal experience and from what they heard from Granny Aileen and their parents. The schools were good and although there wasn't much money, holidays were enjoyable, especially trips out into 'the camp' (Argentinian bush). There was much talk of 'home' which was referring to England not Ireland. Aileen was a woman of her times, very fond of the British monarchy, but then again so was my grandmother Cissy (Jack's younger sister) who spent all her life in Cork. When Ireland was discussed, the main topic of conversation was the photograph of the *Titanic* taken by Jack in 1912. His participation in the 1916 Rising was confined to passing comments only. Ireland was relegated in the Morrogh family to a distant and pleasant memory, absent of bitterness and regret.

Jack Morrogh remained very secretive about his activities in the 1916 Rising, despite his significant role in events. This in itself is not very surprising because soldiers returning from war frequently remain quiet about what happened to them. Had things transpired differently for Jack Morrogh he might have remained in Ireland with his extended family in Cork – sailing at the Royal Munster Yacht Club and pottering about, as his brothers did.

However, the events of Easter week would appear to have changed his life irrevocably. He was heavily involved in the fighting right up to the bitter end, he led a group that wounded James Connolly, and he may well also have participated peripherally in Connolly's execution; all which information may have been gathered by the IRA for further attention. My feeling is that Jack Morrogh's fate changed with the capturing of the Sinn Féin flag and the subsequent photograph of the British officers with the flag.

Twenty British officers are shown at the Parnell monument with the captured Sinn Féin flag hanging upside down, itself a sign of contempt, on a pole strapped to a Tommy's rifle. Only two of the twenty officers have been identified, Jack Morrogh standing in the back row in the middle with a walking stick in his right hand – clearly the star of the photoshoot. The other is Lt Dick Burke, who is on the extreme right of the photograph, far less conspicuous. Dick Burke returned to the front after the Rising, was wounded and awarded the Military Cross for bravery. At the end of the war he returned to live peacefully in Killester, Dublin, with his wife and two daughters.[16] Since both of the officers are members of the Royal Irish Regiment, it is reasonable to presume that they all are. Private Desborough did say that on Sunday, 30 April, 'the high-ups of the regiment stood up and were photographed', so it is likely he was referring to this photograph, among others.[17] Two other officers in the photograph are holding rifles, which were not normally carried by First World War British officers – their weapons were confined to the sidearm and the cane! The presence of the rifles could indicate that Jack's group of sharpshooters (that had wounded James Connolly) had contained not only soldiers but also officers with experience in trench warfare, where sniping was a feature.

If the photograph had been taken by one of Jack's colleagues or by the regimental photographer, it would most likely have been lost from public view

16 Tom Burke, 'Fancy the Royal Irish captured Moore St', *The Blue Cap,* 16 (Dec. 2009), pp 1–17. http://www.greatwar.ie/wp-content/uploads/2016/03/The-Blue-Cap–16.pdf, accessed 10 July 2017.
17 BMH WS 1604 (Albert Desborough), p. 11.

and catalogued away in the regimental records, all of which were stored in London and subsequently destroyed during the Second World War by German bombing. So why did the photograph become one of the iconic images of the 1916 Rising? In the coverage of the Rising by RTÉ's *Nationwide* in 2016, the photograph can be seen for a few seconds as the credits were rolling.

I was intrigued by the fact the photograph was entitled 'Irish Rebellion – *May* 1916 (my emphasis) and not *April* 1916, when the rebellion occurred. I thought perhaps that the photograph had appeared in some publication, like a newspaper or magazine that came out in the month after the Rising. Following a little research, I discovered that the photograph was taken by a photographer from a popular UK newspaper of the time called the *Daily Sketch.* It was published on Wednesday 3 May in a montage of eight photographs headed 'How the soldiers barricaded and held the streets of Dublin against the rebel mob'.

The caption under Jack Morrogh's photograph was 'A group of officers with captured rebel flag. The trophy taken from the roof of the General Post Office in Sackville Street bore the symbol of the Irish Republic of the Sinn Feiners' foredoomed dreams'! Publication of Easter week photographs would have been seen by many in Ireland, so Jack Morrogh's association with the events would have been widely known. So popular did these Easter Rising photographs prove to be that several of them were made into postcards by Eason and Sons, for sale throughout the country. Included in those was a postcard of Jack's group with the captured flag. An original of the postcard of Jack and the Sinn Féin flag can be found in the Curran postcard collection, housed in the Special Collections at the James Joyce Library, UCD, Dublin.

By the end of the First World War, attitudes in Ireland had changed dramatically. Nationalism had grown among the people and Irishmen who had served in the British army and their families were often viewed with suspicion. The attention Jack and his family received at the hands of the IRA may well have been simply part of the reaction at the time. The Morroghs were a pro-British family who would have been well-known by the Carragaline Company of the IRA. However, I cannot but help feel that the photograph may well have played a role. In the days when photography was relatively rare, a photograph of Jack with the captured 1916 Sinn Féin flag was published in a popular newspaper and as a postcard. It is therefore of little wonder that republicans were aware of Jack Morrogh's role in the 1916 Rising and that they were probably waiting for an opportunity to exact revenge. Their opportunity came during the War of Independence and was inflicted in 1921. I can just imagine the postcard being passed around the members of the Carragaline

Montage of eight photographs headed 'How the soldiers barricaded and held the streets of Dublin against the rebel mob', *Daily Sketch*, 3 May 1916.

company of the IRA – 'See that man directly under the flag, well his name is Major Jack Morrogh. Keep an eye out for him'. The net result was that Jack and family were banished from Ireland, in perpetuity, and that this was his fate from the moment his photograph was taken at the foot of the Parnell monument on Sunday, 30 April 1916.

Acknowledgments

I wish to thank Jack Morrogh's grandchildren, Aphra Peard, Julyan Peard and Arabella Bugliani for their enthusiastic support and source of family stories and photographs. A special thanks to Mr Stuart Purcell, Whyte's Fine Art & Collectibles Auctioneers & Valuers, Dublin, for providing me with the photograph from the *Daily Sketch,* to Mr Jonathan Maguire, Royal Irish Fusiliers Museum, Armagh, for background information, and to Mr Declan MacDevitt, Archives, Castleknock College, for providing me with extracts and photographs from Castleknock College's *College Chronicle.* I would also like to thank Special Collections, James Joyce Library, University College Dublin, for allowing me access to the Curran Postcard Collection.

'Ireland will soon be free': Paddy Maher and the Knocklong Raid

LIAM Ó hAISIBÉIL

During the Irish War of Independence (1919–21), Patrick Maher, my great grand-uncle, was one of a group of ten Irish Volunteers executed by British forces in Mountjoy Jail between November 1920 and June 1921. These Volunteers, popularly referred to as 'The Forgotten Ten', were: Kevin Barry, Thomas Whelan, Patrick Moran, Patrick Doyle, Bernard Ryan, Thomas Bryan, Frank Flood, Thomas Traynor, Edmond Foley and Patrick Maher. They were tried and executed under an extension of the Defence of the Realm Act, known as the Restoration of Order in Ireland Act, 1920, which permitted the trial of civilian prisoners in Ireland by military court-martial, rather than granting a trial by a jury of their peers. Patrick Maher and Edmond Foley were the last two Irishmen to be executed in the Anglo-Irish war, just one month before the declaration of a truce between both sides on 11 July 1921.[1]

Patrick (Paddy) was born *c.*1889 in the townland of Knocklara, a short distance from the village of Knocklong in east Co. Limerick.[2] His father emigrated from Ireland to America and died there sometime in the late nineteenth century. In 1895, his mother Ellen (née Quish) re-married and had three children with her second husband, Edmond Quinlan; a set of twins, Thomas (my great-grandfather) and Maurice, were born in April 1897, and a daughter Ellen, who was born in 1899. The family lived in a one-roomed labourer's cottage in Knocklara which, according to the census enumerator's report, was in very poor condition in 1901. Paddy attended school at Glenbrohane national school and was described as being of 'quiet, gentle, and good' disposition.[3] By 1914, Paddy was employed as an egg grader and packer at an egg and poultry store, managed by John O'Riordan, in the village of Knocklong. His role was to 'attend the egg market at the railway station, and to keep a book of all the sales and purchases'.[4] In correspondence some years later, O'Riordan remarked that Paddy's prospects for continuous employment

I am indebted to Dr John O'Callaghan who provided me with several useful documents from previously unseen archival sources relating to Maher, and for additional information on the Knocklong raid, drawn from his extensive research on the War of Independence in Co. Limerick. 1 Seán McConville, *Irish political prisoners, 1848–1922: theatres of war* (London, 2005), p. 697. 2 Officially rendered Knocklary, see https://www.logainm.ie/30945.aspx. 3 Tim Carey, *Hanged for Ireland: the forgotten ten: executed, 1920–21: a documentary history* (Dublin, 2001), p. 160. 4 Ibid., p. 167.

and improved remuneration at the store were excellent.[5] As his duties were based in and around the area of Knocklong train station, Paddy would have been well-known to those frequenting the station. His employment with O'Riordan caused some difficulty for him and his family in the spring and early summer of 1919, when he was ostracized and later threatened by members of the local community for not participating in a strike at the local creamery, then under management of O'Riordan.[6]

According to Patrick O'Donnell, the officer in command of the local Irish Volunteer branch during the War, Paddy enrolled as a member of Cush Company, East Limerick Brigade, in December 1915.[7] While there is some confusion regarding his level of activity with the local branch, a number of members of the East Limerick Brigade and other individuals provided statements in the years following his execution, identifying Paddy as a member of the Volunteers, and as having taken part in drills with Cush Company. In a letter, dated 27 February 1926, Colonel Eamonn Ó Cearbaill stated that:

> The position in most country districts in Munster at that time was that practically every male resident of a locality was nominally a member of the Volunteers. Of these about fifty per cent were entirely inactive; not more than twenty per cent took part in active operations against the British Forces, and the other thirty per cent were employed in various non-militant capacities such as obstructing roads and minor activities of that nature.[8]

Ó Cearbaill continues by saying that at the time of Paddy's arrest in September 1919, these 'minor activities' had not developed to any great extent in the area.[9] It may have been the case that Paddy and other members of his company had no opportunity to participate in such activities prior to the notable increase in hostilities during 1919. Following the Soloheadbeg ambush in Co. Tipperary on 21 January 1919 and events in Limerick city that April, the level of hostility encountered by the Limerick RIC increased and by June of that year the morale of the constabulary 'was nearing breaking point'.[10] What is clear from

5 O'Riordan to Army Pensions Board, 9 May 1935 (Military Archives Ireland, Military Service Pensions Collection, 1/D/343). (MAI, MSPC, hereafter). **6** Carey, *Hanged for Ireland*, pp 168, 170, where it is stated that Paddy, although not employed at the creamery, crossed the picket line to fulfil his duties at the egg and poultry store. This is also alluded to in a statement by Dr Joseph Kearney (Military Archives of Ireland, Bureau of Military History, Witness Statement 0704). (MAI, BMH, WS hereafter). **7** Statement by Patrick O'Donnell to Army Pensions Board, 2 Dec. 1926 (MAI, MSPC, 1/D/343). **8** Letter from E. Ó Cearbaill to Lieut. F.J. Tully, 27 Feb. 1926 (MAI, MSPC, 1/D/343). **9** Ibid. **10** For more on the significance of the rescue, see John O'Callaghan, *Revolutionary Limerick: the republican campaign for independence in Limerick, 1913–1921* (Dublin, the Military Service Pensions Collection files is that Paddy's arrest, detention, and execution caused significant hardship for the family in subsequent years, who were entirely dependent on him at that time.[11] His two half-brothers were only able to obtain occasional work in the locality as labourers and, as such, their wages were uncertain. Indeed, Ned O'Brien, who participated in the Knocklong Raid of 1919, stated that 'there isn't the slightest doubt but he was a Volunteer' and that Paddy could not devote much time to Volunteer activities due to his duties at home.[12] Whatever his level of participation in the activities of Cush Company prior to his arrest, he spent almost the entire active Volunteer period (1919–21) in prison.

Seán Hogan, from Greenane, Co. Tipperary, along with Dan Breen, Seán Treacy and others, took part in the Soloheadbeg ambush on 21 January 1919 during which two RIC officers were killed. The first Dáil was convened on the same day in Dublin and the events in Soloheadbeg were central to the outbreak of armed hostilities between crown forces and the Irish Volunteers. Hogan went on the run but was eventually tracked down and arrested by the RIC in Annfield, Co. Tipperary, on 12 May of that year. He was held overnight at Thurles RIC barracks. On 13 May, while being transferred to Cork Gaol by train, a successful attempt was made to free Hogan from custody when the train had stopped at Knocklong Station. Seán Treacy, Dan Breen and Séamus Robinson, along with local men from the East Limerick Brigade – Ned O'Brien, John Joe O'Brien, James Scanlon, Seán Lynch and Edmond (Ned) Foley – took part in the rescue. Four of the group boarded at Emly Station to confirm that Hogan was indeed aboard the train.[13] Seán Hogan was guarded by four policemen: Sergeant Wallace, Constable Reilly, Constable Enright and Constable Ring. Two of the policemen were fatally wounded in the attack. Constable Enright died on the train after being shot in the stomach and Sergeant Wallace died of his injuries the following day at Kilmallock Hospital. Although Breen, Treacy, Scanlon and Ned O'Brien were injured during the struggle, none of the rescue party were fatally wounded. All four were treated in secret by two local doctors before the following morning.[14] This event became known as the Knocklong Raid and graphic accounts of the raid and its aftermath filled columns in Irish newspapers in the following days and weeks.[15] The deaths of the two policemen and the brutality of the attack

2010), pp 123–5. **11** Report by the Chief Superintendent, Bruff, Co. Limerick to Army Pensions Board, 24 June 1924 (MAI, MSPC, 1/D/343). **12** Letter from Edmond O'Brien to Army Pension Board, 6 Jan. 1926 stating: '... and Poor Maher especially could ill afford any time (though he gave it ungrudgingly) as he was the sole earner for the House-hold' (MAI, MSPC, 1/D/343). **13** John J. O'Brien (MAI, BMH, WS 1647). **14** Tadhg Crowley (MAI, BMH, WS 0435). **15** *Freeman's Journal,* 15 May 1919 – 'Almost simultaneously three shots rang out, and Constable Enright was seen caused a stir at the time, and the actions of the Volunteers were openly condemned.[16] Local members of the Volunteers, however, thought it 'a great day's work for the East Limerick Brigade and [...] for all Ireland'.[17]

The RIC and British military forces conducted extensive searches of the area over the summer of 1919, but were unable to apprehend any members of the rescue party, the majority of whom had dispersed across counties Limerick and Tipperary and Dublin city; two members secured passage to America.[18] Statements collected from local Volunteers at a later date indicate that there was at least one suspected informer in the area who may have been providing the RIC with information, however inaccurate, on those who were present at the Knocklong Raid.[19] The only member of the rescue party to be picked up was Ned Foley, who was arrested at his home in Galbally on 24 September 1919. All accounts from those who took part in the raid indicate that he was not in the carriage when the shooting broke-out aboard the train, and played no part in the shooting of the policemen. Paddy Maher, who was not involved in the attack, nor had prior knowledge of it, was also arrested by the RIC on 24 September. By December 1919, a total of six men had been arrested as a result of this large-scale manhunt. The other men were: Tom and Mick Shanahan, brothers, who owned the Coal Stores at Knocklong; Patrick Murphy, a porter at Knocklong railway station, and Michael 'Mixie' O'Connell, a shop-owner and member of the Volunteers from Thurles who was already known to the authorities for his associations with Sinn Féin and the Volunteers.

Paddy Maher and Ned Foley were first held at the RIC barracks on William Street in Limerick, but were later transferred to Limerick Prison. Four of the six men appeared before a special sitting of the court on 24 October 1919. At this sitting, Paddy was identified as having been a member of the rescue party by two witnesses, namely Arthur Norris and John Farrington.[20] Norris also identified Ned Foley as a participant. This was to spell the beginning of the end for Paddy who, up until that point, had not been formally identified by any witness to the attack. The men were then held repeatedly on remand at Limerick Prison over the next few months while the investigation continued.

to collapse in his seat'; *Skibbereen Eagle,* 17 May 1919 – 'The woodwork [...] was covered with blood stains, a gruesome indication of the terrible struggle which had taken place'; *Kilkenny People,* 17 May 1919 – 'Great excitement and alarm prevailed amongst the passengers during the progress of the sensational occurrence'. **16** *Freeman's Journal,* 15 May 1919; Dan Breen, *My fight for Irish freedom,* 2nd ed. (Dublin, 1924), pp 75, 81. **17** Edmund Tobin (MAI, BMH, WS 1451). **18** John J. O'Brien (MAI, BMH, WS 1647). **19** Statement by Seán Howard, Glenbrohane to Daniel O'Shaughnessy (MAI, BMH, WS 1435). 'My father had him spotted and always maintained that it was he [who] got the information that ultimately led to the arrest and execution of Foley and Maher': name of suspected informer, who was a local farmer, redacted. **20** David Dineen, 'Paddy Maher: a judicial murder', *History Studies: University of Limerick History Society Journal,* 16 (2005), p. 33; *Limerick Leader,* 27 Oct. 1919.

The four men appeared before the magistrate at Limerick Prison on 15 November 1919. On this occasion, Maher complained about the length of his detention, seeing as he was innocent of the charges.[21] All six men were brought before the court on 27 December 1919, at which stage they were further remanded in custody to allow District Inspector Egan to conduct further enquiries.[22] There was another court appearance scheduled for the 24 January 1920 and on this date, further depositions were taken by the prosecution from witnesses and these were completed on the 26 January 1920. The accused were remanded in custody again for trial at a later date.

The final court appearance (following another adjournment) was held at the Armagh Assizes on 6 July 1920 and approximately forty witnesses for the defence travelled from Knocklong to Armagh.[23] On this date, five of the accused including Paddy appeared for trial. Subsequently, the grand jury didn't find enough evidence to proceed with the cases of the Shanahan brothers and O'Connell. It appears that Mixie O'Connell, who was involved in sending telegrams that were sent to Knocklong regarding Hogan's departure from Thurles, had been released from custody in the interim, having gone on hunger strike at Mountjoy Jail. Once released, he went on the run and was not re-arrested.[24] The case against Paddy was then adjourned until the following March, as were the cases against Ned Foley and Patrick Murphy, due to the absence of a prosecution witness, who was also, according to the defence, a key witness in their case. In an unusual and somewhat mysterious turn of events, Sergeant Reilly, one of the four policemen guarding Hogan at Knocklong, was kidnapped by armed men in Armagh while on the way to visit his brother the night before his court appearance.

Reilly reappeared two days later at an RIC barracks in the village of Killylea, six miles from Armagh, apparently unharmed.[25] The three remaining accused had now spent almost nine months in custody and would not see trial for another eight months. Those eight months were to become the most significant period in the case.

The Restoration of Order in Ireland Act was passed on 9 August 1920 and the implementation of this act had dire consequences for the accused who, despite several court appearances, had yet to be convicted of their alleged crimes. It also resulted in a significant departure regarding the body of evidence that had to be assembled to attempt to secure a conviction.[26] The men were recharged for both manslaughter and murder under the auspices of the Act and

21 *Limerick Leader*, 17 Nov. 1919. **22** *Limerick Leader*, 31 Dec. 1919. **23** Dr Joseph Kearney (MAI, BMH, WS 0704). **24** *Belfast Newsletter*, 8 July 1920; *Irish Independent*, 8 July 1920. **25** *Belfast Newsletter*, 9 July 1920. **26** Colm Campbell, *Emergency law in Ireland, 1918–1925* (Oxford, 1994), p. 122.

KIDNAPPED

Sensational Development in Knocklong Trial

SERGEANT SPIRITED AWAY

Set Upon While Enjoying Midnight Stroll

Image from front page of the *Evening Herald*, 7 July 1920.

would no longer face a civil court but instead appear before six British army officers at a military court martial.[27] Of the twenty civilians who were court-martialled under the act, ten were sentenced to death and this group later became known as 'The Forgotten Ten'. In January 1921, Tadhg Crowley, a neighbour of Paddy and Ned from Ballylanders, Co. Limerick, met the pair in Mountjoy Jail as he was awaiting transfer to Portland Prison in Dorset, England. He wrote: 'Foley and Maher seemed to be under the impression that there was no hope for them, and I tried to satisfy them that when they had not been executed already there was no fear that it would happen now, but they said they were prepared to go […] Eventually I said good-bye to them, and did not hear about them until many months afterwards when they were executed'.[28] This is very much in contrast with the account of their demeanour described by Bridget Ryan (née FitzPatrick) following their trial at the Armagh Assizes in July 1920 where she states that Foley and Maher 'did not take part in the hunger strike with O'Connell for, being innocent of the charges which had been preferred against them, they felt confident that they would not be found guilty when their next trial took place'.[29]

The case came up for trial on 15 March 1921 before a General Court Martial consisting of six British officers at City Hall in Dublin, which was

27 Dineen, *Paddy Maher: a judicial killing*, p. 34. **28** Tadhg Crowley (MAI, BMH, WS 0435). **29** Bridget Ryan (MAI, BMH, WS 1488).

adjacent to Dublin Castle. The court martial lasted for five days. Several witnesses from Knocklong, and others who were aboard the train on the day were requested to attend as witnesses for the defence. Early depositions, taken at Limerick Prison before Paddy had legal representation, were used by the prosecution to prove that he was at the scene of the raid at Knocklong Station, and could be accurately identified by multiple (mostly military) witnesses.

Both Paddy and Ned were given the opportunity to each make a statement before the court. Paddy's own account of his whereabouts around the time of the raid, and a summary of all he had experienced over the subsequent eighteen months is outlined in this statement.[30] He stated that he 'never had a rifle or revolver in my possession' and said 'everyone who knows me, knows that if a policeman was shot it is God's truth I never shot him'.[31] Paddy left work in Knocklong for home after 6 p.m. on the day of the raid, accompanied by a young colleague named William Riordan. The pair stopped for a drink at Mulvihill's public house in Garryspillane and were there for a quarter-of-an-hour or so. They left the public house together and parted ways at Pinkers Cross. Throughout his statement he names individuals he met at various places on his way home and outlines how he first heard of the raid that evening. Indeed, based on enquiries made by An Garda Síochána at Bruff in 1924, 'five or six witnesses were examined and proved that Maher was at or near his own house at the time the shooting occurred, and could not possibly have been there'.[32]

A series of events conspired against Paddy Maher, besides his supposed physical resemblance to some of those who participated in the raid, or who were passengers on the train at Knocklong Station. Dan Breen, who was a central member of the rescue party, writing in 1924 stated: 'Paddy Maher went to the scaffold with [Ned Foley] for the same "crime" even though he had not taken hand, act or part in the rescue of Seán Hogan'.[33] According to Tadhg Crowley, who was involved in getting medical assistance for the injured members of the rescue party: 'Ned Foley took part in the attack on the train at Knocklong, but that Paddy Maher had no knowledge of the event at all, and he was not present'.[34] The following was also recounted by Joseph Kearney, then a medical student at University College Cork, who was a passenger on the train when the raid occurred:

> Mr Lynch [Solicitor for the Defence] explained to me that the prosecution's case was that Maher took part in the shooting, that, before the

30 The full text of the statement has been reprinted in Carey, *Hanged for Ireland,* pp 167–71. **31** Ibid., p. 167. **32** Letter from Einrí Ó Frigil to The Secretary, Department of Finance (MAI, BMH, MSPC, 1/D/343). **33** Breen, *My fight for Irish freedom,* p. 71. **34** Tadhg Crowley (MAI, BMH, WS 0435).

> train left Knocklong, he ran across the field, went through an opening in the hedge, over the paling and was helped into the train and that my evidence would be very important because I was the person who came by that route. He also remarked, in passing, that I was very like Maher, and I did not feel at all too happy about that situation.[35]

It was also stated by a 'British soldier who was on the train' (i.e. Arthur Norris) that he saw Paddy going down the platform with some of the attackers, but Maher did resemble one of the men who took part in the attack.[36]

As well as the issue of physical resemblance – Paddy's own alibis changed their statements on a number of occasions. Mr Mulvihill, owner of the public house in Garryspillane, stated that he could not recall any particular person who was in the bar that evening.[37] Paddy's colleague from the Knocklong store, William Riordan, changed his statement before the final trial, denying that he had a drink with Paddy in Mulvihill's and that he had walked with Paddy as far as Pinkers Cross.[38] Both later changed their statements. Dineen speculates that either the witnesses feared for their safety around the time of the trial, or there was some element of revenge or malice directed towards Paddy as a consequence of the creamery strike in 1919.[39] Neither surviving constables (Reilly nor Ring) could initially identify anyone who participated in the raid, but this changed as time progressed.[40] Edmond Crawford, a local man and Lieutenant in Cush Company, was going to testify to Paddy's whereabouts on the evening of the raid to clear him of any involvement in the incident but he was shot by British forces on 25 March 1921, and died from his injuries the following day at Kilmallock Hospital. It was later suggested that he was singled out because of his involvement in the defence of Maher.[41] In any case, his testimony would have come too late for the final court martial.

Despite all the evidence for the defence, admittedly from members of the Volunteers and family friends, Lieutenant John Basil Jarvis, director of intelligence for the Oxford and Buckinghamshire Light Infantry in counties Clare, Limerick and Tipperary in 1920–1, lists Patrick Maher as the 'Chief Assassin' in the raid to free Hogan.[42] This assertion is questionable considering the testimonials of those who took part in the raid, including Dan Breen and local man

35 Dr Joseph Kearney (MAI, BMH, WS 0704). Kearney also states (ibid.): 'Maher had neither hand, act nor part in it. Maher was employed, I think, in a store in Knocklong.' **36** Letter from Einrí Ó Frigil to The Secretary, Department of Finance (MAI, BMH, MSPC, 1/D/343). **37** Dineen, 'Paddy Maher: a judicial killing', p. 39. **38** Ibid., p. 39; Letter from Einrí Ó Frigil to The Secretary, Department of Finance (MAI, BMH, MSPC, 1/D/343). **39** Dineen, 'Paddy Maher: a judicial killing', p. 36. **40** Ibid., pp 36–7. **41** Edmond Crawford (MAI, BMH, MSPC, 1/D/276). **42** John Basil Jarvis, *Lt John Basil Jarvis, May 1921* (Bicester, 1921), Oxford and Buckinghamshire Light Infantry Intelligence Notes, 3/7/A/1, The Soldiers of Oxfordshire Trust Archive (Bicester, 1921).

Ned O'Brien. Paddy's inevitable fate is outlined in the following exchange, which supposedly took place between the solicitor for the defence, Jack Power of Kilmallock, and the prosecuting counsel for the state at lunch hour during the trial:

> 'Whatever about Foley I can tell you that Maher is completely innocent and wasn't there at all'. The Prosecuting Counsel replied: 'I may as well tell you Mr Power that if these two men are not found guilty in this case, I have instructions to issue a warrant for their arrest the moment they leave the Court for the murder of D.I. Potter at Thurles'.[43]

It seems that regardless of the facts of the case, the prosecution and military administration were intent on securing convictions for both men, regardless of their guilt or innocence in the alleged crime. On 22 March, Patrick Murphy was acquitted of all charges. Paddy Maher and Ned Foley were found not guilty on the charge of manslaughter, but were convicted on the charge of murdering the two policemen and subsequently sentenced to death by hanging.

I first became aware of the full extent of my great grand-uncle's story shortly before October 2001, when a decision was made by the coalition government of Fianna Fáil and the Progressive Democrats to hold a state funeral for 'The Forgotten Ten'. This decision, though criticized as 'an act of denial' by some sections of the media in Ireland and in the United Kingdom at the time,[44] brought an end to an eighty-year campaign by relatives of the men, and local memorial committees, supported by the National Graves Association, to have the remains of the dead men returned to their families. The graves were located within the grounds of Mountjoy Jail, and the exhumation of the remains had been the subject of repeated requests from relatives since 1921. Families were initially told that under the Capital Punishment Amendment Act 1868, the bodies of those executed had to remain buried

43 Daniel O'Shaughnessy (MAI, BMH, WS 1435). Gilbert Potter was shot in revenge for the hanging of Thomas Traynor – one of the 'Forgotten Ten' – on 25 April 1921. 44 Fintan O'Toole, writing in the *Irish Times,* referred to the event as 'an act of denial' and 'a great boost to those who want us to feel that the only difference between a terrorist and a patriot is the passage of time' and described the timing of the event as 'grotesque', particularly in the wake of the 11 September attacks in New York, *Irish Times,* 2 October 2001. See also *Sunday Independent,* 21 October 2001, where then Minister for Justice, John O'Donoghue, condemns attempts made by some to link the ten men with the IRA campaign in Northern Ireland: 'They make a false link between the actions of soldiers of the Republic during the War of Independence and the actions of a tiny minority who today have no democratic mandate for their actions and who deal in the currency of terrorism'.

within prison grounds. Paddy's mother, Ellen, wrote to Emmet Dalton in January of 1922 requesting that Paddy's remains be removed from Mountjoy and returned to her. This request was considered but all action on the issue ceased once the Civil War broke out in June 1922. Following the Civil War, it proved a divisive topic among successive governments and the graves remained in situ at Mountjoy.

Although I was aware of the role of my great-grandfather, Thomas Quinlan, in the War of Independence, I heard very little of Paddy's when growing up. I don't recall my grandmother, Paddy's niece, ever mentioning it to me and I can only speculate as to why this was the case. My cousins in Limerick, however, grew up hearing stories about Paddy and this proved instrumental in the campaign for the return of his remains. Paddy Quinlan, a nephew of Paddy Maher, and Geraldine Quinlan, Paddy's grand-niece, along with members of the Paddy Maher Memorial Committee, were central to the campaign to have Paddy's remains returned to the family and brought back to Limerick. I had the privilege of being present for the state funeral in Dublin on Sunday, 14 October 2001 when an estimated crowd of 30,000 people lined the streets of Dublin to pay their respects to the 'Forgotten Ten'. While this was the name popularly given to the ten men, their relatives certainly had not forgotten them over the eighty-year period since their executions. Paddy was the only one of the ten not to be re-interred in Glasnevin Cemetery on that day and, instead, was buried in the republican plot in Ballylanders Cemetery, Co. Limerick.

Paddy, and several of the Forgotten Ten, played no part in the crimes for which they were convicted and subsequently executed. It was well known at the time, and evidenced in various witness accounts provided since 1919, that Paddy didn't play any part in the events at Knocklong and fell victim to the efforts of the British authorities to supress revolution in Ireland, and to find someone accountable for the attacks against the RIC and military forces. Either way, Paddy was a condemned man as soon as he was detained, and regardless of his involvement someone had to go to the scaffold. His demeanour and composure throughout his court appearances, even on the morning of his execution, were admirable. I cannot imagine how Paddy and his family must have felt at the time, realising that all efforts to secure a reprieve were in vain. The reinternment and state funeral certainly played their part in securing closure for the family, and for recognising that he died as a Volunteer, though condemned for another's crime. Government and public attention during this 'Decade of Centenaries' has tended to focus on those who actively fought on both sides of the conflict, particularly during the First World War and the Easter Rising, and thus it is easy to neglect the memories of those who were innocent of any crime, yet were condemned and suffered the same fate as

Paddy Maher (l) and Ned Foley (r).

those killed in battle.[45] The injustice that Paddy suffered should not be forgotten.

In the days before the executions, a memorial for the reprieve of Paddy and Ned was signed by over 2,000 people from Co. Limerick but it was to no avail. The following account of Patrick's final meeting with his mother and sister was printed in the *Freeman's Journal:* 'The aged mother of Patrick Maher and his sister saw him in his prison cell for the last time. Mrs Maher, in a conversation with our representative, said her son was extremely happy and cheery. He was ready and prepared to die. His life would be given gladly for his country'.[46]

Their executions went ahead as scheduled at 7 o'clock on Tuesday morning, 7 June 1921. The two men 'walked with firm step to the scaffold and met their deaths with courage and fortitude. They stood side by side in the trap of the execution chamber, and were launched into eternity simultaneously. The death in each case was instantaneous'.[47] Upon entering the chamber, Paddy stated: 'I am innocent'.[48]

Paddy Maher was only thirty-two years of age when he was executed. The pair issued a joint final statement before their execution. It read:

45 Decade of Centenaries, http://www.decadeofcentenaries.com/. There is, as yet, no mention of the 'Forgotten Ten' as part of this programme of commemoration. **46** *Freeman's Journal,* 7 June 1921. **47** *Kildare Observer,* 11 June 1921; *Southern Star,* 11 June 1921. **48** Carey, *Hanged for Ireland,* p. 177.

> Fight on, struggle on for the honour, glory and freedom of dear old Ireland. Our hearts go out to all our dear old friends. Our souls go to God at seven o'clock in the morning, and our bodies, when Ireland is free, shall go to Galbally.
>
> Our blood shall not be shed in vain for Ireland, and we have a strong presentiment, going to our God, that Ireland will soon be free. We gladly give our lives that a smile may lighten the face of our dear 'Dark Rosaleen'. We will see that Ireland will be free. Farewell! Farewell! Farewell![49]

In accordance with his final wishes, Paddy Maher was reburied at Ballylanders in Co. Limerick on 20 October 2001. Tom Quinlan, my great-grandfather, and Paddy's half-brother, lived to be nearly 102 years of age, but unfortunately passed away in January 1999, just two years before Paddy's remains were brought home to Co. Limerick.

49 Ibid., p. 176.

Dan McCann: IRA artificer and a 'dangerous man'

CHRIS McNAIRNEY

The history of Irish republicanism during the Easter Rising and the War of Independence in what would become the North of Ireland has received limited attention until recent years.[1] Exceptions include Robert Lynch's *The Northern IRA and the early years of partition, 1920–22*;[2] as well as work by Margaret O'Callaghan, Mary Harris and Fergal McCluskey. In 2005, the historian Peter Hart noted that 'the Irish border cut through the historiography with historians working in the south ignoring the north and vice versa';[3] while Diarmaid Ferriter[4] cites an interned teacher writing to the Free State Minister of Education Eoin MacNeill in January 1923 – 'the bitter part is the reflection that when I do get out I shall probably be forgotten' and wryly comments 'he was right'. This coupled with the failure of the IRA to make any impact on partition lead to what Paul Bew has termed a partitionist history.[5] Looking forward, historians like O'Callaghan have argued that even the recent past remains contested along sectarian lines; while Harris notes the role of the Catholic Church in significant areas like education which aided in creating what she refers to as a self-contained Catholic community.[6]

This chapter will look at one actor, Dan McCann, acknowledging the complicated history of the North, the impact of revisionism and later events during the Troubles on the historiography, and the importance of personal/micro histories to this history. After an initial discussion of Dan McCann's involvement in the War of Independence, I will reflect on the connections with the Troubles and the importance of family history and life course to my understanding of both time periods.

Dan McCann

Daniel (Dan) McCann, my grandfather, was born in 1897 in Catherine Street in the Markets area which was, and remains, a small nationalist enclave

1 In this chapter, the North will refer to the six counties that were partitioned in 1925. 2 Robert Lynch, *The Northern IRA and the early years of partition, 1920–22* (Dublin, 2006). 3 Peter Hart, *The IRA at war, 1916–1923* (Oxford, 2003), p. 9. 4 Diarmaid Ferriter, *A nation and not a rabble: the Irish revolution, 1913–1923* (London, 2015), p. 316. 5 Paul Bew, *Ideology and the Irish question, Ulster unionism and Irish nationalism* (Oxford, 1994). 6 Mary Harris, *The Catholic Church and the*

surrounded by the loyalist areas of east Belfast. To this day, it remains a divided area, as it was in the revolutionary period. The McCanns were a republican family, and we believe Dan's father, my great-grandfather, was connected to the Irish Republican Brotherhood. We do know that Dan joined Na Fianna Éireann as a youth, most likely in 1910. The Belfast Fianna had a strong socialist ethos under the leadership of Cathal O'Shannon (a close colleague of James Connolly in the ITGWU) who delivered a series of lectures on European history and organized debates with political opponents in the United Irish League branches. Indeed, the Belfast Fianna included a girl's corps, the Betsy Gray Sluagh, led amongst others by James Connolly's daughters Nora and Ina. Certainly they were a critical part of the revolutionary forces in Belfast and most of their members graduated to the ranks of the Irish Volunteer Force (IVF) and eventually the Irish Republican Army (IRA), forming much of the Belfast leadership.

On the wider stage figures of national importance like Liam Mellows emerged as important republican leaders from the ranks of the Fianna and Dan also followed this path, and he remained a committed republican until his death in 1934. By 1916, Dan was an active member of the Irish Volunteers and as with his comrades across the country prepared to take up arms at the appropriate time. However, the republican leadership in Dublin, notably Connolly and Seán Mac Diarmada who had both lived in Belfast, were acutely aware of the bitterly sectarian nature of that city, and Connolly issued a direct order that no shot was to be fired in Belfast. When the mobilization order was issued for Easter week, the Belfast Volunteers were ordered to travel to Dungannon where they were to join with the Tyrone Volunteers and then make their way to Galway where they were to place themselves under the command of Liam Mellows. Connolly's order was given to Dennis McCullough, a member of the IRB's Supreme Council and leader of the Belfast Volunteers who recounted the meeting as follows:

> I suggested that we would have to attack an R.I.C. barracks on our way through, to secure arms, which we required. Connolly got quite cross at this suggestion and almost shouted at me, you will fire no shot in Ulster: you will proceed with all possible speed to join Mellows in Connaught ... if we win through, we will then deal with Ulster.[7]

Consequently, Dan and 131 of his comrades travelled in three groups to Dungannon over the period of Good Friday and Easter Saturday, apparently as

foundation of the Northern Irish state (Cork, 1995). 7 BMH WS 915 (Denis McCullough), p. 15.

part of a routine training exercise. They were issued with single tickets and brought with them their entire weaponry which consisted of one short arm per Volunteer and forty assorted rifles. On arrival in Dungannon, they were informed of the countermanding orders from MacNeill and instructed to make their way back to Belfast however they could. A Cumann na mBan contingent including Winifred Carney and Nora Connolly separated from the Volunteers and managed to find their way to the GPO in Dublin. From a northern perspective the fallout from the Rising was a disaster; morale hit rock bottom, many of the leadership were arrested and interned and the movement was thrown into disarray.

In a further ironic connection with Galway one of the group of RIC men who arrested Liam Mellows was Constable John William Nixon from Co. Cavan.[8] It was widely believed that as the district inspector of the Browne Square Barracks in Belfast Nixon led an infamous murder gang of RIC men and B Specials. This gang carried out 'reprisal killings' and was responsible for the murder of five members of the innocent McMahon family in north Belfast, in response to the IRA killing of two members of the Specials. Nixon went on to become a member of the Stormont parliament.[9] Other members of the Cromwell Club were targeted by the IRA including Constable Christy Clarke who was killed in March 1922, and in testimony to the internecine nature of the conflict he is buried in Milltown Cemetery yards from where Dan is interred and adjacent to the republican plot.[10]

In the immediate aftermath of Easter week public sentiment among Belfast nationalists to the Rising was similar to that in Dublin and we know that Connolly's family house on Glenalina Terrace on the Falls Road was attacked by 'irate dockers and their wives';[11] as with the rest of the country, this sentiment changed quickly as the executions of the leadership proceeded, and the Volunteers began to regroup and reorganize across the North as prisoners were released from internment. Nationally, the GAA was theoretically non-aligned to any political party or movement but in practice its membership substantially overlapped with the Irish Volunteers[12] and by the middle of 1917 Belfast Volunteers had effectively regrouped around the notional membership of GAA clubs and, oddly, pipe bands. For example, John Mitchell GLC was de facto B Company of the 1st Battalion, Belfast Brigade, while the Clann

8 Tim Pat Coogan, *The IRA* (London, 2000), p. 721. **9** Eamon Phoenix, *Northern nationalism: nationalist politics, partition and the Catholic minority in Northern Ireland, 1890–1940* (Belfast, 1994), p. 195. Tim Pat Coogan, *Ireland in the twentieth century* (London, 2009), p. 126. **10** Tom Hartley, *Milltown Cemetery* (Belfast, 2014), p. 153. **11** Jim McDermott, *Northern divisions, the old IRA and the Belfast pogroms, 1920–22* (Belfast, 2001), p. 11. **12** Gearóid Ó Tuathaigh, *The GAA and the Revolution in Ireland, 1913–1923* (Cork, 2015), p. 130.

Uladh Pipe Band was D Company. In fact, the GAA was an integral part of the republican network in Belfast and club rooms frequently doubled as meeting rooms.[13]

In parallel with the rebuilding of the Volunteer movement, the number of loyalist paramilitary groups were increased, to seize what Carson called the 'irreducible minimum' of the six counties. These groups included the Ulster Volunteer Force, the Ulster Ex-servicemen's Association, the Imperial Guards, Crawford's Tigers and the Cromwell clubs, which were frequently centred in RUC/RIC barracks. The RIC official estimates suggest that UVF membership in Belfast alone stood at six battalions comprising 10,000 men. The UVF in particular were considered to be a significant military force with many of its members having served in the British army. Irish Department of Defence reports assessed the strength of the Belfast IRA as under 600 men and women.[14] Against this backdrop what passed for normal life continued and Dan, a skilled joiner by trade, apparently found work relatively easy to come by, unlike most of his community who were not welcomed in the major employment centres of Harland and Wolff Shipyard, Mackie's Foundry or the Short Brothers engineering factories. Although the city remained bitterly divided there was from time to time a temporary increase in the need for workers, and Catholics would be employed to meet this short-term demand, most famously during the building of the *Titanic*.

In this environment Dan married Susan in St Peter's Pro-cathedral on the Falls Road in 1918 and moved to 71 Albert Street in West Belfast, where he was assigned to the 1st Battalion of the IRA's Belfast Brigade. On 11 July 1921 an RIC raiding party entered Raglan Street, yards away from Dan's home. IRA lookouts reported that the raiding party had 'blackened faces', which was seen as an indication that they were intent on reprisal shootings rather than a standard raid. The raiding party was attacked by the IRA who killed one RIC officer and wounded two others including a B Special. The following day loyalist mobs led by RIC and B Specials launched a series of attacks[15] against Catholic areas that became known as Belfast's Bloody Sunday. In the fierce street fighting that followed 16 people were killed, 11 of them Catholics, while 160 Catholic houses were razed to the ground. By this stage Belfast had descended into open intercommunal war. Between July 1920 and July 1922 the estimated death toll for Belfast was 453: 257 Catholics, 157 Protestants, 2 of unknown religion and 37 members of the security forces. Between nine and eleven thousand Catholics lost jobs, tens of thousands were forced to flee their

13 McDermott, *Northern divisions*, p. 7. **14** Ibid., p. 15. **15** McDermott, *Northern divisions*, p. 95.

homes and 500 Catholic businesses were destroyed. This was on a scale unmatched elsewhere on the island.

On 22 June 1922, Dan was travelling across Belfast by taxi on IRA business when he was stopped by a military patrol. He was immediately arrested and taken to Roden Street Barracks for interrogation. From there he was taken to Crumlin Road Gaol for processing. This process involved an RIC inspector making a recommendation to Dawson Bates, the Minster for Home Affairs in the Stormont administration, that a named individual should be interned. The recommendation drew on local intelligence and in Dan's case the report was drawn up by a Sergeant McQuaid of Roden Street Barracks and concludes:

> Daniel McCann is an active member of the IRA and from observation of him, he is strongly suspected of being engaged in organising work. His associates are all regarded as being dangerous men. Nothing is known against him as far as the ordinary law is concerned.[16]

The subsequent recommendation for his internment records his IRA rank as an artificer and notes 'this man has been plying his trade as a joiner for making secret receptacles for the concealment of arms'. The actual internment order was signed by Dawson Bates and Dan was taken from the jail to the prison ship, the HMS *Argenta,* which had been moored in Belfast Lough, to be interned until further order. There, along with hundreds of his comrades, he was held in appalling conditions. Prisoners were locked in cages below the deck where there was neither natural light nor fresh air. Two exhaust fans pulled air down from the decks and pumped it around the dimly lit hold. Two banks of four cages had been placed on each side of the boat, separated by a narrow two-foot passage, which was patrolled by guards drawn from the A Specials.

Sanitary conditions on the ship were terrible and prisoners became seriously ill on a regular basis. Klenrichert has characterized it as a floating gulag. Medical support was virtually non-existent, and in particular the internees complained about one medical officer, Dr Robin Hall, who, it was reported, seemed to take pleasure prescribing the same dosage of castor oil regardless of the condition of the prisoner.[17] Eventually the prisoners refused to go to the medical officers and conditions continued to deteriorate, culminating in an outbreak of tuberculosis. The authorities' response was not to provide treatment for the prisoners but rather, as individuals became critical, they would be hospitalized in Larne workhouse or, on occasion, released. A number

16 Papers obtained from Public Records Office Northern Ireland. **17** Denise Klenrichert, *Republican internment and the prison ship* Argent,a *1922* (Dublin, 2001), p. 111.

of prisoners were carried off the *Argenta* on stretchers, at least one of whom died shortly after being removed from the ship.

Keeping warm was also a problem. Prisoners were supposed to be issued with a standard set of clothing but frequently this did not happen and many were dependent on what their families could provide. Some individual internees had only the clothes they were wearing when arrested. In Dan's case his wife Susan sent a suitcase of clothes to the ship, which records show was delivered but which Dan never received. After his release Dan sought recompense from the Minister for Home Affairs for this loss and we know from the documents released by the Public Records Office that Dan engaged in a lengthy correspondence with the Ministry of Home Affairs over a period of years, seeking compensation for the loss of 'the case and its contents which were valued at six pounds, eighteen shillings and nine pence'. Dan seemed to take pleasure in challenging what he viewed as a particularly petty harassment and three years later rejected an offer of 'one pound and 10 shillings as compensation for the brown suit and shoes neither of which were new at the time of their loss'. The correspondence gives us an insight into Dan's personality and his refusal to accept the new dispensation.

As tensions on the ship reached breaking point a mass hunger strike was declared on 25 October 1923, the anniversary of the death of Terence MacSwiney and in parallel with the hunger strikers in Mountjoy Prison in Dublin. On the *Argenta,* 130 hunger strikers were drawn equally from pro- and anti-Treaty prisoners. Most of the IRA prisoners held on the *Argenta* supported the Treaty, reflecting the high regard that the Volunteers had for the leadership of Michael Collins. Dan was one of the anti-Treaty volunteers to take part in the hunger strike. Reaction from the Stormont regime was swift and brutal. Two days after the strike commenced Dan and his comrades were dragged from their beds, manacled in pairs, and dragged to the deck where they were made to stand in the freezing rain for hours before being beaten and forced to run between rows of A and B Specials towards a tender that would take them to shore. Prisoners complained of 'running the gauntlet' and of being 'kicked liked footballs'. Once ashore the internees were transferred to Crumlin Road Gaol. Many of the strikers were already weak and ill and the health of some individuals became critical very quickly. Dan fell unconscious on 7 November and the prison chaplain and his wife were sent for by the governor of the jail. Dan was taken off the strike and returned to the cages on the *Argenta.* Dan never fully recovered from his experiences on the ship and died a relatively young man in 1934, leaving six orphaned children.[18]

18 Klenrichert, *Republican internment and the prison ship* Argenta, p. 222.

Impact and legacy

It is difficult to assess the impact that Dan had on me or my siblings; on one level the few colourful stories we heard we didn't take seriously. His physical legacy consisted of a notebook signed by each of his fellow internees, which had been smuggled from the prison ship, the tricolor used at the burial of Joe McKelvey – both of which were taken from the house by a British army raiding party in 1972 – and an incongruously large wardrobe big enough to be a favourite hiding place during games of hide-and-seek. The wardrobe, we were frequently told, was made by Dan without the use of nails, a tribute perhaps to his skill as an artificer. Apart from that we learnt that Michael Collins was actually a republican hero while de Valera was not, an especially northern nuance reflecting the ongoing support Collins provided to Belfast Volunteers after the truce. The *Sunday Press* could be read while the *Sunday Independent* could not. Apart from that there was the occasional story my mother would tell us – for example, that when Dan confessed to shooting a B Special his priest advised him that there was no need to confess venial sins, which we dismissed as an urban myth.

But it seems there may be some truth attached to this tale. It is a fact that Father Charlie O'Neill did indeed write 'The Foggy Dew' after listening to the roll call of the first Dáil. He was the curate in St Peter's parish on the Falls Road were Dan was married. He actively supported Belfast republicans and we know he provided one IRA officer, Jim McDermott, with a suit of his clothes so that he could escape Belfast dressed as a priest.[19]

In general, Dan was in many ways a remote character and we did not have much to relate to him. When he died my mother, the youngest of the McCann children, was seven years old and her memories of Dan were scant. We learnt that our grandfather was an IRA man who had played an active part in the War of Independence. We knew that he had been interned on a prison ship and that he had been a hunger striker. Rather bizarrely we knew the story of his missing suitcase of clothes but very little about his actual IRA activity. Of his personality we had a sense that he was a stubborn individual regularly refusing to address RUC men in English, which usually resulted in him being arrested. My mother would tell stories of a man who read voraciously and encouraged his children to read but who also drank too much and was quite bitter. We knew that his wife had died in childbirth and that he struggled to keep the family together, and that because of his republican background work was scarce and money scarcer. I suspect that today he would be seen as suffering from post-

19 McDermott, *Northern divisions*, p. 13.

traumatic stress disorder but in the 1920s there was little solace to be had for defeated revolutionaries. In truth Dan resonated deeply with all of us not because of the vague stories we had heard but because of what was unfolding in the streets in front of us.

I was born and lived in 71 Albert Street and grew up in the same house as Dan and played in the same streets that he had lived and fought in. It was as if time stood still in Belfast and RUC officers and members of the B Specials could be seen through my bedroom window. Even then it seemed there was a direct line of sight between the little I knew of Dan's fight and what was happening on the street outside my bedroom window. In that sense, his life provided a lens through which the unfolding events after 1969 could be viewed if not fully understood. Dan's real legacy and that of his comrades was the fact that many in the nationalist community seemed to have an appreciation that these events were predestined to happen and as appalling as they were, it could not be a surprise. Nor was it a surprise a year later to see the black-and-white image of my mother on the front of the *Irish News* as, along with a group of other working-class women, she pushed past ranks of British soldiers to bring food to the people of Albert Street who had been under military curfew for four days. While the BBC reported the events unfolding on the streets as being solely about religious/sectarian differences, we knew that ultimately the real question was political. Connolly had not 'won through' and Ulster had not been dealt with. By 1972, fifty years after the *Argenta* sat in Belfast Lough, once again a prison ship, the *Maidstone*, was moored in Belfast harbour as an internment camp for Belfast republicans and Dan's ghost seemed to stalk the narrow terraced streets of west Belfast.

For northern nationalists and republicans the events of 1916 to 1922 did not just reverberate; they repeated themselves with awful and terrible consequences, while for most people living in the Republic, the Easter Rising and the War of Independence were simply events from recent history. I believe that when all is said and done the message of Dan's life and the impact his life had on me is a deep sense that it is all too easy for ordinary people to find themselves responding in an extraordinary way to extraordinary circumstances.

Peadar O'Donnell: a rebellious relative

TOM BOYLAN

I have very clear memories, from a very young age, of overhearing my late mother, whose maiden name was Mai O'Donnell, recounting memories of visits to her home in Derry city from 'her relative from Donegal'. He was a frequent visitor and she always spoke of him with deep affection describing him as 'wild, mischievous and great fun who always managed to turn the house upside down.' The visitor, I was to learn later, was Peadar O'Donnell. So from an early age I became acquainted, in a manner of speaking, with this relative of my mother's through her very funny anecdotes of his escapades. This was a benign introduction to one who was to emerge as one of the leading radicals and combative activists in twentieth-century Ireland. The period from 1913 to 1923, which corresponds roughly to the period of interest of this volume, represents just one episodic decade in a career that extended over the course of seventy years and included his time as teacher, trade union organizer and military commander during the War of Independence/Civil War, radical political agitator, writer and social critic.[1]

Peadar O'Donnell was born in the townland of Meenmore, near Dungloe, in February 1893, where his parents, James Sheáin Mór and Brigid O'Donnell, and their nine surviving children of six boys and three girls (four other children died in infancy) lived on a five-acre holding, the source of their food supply of potatoes and oats, which was complemented by access to the turf on the surrounding bogs and fishing in Dungloe Bay. As one biographer succinctly and prosaically put it, O'Donnell's parents 'supported themselves and their nine children … in the standard manner of their class in the area at this time.'[2] Integral to the 'standard manner for their class' was the endemic emigration from rural Ireland. In the case of west Donegal the unique feature of migration was the annual exodus of the male population along with single women to pick potatoes in Scotland, the famous 'tatie hoking' activity, for several months of

I would like to dedicate this chapter to my sisters Colette, Ethna and Stephanie and my granddaughters Aifric and Lara, both of who were born during the writing of this piece in 2016. They represent the next generation of relatives of Peadar O'Donnell. 1 O'Donnell himself produced these autobiographical works covering different episodes of his life and career: *The gates flew open* (London, 1932); *Salud! An Irishman in Spain* (London, 1937); *There will be another day* (Dublin, 1963). In addition there are four biographical works on Peadar O'Donnell: Grattan Freyer, *Peadar O'Donnell* (Lewisburg, 1973); Michael McInerney, *Peadar O'Donnell: Irish social rebel* (Dublin, 1974); Peter Hegarty, *Peadar O'Donnell* (Cork, 1999); and Donal Ó Drisceoil, *Peadar O'Donnell* (Cork, 2001). 2 Ó Drisceoil, *Peadar O'Donnell*, p. 4

the year.[3] Peadar's father took part in this annual migration, while his mother undertook piece-work at exploitative wages as a knitter in the local clothing industry. Running parallel to this 'tatie hoking' activity in Scotland were the notorious 'hiring fairs', where young men were hired by the larger farmers in eastern Donegal. None of this was lost on the young Peadar and the plight of the 'tatie hokers' and the struggle for their rights became an abiding target of his later political activities.

The communal approach, or 'gatherings', which characterized the environment of his youth inculcated and nurtured a spirit of community solidarity and good neighbourliness. O'Donnell came to enshrine this communal model of interaction over that of the individualistic, a theme that became a pervasive motif in his later political and literary works. He also arguably found within this framework of communal effort and community support for the embryonic model of a future socialist society, or more specifically his socialist republicanism, which was the informing animus of his later political philosophy. In addition to the impact and formative influences of his social class and the social values he absorbed, there was a third and very potent influence, namely his mother Brigid. Peadar was lucky in his parents. His father was a quiet, retiring man of gentle disposition, and in every sense 'a good man'. He was also an extremely talented musician. Their house, a two-roomed thatched cottage, was a centre of activity – of music provided by Peadar's father along with reading and learning centred on Brigid. Locally their home was known as a 'reading house', where neighbours, many of whom were illiterate, came to have their letters read and written for them. Brigid was a formidable woman, who placed great value on education. Their house was, in Peadar's recollections, well stocked with books, which included an extensive array of the established classics, all enthusiastically read and re-read by the young Peadar. In conversation he would describe his mother, with justification, as 'an advanced thinker'.[4] This accolade would apply not only to her progressive disposition to education in general, but would apply with particular force to her politics. Brigid was a highly politicized woman who espoused the position of Jim Larkin, founder of the Irish Transport and General Workers' Union (ITGWU). Brigid was in Peadar's words not only a 'fervent Larkinite' but an 'evangelist' for his cause.[5] This was complemented by Brigid's sister, Madge, a teacher by profession and a union activist within the Irish National Teachers' Organization (INTO), who also enthusiastically supported Larkin. Their brother Peter, who returned to Donegal in 1913, contributed an additional

3 Anne O'Dowd, *Spalpeens and tattie hokers: history and folklore of the Irish migratory agricultural worker in Ireland and Britain* (Dublin, 1990). 4 Ó Drisceoil, *Peadar O'Donnell*, p. 5. 5 Ibid., p. 8.

element to Peadar's education in the politics of trade union activism. Peter had been an active member of the syndicalist Industrial Workers of the World, or 'Wobblies' as they were termed, during his time in America, and imbued Peadar not only with his valuable insights into the values and working of the syndicalist movement, but also greatly influenced his 'awareness of the class struggle'.[6]

The invaluable insights from the harsh reality of his social environment ('tatie hoking' in Scotland/hiring fairs); the richness of the lessons of solidarity, mutual and reciprocal support through communal and group effort rather than the valorization of individualism; and the incipient political resistance and independence of thought inculcated by the formidable women in his early life and complemented by his uncle Peter, all contrived to etch an indelible political mark on O'Donnell. These formative influences shaped his social and class consciousness, and provided him with a deep and abiding commitment to the primacy of community over individualism and an unflinching commitment to the role and status of women in any envisaged future of Irish society. These commitments, among others, represent the abiding and durable themes that pulsate through his political, social and literary writings and activity for the remainder of his long and celebrated life.

O'Donnell had started school at the age of three, attending Rampart national school, and remained until the age of fourteen. He was an outstanding pupil and from an early age displayed a rebellious streak that on more than one occasion invoked the wrath of his teachers, including on one occasion a severe censoring of an essay on the local St Patrick's Day parade in which the young O'Donnell lamented the absence of a banner objecting to British rule in Ireland. Many years later he reflected with characteristic frankness that 'I wouldn't say I was better than many others. Fellows like Paddy John Jack and Eddie James Charlie were much brighter, but I was lucky'.[7]

In 1907, at the age of fourteen he was appointed a monitor at Roshine national school near Burtonport, and in September 1911 O'Donnell began his two-year teacher training course at St Patrick's Training College in Drumcondra. The training college was not much to his liking. The trainee teachers were subject to a strict disciplinary code, which included restrictive curfews; the library he described as 'a dump'; and in general the intellectual stimulation on offer was decidedly underwhelming to O'Donnell. Notwithstanding his disposition to the college, his academic ability was clearly evident. His results for both years were in the first division, and many years later one professor in the college spoke of O'Donnell as being among the three best students he had known during his tenure there.

6 Hegarty, *Peadar O'Donnell*, p. 30. **7** Joe McGarrigle, *Donegal profiles* (Ballyshannon, 1986), p. 185.

On graduation from St Patrick's College in 1913, O'Donnell returned to the Rosses to take up his first teaching appointment on Innisfree Island. From the outset as a teacher O'Donnell would display that spirit of recalcitrance, impatience and active hostility to authorities against who he felt it was necessary to act. This is well illustrated by an incident that occurred following his appointment as head of the two-teacher school in Derryheny on the mainland about nine miles from Dungloe, following his period on Innisfree Island. The Derryheny schoolhouse was, in O'Donnell's estimation, 'a hovel' and the barbed sarcasm of his annual returns to the Department of Education conveyed O'Donnell's annoyance and impatience with the authorities ('How often was the school floor washed during the year?' Answer: 'Every time it rained heavily'; 'Is there a school museum?' Answer: 'No, but the school should be in a museum').[8] Running out of patience with this charade, in early 1916 O'Donnell organized a group of friends and proceeded to demolish the 'hovel' that was the Derryheny national school, thereby forcing the authorities to fund the building of a new school. O'Donnell the activist in all things had emerged in no uncertain terms. Many years later during a conversation in Galway in 1984 I asked him if this episode of the school at Derryheny resonated with the momentous events that occurred in the same year with the destruction of the GPO and the centre of Dublin during the Rising, he quickly and mischievously retorted, 'I got there first'.

Before leaving Derryheny, his recorded last entry in the school day-book read: 'This ends the first chapter of my life. I wonder when Autumn comes will it bring those lovely things that Spring has promised'.[9] This comment was indeed prophetic in that while O'Donnell would remain a further two years in the teaching profession as headmaster of one of the two national schools on Arranmore island, it was also here that a number of developments occurred that heralded new directions for him and it was at this time that he abandoned any prospect of teaching as a life-long career. He developed an interest in writing and allocated a dedicated period of time each day to this pursuit. But it was also in Arranmore that O'Donnell entered what he might have called 'the second chapter' of his life, that of trade union activist, an activity which led him out of teaching in the summer of 1918 to become a full-time union official.

This was a period that witnessed a major resurgence in union activity in general along with the emergence of an increasing militancy motivated by the desire for separation from Great Britain, under the political rubric of Sinn

8 Hegarty, *Peadar O'Donnell*, pp 29–33. **9** Anton McCabe, '"The stormy petrel of the transport workers": Peadar O'Donnell, trade unionist, 1917–1920', *Saothar*, 19 (1994), p. 41.

Féin. O'Donnell was elected the secretary for the Donegal branch of the Irish National Teachers Organization (INTO) and quickly made his mark as an outspoken, effective and militant spokesman for the union. In an address to a meeting of teachers in Letterkenny in February 1918, he unveiled his emerging revolutionary mind-set when he exhorted his fellow teachers to 'convert our schools into hotbeds, where working men's interests are fostered. Let us fling ourselves among the most fervent of social and economic revolutionists'.[10] His ability, commitment and effectiveness within the INTO was not lost on the wider labour movement, including the Irish Transport and General Workers Union (ITGWU), and in the summer of 1918 he left teaching to become a full-time union official.

O'Donnell moved to Liberty Hall in September 1918, then the headquarters of the ITGWU. He was given a difficult and challenging assignment, namely to organize the ITGWU in Ulster, apart from Belfast and the counties Antrim and Down. The ITGWU had a very weak and poorly developed presence in the province, contributed to by the suspicion of Protestant workers that a close relationship existed between the ITGWU and Sinn Féin. Arising from the poor presence of the ITGWU both Protestants and Catholics belonged predominantly to British-based unions that dominated the unionized labour force in the province. O'Donnell's activities in Ulster constitute an involved, complex and extensive programme of activity on his part, in which he displayed an extraordinary capacity for confrontation and militancy on behalf of the workers within his area of responsibility. One celebrated episode, led by O'Donnell, involved the occupation of the lunatic asylum in Monaghan. This arose from a dispute between the staff and management. When negotiations broke down on O'Donnell's demand for equal pay increases for women workers, the nurses and attendants went on strike on 23 January 1919. Fearing retaliation by police and military with a view to breaking the strike, O'Donnell devised a daring and innovative tactic. On 28 January he led the workforce and occupied the entire asylum, which was now run by O'Donnell as 'governor' and a newly appointed management committee. The red flag was hoisted over the asylum and this conveyed a highly charged political resonance in the circumstances of 1918–19. Negotiations ensued and by 3 February the occupation and strike ended in a resounding victory for the workers, with a new fifty-six hour working week and equal pay rises for men and women agreed. It was a personal triumph for O'Donnell and for his union, the latter being much more important to him. However, he also was to suffer bitter defeat later in 1919 in the Caledon Mill strike in Co. Tyrone.

10 Ibid., p. 42.

During his time as trade union organizer, O'Donnell displayed two salient attributes that, in retrospect, characterized his whole career. The first was an uneasy relationship with authority, which led him to frequently act without any authorization from his union as in the case of the Monaghan asylum. Allied to this was his increasing disdain for the conservatism of both the trade union leadership in many cases and the Labour movement in general.[11]

In January 1919, on the day that the first Dáil convened in Dublin following the general election in late 1918, an attack on a police convoy at Soloheadbeg in Co. Tipperary in which two RIC men were shot dead is generally taken as the incident that marked the beginning of the War of Independence. It was at this time that O'Donnell formally joined the IRA. In late 1920, O'Donnell set up a 'flying colum' to operate in Donegal and his active involvement in the War of Independence began. His 'flying column' quickly engaged the British forces, derailing a troop train, blocking railway tracks and attacking the RIC barracks at Falcarragh. The reprisals were swift. British troops descended on Donegal town and proceeded to wreck it, burned a local creamery, and killed a civilian in Malinbeg. This would become the standard pattern of the war. Meanwhile, the IRA regrouped their four brigades in Donegal into the First Ulster Division. O'Donnell was appointed Officer Commanding of the Second Brigade, with responsibility for East Donegal, the Inishowen peninsula and Derry city. What follows is a complex and strained set of relations between O'Donnell and other commanders, which arose from O'Donnell undertaking activities without consultations. Soon his superior officers tired of O'Donnell's refusal to take orders, something of a life-long characteristic. He was suspended from his command of the Second Brigade while his insubordination was investigated. Notwithstanding a negative assessment of his behaviour, Michael Collins retained O'Donnell as Brigade Commander.[12]

But O'Donnell was fighting on two fronts, the military and the political, and of the two the political was paramount for him. His political aim was to make government inoperable and that included not only the British government structures, it also extended to the emerging Irish government that was now replacing the British administrative structures and processes. Sinn Féin increasingly extended its influence and grip on the administrative machinery of the state. Land courts, labour courts and courts of justice were established

11 For extended studies of the general circumstances of labour and politics at this time, see C. Desmond Greaves, *The Irish Transport and General Workers Union: the formative years, 1909–1923* (Dublin, 1982) and Emmet O'Connor, *Syndicalism in Ireland, 1917–1923* (Cork, 1988) and *A labour history of Ireland, 1824–2000* (Dublin, 2011) by the same author. **12** Ó Drisceoil, *Peadar O'Donnell*, p. 19.

during 1919 and 1920. O'Donnell quickly detected and opposed what he considered the deep conservatism within Sinn Féin as revealed in the activities of its courts, particularly in the way they dealt with smallholders and landless labourers who had been involved in land seizures and cattle drives. These newly established courts in general sided with the landlords and the IRA was used as a police force to enforce the decisions. O'Donnell was opposed to these developments and within his brigade area jurisdiction of north-east Donegal he forbade the use of the IRA men in his brigade to be deployed in this activity, which resulted in the inability of the Dáil courts to function in this area.

By mid-1921 the conflict was not going well for the IRA in general and Donegal was no exception. Problems of imprisonment, arrests, deaths and chronic shortage of ammunition were inflicting a heavy toll on the activities of the IRA. The issue of ammunition shortages was significant, something that was confirmed for me on overhearing my father, who served in the North Mayo Brigade of the IRA and later in the Civil War fought on the side of the Free State, replying to an American visitor to our home in Dublin who asked 'why did the delegates and in particular Michael Collins sign the Treaty in 1921?' My father's reply, to which I was acutely alert, was 'whatever of the politics, in our brigade we didn't have five rounds between us to continue the fight. Collins knew this very well. I cannot speak for the others.' It was a telling insight into the reality of the situation on the ground. Parenthetically, I might add that my father, like many of his generation, maintained a resolute and absolute silence on anything to do with his activities or experiences in the War of Independence and Civil War. Months before he died in 1971 (he was at this stage very ill with cancer) I broached the subject one last time with respect to his activities in 1920–3, but my question was quietly despatched with the reply 'we did what we had to do then, why don't you do what you have to do now'. Reflecting on his reply to me all those years ago, it came across not as a rebuke, but as a quiet admonition to leave certain aspects of the past alone while at the same time resonating as an inter-generational wish on his part perhaps that in a new and different set of circumstances we would see our way to enhance what had been bequeathed to us.

Meanwhile back in Donegal in 1921 and against the background of the difficulties being experienced by the IRA, O'Donnell was forced to disband his 'flying column'. A truce was called on 11 July 1921 and the Treaty signed on 6 December 1921. The terms of the Treaty divided Sinn Féin, the Dáil and the IRA. While nine of the thirteen members of the General Headquarters staff supported the Treaty, the majority of the field commanders, O'Donnell among them, rejected the terms of the Treaty out of hand, while up to three-quarters of the rank-and-file opposed the Treaty. The scene was set for the resulting bitter and divisive Civil War. Not that this outcome would have hugely surprised O'Donnell. He had a low opinion of Arthur Griffith as the elder statesman in the Treaty negotiations, whom he viewed as an advocate and defender of the bourgeois propertied class, while Collins in his estimation 'had emerged from the Tan struggle with the outlook of a "Fenian Home Ruler" and the code of a tinker swapping donkeys at a fair; he was suspicious of what he was getting but contented himself that what he was giving was not an honest beast'.[13]

In March 1922 control of the IRA, or that part of it opposed to the Treaty, passed to a newly established executive of sixteen members, which included O'Donnell, who was appointed commander of the newly established First Northern Division. The following month the Four Courts in Dublin was occupied by the IRA where they established their headquarters. O'Donnell returned to Donegal to pursue his military responsibilities but relocated to the Four Courts in June 1922 to participate more fully in the executive. O'Donnell was not impressed with the quality of the IRA leadership at this time, which he later described as 'rather pathetic; bankrupt of ideas; uninspired, confused and feckless'.[14] This assessment was motivated by their inability, in O'Donnell's view, to provide an alternative programme that went beyond mere opposition to the Treaty. In his view, neither the IRA executive or the political opposition led by de Valera articulated 'what play of social forces constituted the Treaty in terms that made sense to the republican mass'. They were he argued 'the stuff that martyrs are made of, but not revolutionaries'.[15]

On the ground events moved rapidly. With the assassination in London of Unionist MP Sir Henry Wilson in June 1922, the British government insisted on action by the Free State government in Dublin, in the absence of which they threatened an assault by the British army. This was quickly followed by the kidnapping of the Deputy Chief-of-Staff of the pro-Treaty army by the IRA in response to the arrest of a senior IRA commander. This triggered the attack by the Free State government on the Four Courts by an artillery bombardment by eighteen-pounder guns supplied by the British authorities on 28 June 1922. Two days later, with the building in flames, the garrison surrendered, which included the executive and O'Donnell among them. For the next twenty-one months O'Donnell would spend his time in a number of jails and internment camps, including Mountjoy, the Curragh and Finner Camp in Donegal, from which he escaped wearing the uniform of a Free State officer on 16 March 1924. During his term in prison he was elected TD for Sinn Féin in the general election of 1923 when he topped the poll in Donegal and later in the same year

13 O'Donnell, *The gates flew open*, p. 17. **14** Ó Drisceoil, *Peadar O'Donnell*, p. 25. **15** Tom Boylan, Notes from Private Conversation, Galway, 1984.

he participated in a hunger strike in Mountjoy, which led to the death of two of the hunger strikers, and for him lasted for forty-one days. Thus ended what he may have called 'the third chapter' of his life, coinciding with the so-called 'decade of revolution'.

Emerging from that period, I would like to note briefly two events that greatly affected O'Donnell in rather different ways. One was the execution of Liam Mellows on 8 December 1922 along with three other prominent republicans. O'Donnell's execution was widely expected to follow shortly afterwards. Mellows and O'Donnell were very close personal friends and ideological soulmates. He was devastated by the loss of Mellows whom he described as 'the richest mind our race had achieved for many a long day had been spilled', adding that 'the future now seemed to stretch in a grey dull waste to the edge of the years that had been so alive'.[16] It was Mellows, in fact, who was instrumental in launching O'Donnell's writing career in Mountjoy when he began a prison magazine, facetiously called *The Book of Cells,* which served as an outlet for the republican prisoners to parody members of the government and prominent Free Staters.

The second event was an altogether happier one. During his imprisonment O'Donnell was in charge of the communication lines between the republican prisoners and the outside contacts in the IRA. The person on the outside in charge of conveying these communications was Lile O'Donel, an activist in Cumann na mBan and member of the Communist Party of Ireland, whose father, Ignatius O'Donel, was a substantial landowner in Mayo. When he escaped in March 1924 he finally met Lile and they married in June of that year. This was to be a singularly happy marriage, which lasted until she died in 1969, leaving him with an abiding sense of profound loss. They had no children of their own, but they raised a nephew of Peadar's, the son of his brother Joe who died in a car accident in New York in 1939. In 1924, O'Donnell was a young man of thirty-one and over the next sixty-two years he would write an intriguing series of 'chapters' of his life, which can only be briefly addressed here. O'Donnell's aim was to establish a thirty-two county socialist republic. During the 1920s he exerted considerable influence on the IRA, through his editorship of *An Phoblacht* (1926–9) where he attempted to redirect the IRA from their predominantly militarist preoccupations and to adopt a socialist republican philosophy.[17] In the 1920s and early 1930s his activities were increasingly directed to the campaign of the non-payment of the land annuities, which he initiated, and through his political acumen he later

16 MacEoin, *Survivors*, p. 41. **17** For an excellent study of this topic see Adrian Grant, *Irish socialist republicanism, 1909–1936* (Dublin, 2012).

managed to foist on the Fianna Fáil Party who reluctantly adopted it. It contributed hugely to their electoral success in 1932, and was later the cause of the Economic War during the 1930s.

If the land annuities represented something of a victory for O'Donnell, he was less successful in radicalizing the IRA and following the failure of Saor Éire, a left-wing political organization, tensions between the left-wing of the IRA and its conservative leadership led O'Donnell, along with his close colleagues on the left, George Gilmore and Frank Ryan, to split from the IRA and to pursue a socialist republican political programme. This lead to the establishment of the Republican Congress in 1934, an ill-fated and short-lived endeavour that sought to unify the more radical groups into a Marxist-inspired common front. On the ground O'Donnell in the twenty-six counties and Gilmore in Belfast attempted to mobilize the shared grievances of the small farmers of rural Ireland and the industrial workers of the urban centres. Under the pressure of internal divisions and external hostility from various sources, the Republican Congress collapsed. This was another major defeat for O'Donnell, both personally and politically, and a source of deep frustration for him.

Following the failure of the Congress, O'Donnell, who was in Spain when the Spanish Civil War broke out, was quickly involved in support of the Spanish Republic. He recounted to me in some detail his organization of a gun-running operation through Belgium and France into Spain with the help of a number of writers of his acquaintance in both countries, a group not known perhaps for their prowess in gun-running! This endeavour also ended in failure with the victory of Franco's fascist regime. He was at this time no stranger to frustration, or to physical attacks at political meetings and wholesale condemnation by the Catholic clergy from pulpits the length and breadth of the country. He was banned from entering the United States for several decades (perhaps the ultimate compliment in his view!) and at a more local level was also forbidden entry to University College Dublin.

The year 1940 represented something of a watershed for O'Donnell. The intense activism of the previous two decades delivered little by way of achievement for his political programme of revolutionary change. Irish politics was firmly embedded in the deep conservatism of Fianna Fáil which now included Irish republicanism and the majority of the Irish working class, while the IRA was marginalized to an apolitical and emasculated militarist remnant, and his hopes for an emergent socialist republic were dashed with the collapse of the Republican Congress. Now in his late 40s, but with unimpaired energy, he sought new outlets for his endeavours. At this time another 'chapter' began; that of writer, editor and journalist. His writing career had began, as noted, while in jail. His first novel, *Storm* (1925), was set in the War of Independence. Three years later *Islanders* (1928), one of his most highly regarded books dealing with poverty in rural Ireland, was published, while the most significant of his later novels was *The big windows* (1955). In addition he produced a trilogy of autobiographical work, *The gates flew open* (1932), which covered the Irish Civil War, *Salud! An Irishman in Spain* (1937), in which he described his involvement in the Spanish Civil War, and *There will be another day* (1963), which documented his role in the land annuities campaign. O'Donnell himself always claimed that his writing was always secondary to his political activity, noting that 'my pen was a weapon and I used it as such'.[18] W.B. Yeats, who held O'Donnell in high regard, inverted this claim when he stated that 'he wished Mr O'Donnell would devote his interest entirely to his novels and leave politics for a past-time in old age'.[19] Not perhaps one of Yeats most perceptive insights!

In addition to his own writings, O'Donnell's other major contribution to literary endeavour in Ireland was his establishment of *The Bell*, an innovative literary and political magazine that provided a pivotal role in facilitating a whole generation of Irish writers to publish their work in what was an oppressive, insular and conservative period. Having launched *The Bell*, O'Donnell prevailed on Sean Ó Faoláin to be its first editor, which he was from 1940 to 1946 and was followed by O'Donnell himself as editor from 1946 until 1954 when the magazine was wound up.

O'Donnell continued relentlessly to support every serious radical campaign until his death in 1986 at the age of ninety-three. These included, among others, his life-long campaign on behalf of Irish emigrants. In his 90th year and travelling *incognito*, he undertook a tour of Salvation Army Hostels in England to learn for himself the conditions of the residents, particularly those of the Irish emigrants. On that occasion he told me that he was mugged twice and robbed on a number of occasions. The episode is striking testimony to his enduring commitment and abiding interest in the plight of the marginalized Irish emigrants in Britain, not to mention his personal courage. He was also prominent in the Irish Campaign for Nuclear Disarmament and served as its president for a number of years, and was active in the anti-Vietnam war protests and the anti-apartheid movement. During his first stay in our home in Galway City he presided over a meeting of the Irish–Cambodia Committee in our front-room, a group I must confess I was blissfully unaware of at the time!

I will forever be grateful to the authorities of UCG/NUIG in deciding to

18 'Peadar O'Donnell talks to the Monday Circle', http://politico.ie/archive/peadar-odonnell-talks-monday-circle, accessed 14 February 2017. **19** Cited in Ó Drisceoil, *Peadar O'Donnell*, p. 73.

confer an honorary doctorate on President Ronald Reagan, since they were instrumental in facilitating my meeting with Peadar O'Donnell and hosting him as a guest in our home in 1984. He was then ninety-one years old. The reason for his presence arose from the decision of the Committee of Concerned Academics at UCG, an *ad hoc* group under the chairmanship of Dr Richard Gault of the then Department of Industrial Engineering and including a wonderful group of colleagues, including Professor Pat Sheeran (Department of English) and Dr Tony Christofides (Department of Mathematics), now both sadly deceased. The Committee organized an 'anti-conferring' and three honourable gentlemen, Dr John De Courcy Ireland, a distinguished naval historian, and Dr Austin Burke, former Director of the Irish Meteorological Service, and Dr Aodagán O'Rahilly agreed to hand back their DSc degrees to the NUI as a part of the protest against UCG's conferring of a doctorate on Reagan arising from America's foreign policy activities against a democratically elected government in Nicaragua. Peadar O'Donnell was chosen as a suitable figure to act as the 'Anti-Chancellor' and to receive the handing back of the DSc degrees. A make-shift platform was erected in Grattan Park and Peadar, robed in Professor Tadhg Foley's doctoral gown from Oxford, duly presided with all due solemnity over the occasion on that memorable day in June 1984. His second and more extended stay with us was in January 1985 when Donal Lunny and Moving Hearts presented him with a musical tribute following an extraordinary lecture that he delivered in UCG, published in 1986 as 'Monkeys in the superstructure: reminiscences of Peadar O'Donnell'.

During the course of these two visits in 1984 and 1985 and having the privilege of his presence in our home I availed of the opportunity to converse with him over what looked like extended periods of time, but which now in retrospect seem all too brief and fragmented. Given the vulnerability and fluidity of memory I greatly regret that I was not more assiduous in recording these fascinating conversations. I attempted to raise as many issues as I could and to hear in person his version, opinions and assessment of events. Many of these are now very well documented in the excellent biographies now available of him and cited earlier, along with the extensive academic literature that has addressed his life and work.[20] Here, no more than the briefest reference can be made to a very small number of selected issues which I had the opportunity to raise with him.

I raised the issue of why he chose to destroy his papers, thereby depriving historians of the benefit of their insight. He spoke of his utter insistence that

20 See the excellent 'Guide to further reading' in Ó Drisceoil, *Peadar O'Donnell*, pp 151–4 for some of the best academic work on the different aspects and episodes in O'Donnell's extended career.

for him it was the right thing to do, and one was left with the very clear impression that once he made up his mind it was not easily changed. But perhaps his final word to me on this issue provides the key to his decision, 'I could have started the Civil War all over again if the contents of these papers were made available!' I broached the subject of the relentless condemnation of him by priests and bishops for a great part of his life. A lot of this he regarded as 'humbug'. He provided, he felt, an easy target for them and that their grandiose public condemnations did more to 'enhance their already over-inflated status' than it did personal damage to him. One intriguing story which he related to me concerned his friendship with Dr Con Lucey, bishop of Cork and Ross, whom O'Donnell respected and liked. This arose from their mutual interest in rural poverty and the issues of rural unemployment and emigration. He recounted holidays he spent walking the hills in West Cork with Dr Lucy pursuing their discussions, which he described as 'a most enjoyable experience' but at the time he assured me 'was known to very few people.' If it was known, 'Dr Lucey stood to lose a lot more than I would have had,' but that didn't mean 'that the following week the good bishop would not be most likely roundly condemning me at a confirmation ceremony in Skull or Skibbereen'! But somewhat ironically on his second visit to Galway in 1985 another bishop was involved. On this occasion it was the then bishop of Galway, Dr Eamonn Casey, who contacted me to request a meeting with Peadar, whom he said he had admired for over forty years. Bishop Casey, as Peadar informed me, had done great work for the homeless in London as a young priest and he was very happy to meet him. On his arrival at our house, I ushered him in to meet Peadar, who dispensing with any social niceties greeted the bishop, who was more used to being listened to than spoken to, with: 'Sit down there please. Your heart is in the right place but your thinking is very confused.' What followed was an extraordinary discourse by Peadar on the topic of homelessness in Ireland and as to how the bishop should politicize the issue by establishing a Commission on the Homeless. For the next hour-and-a-half O'Donnell elaborated on how this Commission should go about its business, both tactically and politically. The bishop was, rather unusually, unable to get a word in edgeways, much to my amusement as an observer of this performance, and for a finish the bishop himself realized the futility of adopting any other posture than that of listening.

Peadar O'Donnell died on 13 May 1986 aged ninety-three. The following day he was cremated and his ashes were brought to be placed in the grave of his wife, Lile, on a hillside outside Swinford in Mayo. I attended the funeral by invitation and my travelling companion that day was Michael D. Higgins. The ceremony was simple, sparse and dignified. The chief mourner was his son

Peter (Peadar Joe) who in silence placed the urn in the ground. There were no speeches, no elegies, no ceremonial trappings of any kind and no clergy at O'Donnell's own request. He had never forgiven the Catholic Church for their excommunication of republicans during the Civil War.

Standing at that hillside outside Swinford that day, my mind drifted further west to another graveyard on the edge of the Atlantic on the Mullet Peninsula in Bangor Erris where my parents are buried. My father, to the best of my knowledge, never met Peadar. They both fought to secure the independence of this country during the War of Independence, though their paths diverged in the Civil War. My father fought on the side of the Free State, and was among the first intake into An Garda Síochána, which faced the difficult task of regaining the trust and allegiance of the people following the atrocities of the Civil War. But even if they took different sides following the War of Independence – my father in attempting to contribute to the stabilization of the country, Peader in pursuing his political programme seeking to 'destabilize' and 'reconfigure' the future of Irish society – they nevertheless shared, I believe, a great deal in common in both their background and fundamental values. Both were men of the Atlantic seaboard as they were of the iconic five-acre farms, a harsh environment that bred a resilience and resourcefulness which were prerequisites to survival in these circumstances. But their backgrounds also nurtured and shaped the values of mutual communal support, good neighbourliness and a deep generosity of spirit. They also displayed in their different spheres of activity an abiding commitment of service to others and an intense fidelity to their native place. These values underlay, informed and shaped their behaviour and disposition towards the people they encountered and whom they sought to serve. The final word I leave to Peadar. On his first visit, in 1984, I asked him to sign a copy of one of his books for my son, John, who was then one year old. He wrote:

> To John.
> John two things. Stand alone! Kindness in another's trouble, courage in your own. You will understand later. It is in your breed.
> Peadar O'Donnell, 2/6/1984

This might be as succinct an account of Peadar's own extraordinary life that one could find.

Michael Canavan: an ordinary (heroic) life

JOHN CANAVAN, DOROTHY NÍ UIGÍN
& JIM HIGGINS

Our grandfather, Michael Canavan, from Corrandulla in County Galway, was arrested and imprisoned in 1923 for his part in the activities of anti-Treaty forces during the Civil War, spending time in both Galway Gaol and the Curragh at Tintown B. Like many other young men and women at this time, he was an active participant in the tumultuous events at the beginning of the modern Irish state. Yet, for his children and subsequently his grandchildren, our extended family narrative does not reference this extraordinary experience, either its significance for 'Pop' as a person, or his role in the formation of modern Ireland. He did not talk to his children in any detail about his experiences of this time and did not attend commemorations. He was not in receipt of any pension or other form of recognition for his contribution. Instead, his life was remarkably ordinary, involving work, marriage and parenthood. This chapter aims first to honour Michael's story and in doing so to note the significance of the ordinary and the private in our collective understanding of the Civil War and its consequences, in the context of the many high-profile, public events running from 2016 through the years ahead. The chapter also aims to explore and understand a significant gap in our extended family's narrative inheritance, considering, among other ideas, the heroic in the seemingly ordinary, religious faith and the moral justification of war, and the private versus public.

In the context of an absent overall narrative, our sources for this chapter are threefold. First, we have a small number of individual snippets of information passed on by Michael to family members, and their memories of him. Second, we have three artefacts from his time in prison and third, we have some confirmatory sources in official archives alongside some of the historical accounts of the events of the time. Theoretically, we think that life course theory and the related notion of temporality are useful in framing Michael's story. Thus, we can think of Michael's biography, his own story, his agency and the events, causes and consequences of his early life in particular. Similarly, a focus on historical time is useful; what were the effects of local, national and global history on his life during and subsequent to his involvement in military activities. Finally, thinking in terms of generations allows us to reflect on our own generational link to Michael, and its particular nature. One further quasi-theoretical strand informs the work. Once we began exploring and thinking about Michael's life, his wife Maryanne (Granny) emerged as a key, quite powerful, figure in his life; in its broadest sense, the chapter reflects an imperative to properly include women in history.

We begin the chapter by providing an account of Michael's family background and his involvement in the War of Independence and subsequently in the Civil War, before describing his working and family life in Galway city. Central to this part of Michael's story is the role of his wife Maryanne. In the final part of the chapter we offer some interpretative positions on the absence of a War of Independence and Civil War narrative in his family. As a caveat to this chapter, we note our own struggle in filling the gaps in this part of Michael's life, and that we have only a limited objective knowledge to work with. Thus, beyond the facts of this story is only interpretation; we cannot and do not claim beyond this.

Youth and involvement in War of Independence and Civil War

Michael Canavan was born in 1903 in Bolisheen, Corrandulla, Co. Galway, and was the seventh of the eleven children who survived in the family of Robert and Katherine Canavan. He was born into a farming family, although Michael himself later worked in Cregg Mill near Corrandulla village. Although we have no evidence to suggest that any of his siblings were involved in the War of Independence or Civil War, we know that Michael was involved in the nationalist movement from an early age.[1] Indeed he told one family member that he was secretary of the local branch of Sinn Féin during the tumultuous years between the 1916 Easter Rising and the War of Independence – given his age, such a role would only be feasible for the latter part of this period. In an application for a Service Medal he says:

> I was in the movement since 1918. I was for a period a Court Clerk of the Republican Court of the time.

While we have no reason to doubt his involvement in Sinn Féin or in Óglaigh na hÉireann, we have no corroborating evidence of this, as there does not seem to be any extant records or minutes for the Sinn Féin branch in the area for this period. The only story shared by Michael from the War of Independence period relates to a raid on his workplace, Cregg Mill, and how he and others

1 For a discussion of Na Fianna Éireann and youth during the Revolution, see Marnie Hay, 'An Irish nationalist adolescence: Na Fianna Éireann, 1909–23' in Catherine Cox and Susannah Riordan (eds), *Adolescence in modern Ireland* (London, 2016).

were dragged from the building at gunpoint. Most versions of the story suggest that the raid was carried out by the Black and Tans and in it Michael and a friend were beaten and pushed in the direction of the field opposite the mill – most likely to be summarily executed. However, some witnesses arrived on the scene, interrupting the event, and the Black and Tans boarded their lorry and left.

We have no objective data on Michael's involvement in the Civil War, apart from information on his stay in prison. Records from Galway Gaol show that he was on remand there from 17 March 1923. Why he was arrested, how it related to other activities in the Civil War in Galway, and to subsequent events are something of a mystery. The date of registration in Galway Gaol comes a month after the arrest of a group of eighteen volunteers in Annaghdown and two months after the execution in Athlone of six men attached to the North Galway Brigade. The date is prior to the execution of six anti-Treaty volunteers, subsequent to a raid on Headford Barracks, which housed Free State forces. Subsequently termed the 'Tuam Martyrs', their execution was among the last of the major events of the Civil War. A story known by most of his grandchildren was that when he was arrested, he was saved from execution because his weapon was never found. We were also told of a Free State army officer, who was a former comrade of his during the War of Independence, who vouched for Michael, when other friends and comrades of his were executed. A further story related to us tells of how he spoke to fellow prisoners through a cell-door on the morning of their execution – it is possible that these were the Tuam Martyrs as they were brought from Galway Gaol to Tuam to be executed. One of those executed was Frank Cunnane, whom Michael mentions in his application for a service medal as having been involved in training him and other Volunteers during the War of Independence.

What happened after his time in Galway Goal is unclear. The records suggest a discharge on 29 August and we assume that he was transferred to Tintown at this point. It is worth noting that the War officially ended in May 1923, although there was an extended period before most anti-Treaty prisoners were released, which lasted into 1924. Whatever the timing of their production, some artefacts remain from his time in prison: a tea cosy that he made while incarcerated; a ring hollowed out of a sixpence and a shilling; and a blanket from his time in Tintown. These were physical manifestations of his prison stay, a material representation of these events in the face of a silence surrounding them among family members.

In the process of researching the chapter, we discovered to our surprise that Michael applied for a Service Medal in August 1959, in respect of his role in the

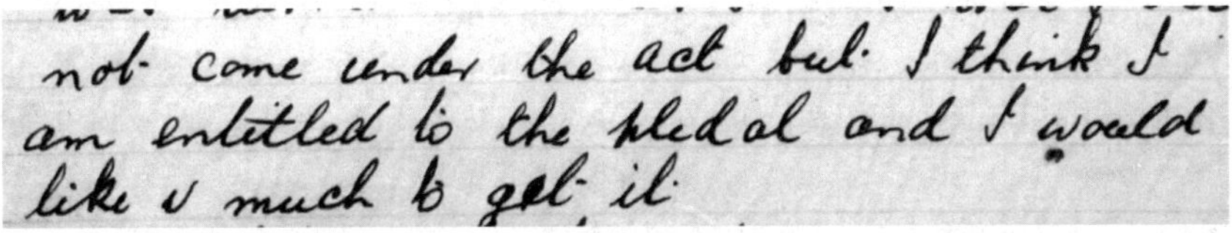
not come under the act but I think I am entitled to the Medal and I would like v much to get it

Excerpt from Application Letter for Military Service Medal.
Text Reads: 'but I think I am entitled to the medal and I would like v much to get it'.

War of Independence. His application letter also refers to having a prior application for military pension being turned down. Michael was also turned down on this occasion.

However, the archival material raises some questions. In his application, he names his company Captain and 1st Lieutenant and the Battalion O/C. It appears that a list of seven individuals was created from whom information would be sought to establish the suitability of Michael's application. Four of those named were senior officers in the Mid-Galway Brigade, one of whom was deceased. Three were officers in the local Annaghdown unit, two of whom were deceased. One of the deceased was the only officer (the company Captain) Michael named in his application that was included in the list of seven. Forms were issued to three surviving senior officers in the Mid-Galway Brigade, and one officer of the local company. Two of the former replied saying that they did not know Michael, and one didn't reply. The two who responded that they didn't know Michael were both living overseas, one in the US and one in New Zealand. The one local officer replied that he did know Michael and supported his application. Intriguingly, this response was sent on 27 December 1964, with an apology that the respondent had been ill. It came too late to influence the decision to turn down Michael's application, which was made in a letter dated 11 December of that year. Reading this material elicited strong emotions for the authors of this chapter, sadness that the application was rejected and disappointment at his treatment by this somewhat dubious process.

Outside of not speaking about his own experiences from this time, Michael talked about some of the key figures of the period. He described Liam Mellows as 'the bravest man who ever lived'; yet he never attended the annual commemoration for Liam Mellows that took place a mere two hundred metres from his home. Despite having remained on the side of the Republic during the Civil War, we recall Michael's admiration for Michael Collins whose military tactics and bravery he admired. However, he disliked William Cosgrave Sr, and was very saddened by the executions of republicans by the Free State forces during the Civil War. Yet it was sadness and not bitterness that tinged these occasional references. In more recent times during the Troubles, he strongly disassociated the activities of his former comrades from those of the Provisional IRA and others.

Maryanne and family life

Maryanne Glennane was from Waterdale, not far from Michael's home, and was born in 1902, one of two daughters of Michael and Norah Glennane. Her mother died when she was quite young, and family lore tells us that she and her sister Delia were considered to be very precious and were dressed in white until their seventh birthday. We are not certain when Michael and Maryanne met but know that they married in 1926, only a short number of years after the Civil War. Notably, they eloped. Following marriage, they moved to Galway city, staying initially with relatives in Forster Street, while they also lived for a time in Flood Street where a number of their children were born. Eventually, they moved to St Bridget's Place in Prospect Hill where they lived for the rest of their lives.

We know that theirs was a strong partnership where Michael was the breadwinner and Maryanne the homemaker. Like Michael, Maryanne proved to be very resourceful and hard-working, and was anxious for the family to do well. We were told that it was Maryanne who approached a local politician about getting this house. Michael and Maryanne had nine children, three of whom entered religious life. Religion was very important for Michael, and he was a daily mass-goer throughout his life. He worked in Thomas McDonagh's firm on Merchants' Road in Galway, until his retirement at the age of seventy-five. When he first started working there, the company was run by 'Máirtín Mór', who was a Cumann na nGaedheal TD from 1927 until his death in 1934.[2] Family lore again suggests that it may have been Maryanne who approached Máirtín McDonagh about a job for Michael. Despite Michael's background in the Civil War, and McDonagh's involvement in the Cumann na nGaedheal government, we recall his describing the McDonaghs as good employers, and he was certainly a hard-working employee throughout his long working life.

After his retirement, Michael attended Mass four or five times daily, attending different churches in the city, and was a well-known and well-liked figure around town. Maryanne suffered a stroke when she was in her seventies and didn't go out very much subsequently, but Michael would return home

2 For a discussion of 'Máirtín Mór' see Jackie Uí Chionna, *He was Galway: Máirtín Mór McDonogh, 1860–1934* (Dublin, 2016).

daily from Mass with news for her. Our memory of our grandparents' house is of one where there was a lot of laughter and fun. There were always visitors, many from the 'country' and it was always busy. While Michael's involvement in the events of the War of Independence and Civil War was rarely mentioned, he had a repertoire of songs – 'The Old Fenian Gun', 'Revenge for Skibbereen', 'The Galtee Mountains', 'The Bold Fenian Men', 'The Boys of Barr na Sráide' – reflecting no doubt an historic interest and a political sympathy for the republican cause.

Our shared memory of our grandparents is a positive one. We remember phrases and sayings that our grandparents both used: for generosity: 'There are no pockets in a shroud'; for tolerance and tact: 'Never ask anyone their politics or what they earn'; democratic history and liberty, equality and fraternity are brought to mind by 'There are no sins in a Republic'. 'Being poor is not a crime – the crime is poverty' was another phrase inherited from them, while 'No one is better than anyone else' was another of the important phrases used. These phrases and the opinions and attitudes they represent are a wonderful historic inheritance. Michael Canavan died in 1997, Maryanne predeceased him, passing away in 1993.

Interpreting a partial narrative inheritance

What we are left with in providing this account is a tension between what was clearly a formative experience in Michael's life as a young adult and its subsequent downplaying in his family life. We remain struck by the absence of a strong inter-generationally shared narrative of this part of his life, apart from relatively randomly shared stories. From undertaking this work, we learned definitively that this was meaningful to him; seeking a service medal indicates a certain pride in his involvement in the War of Independence. In this section, we map out our interpretation of this tension. We also consider what this narrative absence means to us as Michael's grandchildren and reflect on the ethical issues in researching and making it public. We frame our interpretation within a life course orientation following Elder's framework for studying the life course. He argues that the life course is built on four key ideas: the role of time and place in shaping individual biography; how the impact of life transitions relates to their timing; the interdependence of lives and the expression of social and historical influences through these 'linked lives'; and the capacity of individuals to act, within social and historical constraints.[3]

In all our analyses, Michael's relative youth must be considered. Current

3 G.H. Elder, 'The life course as developmental theory', *Child Development*, 69:1 (1998), pp 3–4.

social science understandings of youth in the minority (western) world note the elongation of the idea of youth and that of emerging adulthood with transitions into work, long-term relationships, own accommodation and parenthood more likely to occur in our late twenties and early thirties.[4] In this context, adult identity formation is more gradual with more opportunities for exploration of life opportunities. Like other young people of this time, Michael's transitions were much earlier and briefer than currently, but alongside this was a set of significant experiences in military conflict. We are left to wonder to what extent this featured in his identity as a young adult. From a life course perspective, the significant issue is the nature and timing of Michael's transitions and their consequences for his future biographical trajectory. A transition to adulthood involving participation in a military revolution followed by participation in a civil war, while not unusual, couldn't be described as normative. Similarly, Michael and Maryanne's elopement was non-normative. From a structural or macro-perspective, the risk from these non-normative transitions was their potentially negative impact on their future life course. A wider life course consideration is how Michael's experiences connected with other young men in similar circumstances. It is arguable that such a group exists, a cohort generation, 'a block of people born during a specific span of years who are considered distinct from those who precede or come after them', in this case differentiated from others in the society by the direct impact of the historical events of revolution and civil war.[5]

But following Elder, we have to take account of agency – Michael and Maryanne's capacity to act in the face of the constraints they faced and the risks from prior transitions. Thus, they had to create their biography in the context of the nature of the economy and available low-paid work, the absence of a welfare state, the particular political landscape of the 1920s, and Catholic Church values' hegemony, as they began their life together. In those circumstances, we can imagine their view of the past being the past, and the post-Civil War need to survive and ultimately thrive. This chosen biography may not have accommodated the space and time to reflect and make meaningful Michael's experiences of the time. Similarly, at this individual level of analysis, a likely factor in Michael's reticence about his experiences relates to his strong Catholic faith. As our account indicates, he was a very religious man, with three of his and Maryanne's children entering religious life. He was particularly proud of these children. It is worth remembering the threat of excommunication of those involved in anti-Treaty forces made by the Catholic hierarchy in

4 J.J. Arnett, 'Emerging adulthood: a theory of development from the late teens through the twenties', *American Psychologist*, 55:5 (2000), pp 469–80. 5 R.I. Millar, *Researching life stories and family histories* (London, 2000), p. 30.

1923. We also feel that, in comparison to Maryanne, he seemed more worried about death. This piece of the puzzle leads to at least a potential ambivalence in terms of memories of this early part of his adult life. Alongside the notion of guilt relating to religious beliefs, we can speculate that Michael may have felt some guilt, or trauma about deaths of others. Most likely there were a number among those who lost their lives during this time who were at least well known to him and possibly friends. We have the family stories of his speaking to those going to their death, and a sense that he survived death through two pieces of good fortune – the never-found gun and the former colleague speaking on this behalf.

Of course Michael was on the losing side. Unlike others for whom this had a significant negative consequence, Michael, with the support of his wife, was able to begin a family and working life, ironically in the employ of a Cuman na nGaedheal TD. Perhaps particularly in the immediate aftermath of the Civil War, it was less risky for somebody like Michael to get on with life and not engage in explicit demonstrations of political positions, at least publically. So attendance at republican commemorations was not an option. Maryanne's key role in supporting Michael in relation to work and setting up home hints at the challenges they faced in starting their life together. These practical challenges of life reflect the idea of linked lives and the need to 'get on' with people regardless of profound political differences of the immediate past. It also reminds us of Michael and Maryanne's linked life of love and mutual support.

If this is our interpretation of why we don't have the story in full, what does it mean to us? Drawing on Goodall, McNay defines inheritance as comprising 'the stories and family lore that parents and other relatives pass on to children about the family'.[6] She suggests that they are 'essential to the construction of personal identity, relationships, and fully actualized lives' but also highlights that they may be difficult to access, only partially available or intentionally obscured. In our case, we have a strong overall family narrative inheritance from our grandparents beyond the specifics of Michael's involvement in the War of Independence and Civil War. Accepting that the sources of our identity are manifold, reflecting the sayings mentioned above, our grandparents are part of the 'family we live by'[7] and have been part of our identity formation. Yet it is true that there is part of Michael's life for which there is an 'absent memory', something we have tried to make present in this chapter. We can only ponder what the impact of a story fully told would have been on his own children, in terms of values, political orientations and so on, and in turn on his

6 H.L. Goodall, 'Narrative inheritance: a nuclear family with toxic secrets', *Qualitative Inquiry*, 11:4 (2005), pp 492–513. M. McNay, 'Absent memory, family secrets, narrative inheritance' *Qualitative Inquiry*, 15:7 (2009), p. 1178. **7** J.R. Gillis, *A world of their own making* (Boston, 1996).

grandchildren. Certainly, in the period of national reflection starting in 2016, we would have been placed differently to where we were at the start of our work on this chapter. As a final point in our interpretation we must briefly refer to ethics; we are conscious of the ethical issues in telling a story not told in full by Michael himself. Our private justification is that we are proud of his contribution to the building of our nation, but our public justification is that his reflects many other untold stories from this period – stories that, if told, may help us better understand our individual and social present from our past.

Conclusion

Undertaking this project has required us to make our grandfather 'strange' in the sociological sense, in order to make a particular part of his life historically and sociologically meaningful.[8] While in the absence of a coherent body of evidence, our account is only partial, we can imagine that Michael's experiences of the War of Independence and Civil War were common. They most likely exemplify the transition of many young men of this time in Ireland through extreme adolescent and early adult experiences into ordinary adult work and family life and all its survival struggles. Subjectively, of course, Michael and Maryanne were our grandparents and we cannot escape our feelings of love and respect towards them. We are not 'narratively disinherited' by lacking the full story of Michael's role in the War of Independence and the Civil War. Rather we are honoured to be able to reflect on this extraordinary part of his and Maryanne's seemingly ordinary life, and to shine a light on this ordinary hero.

Acknowledgments

Thanks to Mícheál and Noelle Higgins, and Cormac Ó Comhraí for their assistance in preparing the chapter.

8 C. Wright Mills, *The sociological imagination* (Oxford, 2000).

Caught in the conflict: the predicament of the Irish police force during the War of Independence

MICHAEL LANG

Introduction

In the discussion surrounding the Irish revolution, relatively little consideration has been given to the dilemma faced by members of the Royal Irish Constabulary (RIC), the vast majority of whom were decent men from rural homesteads who joined the police force during peaceful times. Upon the outbreak of hostilities, they found themselves caught in the middle of a conflict that forced them to reconcile their political loyalties and family obligations with their sworn duty to protect the peace. Many of them resigned, either because of conscientious objections, fears for personal safety, or as a result of pressure being exerted upon them or their relatives by Sinn Féin activists. Others stayed on, in many cases because they had wives and children to support and could not afford to forfeit their only source of income.

Even to this day, there is a considerable degree of bitterness towards the RIC. They are often portrayed as brutes and vagabonds, infamously remembered for their association with the crowbar brigades of the Land War and later the notorious Black and Tans. However, on the recent launch of his book *46 men dead*, which draws on his doctoral study of police casualties in Tipperary between 1919 and 1922, Garda Sergeant John Reynolds expressed his view that the popular characterization of the RIC as a 'paramilitary, colonial, oppressive police force' is wide of the truth. That opinion was met with indignation on internet forums where respondents used emotive terms such as 'eyes and ears of the crown', 'oppressors of democracy', 'colluders with British reprisals', 'subjugators of the Irish people' and 'spies and informers'.[1] The RIC is a tainted brand in the eyes of many; its emblem featuring a crown above the harp, which was retained by the Royal Ulster Constabulary after 1922, exudes a different image than the stylized Celtic motif and traditional Gaelic lettering of the Garda Síochána badge. In reality though, the RIC and the early Garda Síochána were more alike than different; indeed, the RIC manual served as that of the Garda Síochána until 1942.[2]

1 http://www.thejournal.ie/ric-book–2743413-May2016/, accessed 1 June 2017. 2 Elizabeth

I come from three generations of policemen who between them gave over a century (1889–1996) of almost unbroken service across all four provinces. Two of my ancestors served in the RIC during the Irish War of Independence. One was my great-grandfather, Head Constable John Dillon; the other was a man whose life story I am drawn to because we share the same name and native county, my great grand-uncle Sergeant Michael Lang. Whereas one of them resigned from the RIC during the conflict, the other served all the way through. This chapter contrasts the tales of these two men and analyses the underlying reasons which motivated them to follow different paths.

Family background and reasons for joining the RIC

The careers of Michael Lang and John Dillon have many similarities but very notable differences. They were both born in the early 1870s and joined the police about the same time, in January 1894 and November 1895 respectively. In the 1910s, they were both promoted to the rank of sergeant. A key difference in their lives, which affected their decisions thereafter, was that John Dillon got married and fathered seven children between 1903 and 1917 whereas Michael Lang remained a bachelor. When things turned hot during the War of Independence in 1920, Michael Lang resigned from the RIC but John Dillon stayed on and ended up as a head constable (equivalent to modern rank of Garda inspector).

Michael Lang was born in 1874, the fifth of ten children of my great-great-grandparents Thomas Lang and Anne Savage. They were tenants on the estate of the O'Haras of Annaghmore who were the only Gaelic family to continue as major landowners in Co. Sligo up to relatively modern times. Major Charles O'Hara was a benevolent landlord but that part of Sligo was then, and still is, a bleak landscape on which to eke out a living as a small farmer. Of those ten children, three died in childhood. Two others emigrated to America, two joined the RIC, two stayed at home and never married, and one married locally. The two who joined the RIC were brothers Patrick, who joined in 1889 but left in 1898 following a series of reprimands, and Michael who joined in 1894. Sometime in the 1890s, their father died. That would have cast Michael into the role of provider for his mother and two youngest siblings. A career in the police force was an opportunity to bring in a dependable income and most likely that was the main reason he signed up. It was also an avenue to a higher level of education because recruits were instructed on arithmetic, algebra, orthography, grammar, geography, book-keeping and first aid.[3]

Malcolm, *The Irish policeman* (Dublin, 2006), p. 216. **3** D.J. O'Sullivan, *The Irish constabulary 1822–1922: a century of policing in Ireland* (Dingle, 1999), p. 62

Of John Dillon's lineage, I have less knowledge. He was born in Tullow, Co. Carlow, in 1871 to parents Anne Bolger and Michael Dillon, a postman. They also had ten children, of whom John was the eldest. Sometime in the 1890s, they moved from Carlow to the Woodquay area of Dublin city. John Dillon worked for a while as a railway porter in Kingsbridge Station (now Heuston Station) before joining the RIC at the end of 1895. His brother Thomas joined the Royal Dublin Fusiliers and served in the Boer War, as did hundreds of other Irish Catholics during that period.

At the time of the 1901 census, Michael Lang and John Dillon were stationed in Wexford town and Belfast respectively. It is interesting to look at those two barrack census returns as an indication of the composition of the RIC. Of the forty-four men including Constable Dillon who were based in Mountpottinger Road Barracks in Belfast, their religious denominations were 59 per cent Roman Catholic, 36 per cent Church of Ireland and 5 per cent Presbyterian. In Wexford, Constable Michael Lang and thirteen others, mostly from the west of Ireland, are listed on the return for the Lower George's Street Barracks. Seventy-one per cent of those men were of the Roman Catholic faith and the remainder were either Church of Ireland or Presbyterian. Taking the two returns together, all but two of those fifty-eight men had as previous occupation 'farmer's son' or 'labourer'. That was quite typical of the RIC as a whole. The majority of the rank-and-file were Catholics from rural backgrounds but the officers of the RIC were almost exclusively from the Protestant ascendancy. There was considerable religious bigotry within the force and several of the senior officers treated their subordinates with disdain.[4] Among the ordinary members, however, there was never any animosity about religion.[5]

To gain insights into the mindset of RIC recruits, it is useful to read the testimonies submitted by former policemen to the Bureau of Military History. J.J. McConnell, who entered the police in 1907, stated that:

> [I joined] at the age of twenty and realized my childhood ambition. Indeed, it was the dream of all my boyhood pals to join the force that was generally admired and respected throughout the country. My parish priest gave me a character [reference] and his blessing, the former being essential. When I left my home for the Depot in the Phoenix Park, I carried with me the regards and good wishes of all and sundry. It never occurred to anyone that I was doing anything unpatri-

4 R. Fennell, *The Royal Irish Constabulary: a history and personal memoir*, edited by Rosemary Fennell (Dublin, 2003), pp 69–77. 5 J.D. Brewer, *The Royal Irish Constabulary: an oral history* (Belfast, 1990), pp 67–71.

> otic, not even the old Fenians and Land Leaguers who still survived, amongst them my father [who was] a veteran of both organizations.[6]

In similar vein, just three years before he founded Sinn Féin, Arthur Griffith's *United Irishman* featured a piece that spoke very admirably of the RIC:

> The Royal Irish Constabulary is a body of Irishmen, recruited from the Irish people. They are bone of their bone, and flesh of their flesh. The typical young constabularyman is Irish of the Irish, Catholic and (as the word goes) Nationalist; the son of decent parents; his father a Home Rule farmer; … he is smiled on by the Irish clergy; he is smiled on by the Irish girls; he is respected by the young fellows of the street corner and the country crossroads.[7]

These contemporary writings dispel the myth that the RIC were all loyal subjects of the British empire. Liam O'Riordan, who served from 1913 to 1918, was anxious to put on record that 'the common belief that recruits at the Depot had to be good Britishers … is utterly untrue'.[8] In his memoirs written in the 1940s, former RIC Head Constable Thomas Fennell appended a chapter to vehemently deny the claims of republican historians that the RIC were steadfastly loyal to the Crown.[9] Recruits were required to take an oath of allegiance but that was looked upon as a mere formality which did not trouble any member.

Life in the constabulary, 1895–1916

The years from the mid-1890s to the early 1910s 'were carefree, peaceful days in Ireland and a policeman's life was then a happy one … duty consisted of maintaining peace at fairs and race meetings, supervising licensed premises, and generally preventing and detecting ordinary crime'.[10] The early careers of constables Michael Lang and John Dillon were largely uneventful; their names are listed in court registers for bringing cases of drunk and disorderly behaviour, unlicenced dogs, unlighted carts or disputes between neighbours.

At that time, the RIC was well integrated within the local communities of rural Ireland. They had become a de-militarized civil police force whose duties included not just law enforcement and revenue collection but also other work

6 J.J. McConnell, ex-Sergeant / District Inspector RIC, Bureau of Military History 1913–21, Witness Statement No. 509, p. 1. **7** O'Sullivan, *The Irish constabulary*, p. 227. **8** Liam S. O'Riordan, ex-Constable RIC, Bureau of Military History 1913–21, Witness Statement No. 888, p. 1. **9** Fennell, *The RIC*, pp 153–75. **10** McConnell, BMH Witness Statement No. 509, p. 1.

such as census returns and agricultural statistics that involved making visits to every home.[11] Many country people were illiterate so constables helped them to fill their returns; they also read and composed letters, completed forms for old age pensioners, and assisted shopkeepers with their books. As relatively well-educated men, they were held in similar regard as school teachers.[12]

My great grand-uncle Michael Lang spent the first eighteen years of his police career in Co. Wexford. He was a keen sportsman and served as assistant secretary of the RIC Cycling and Athletic Club for several years. In 1912, he moved back to the Phoenix Park Depot as a member of the RIC Reserve, a unit of specially selected men who could be quickly dispatched to any place to quell disturbances, such as the annual Orange Order marches in Ulster.[13] In 1913, he attained the rank of sergeant, a popular promotion that received 'the hearty felicitations of his comrades'.[14]

Maybe he preferred to be single or perhaps it was because the constricted life of a policeman was not conducive to marriage but for whatever reason Michael Lang did not marry. In contrast, my great-grandfather John Dillon was not shy when it came to making marriage proposals. As it turned out, he married three times in life. RIC regulations were that a member had to be in the force for at least seven years before he could marry. After moving from Belfast to Longford in the latter half of 1901, John Dillon wasted no time finding a partner. In November 1902, when he had served just two weeks beyond the minimum seven years, he married my great-grandmother, Eileen Collum from Drumlish, a national school monitor. Marriage to a policeman meant having to leave one's native county and move at least fifty miles away and so the newly married couple set off for Co. Mayo where they spent the next ten years of their lives.

Eileen Dillon gave birth to five children in Mayo, including my grandmother Kathleen. It may have been a wish to see her newborn niece that took Eileen's sister Agnes on a fateful visit to Mayo in 1908. One of John Dillon's colleagues in Kilmaine made an impression upon her and so it came to pass that Agnes Collum married Constable Joseph McCormack.

In 1913, John Dillon was transferred to Arvagh, Co. Cavan, just twelve miles from his wife's home place. After a few months there, he moved to the neighbouring village of Ballinagh as sergeant-in-charge. A sixth child was born to Eileen and John Dillon in October 1914. By then, the First World War had broken out and things were also starting to heat up in Ireland. In 1915, Ballinagh had the only active IRA unit in Cavan.[15] The local Volunteers drilled

11 O'Sullivan, *The Irish constabulary*, p. 97. **12** Brewer, *The RIC*, p. 4. **13** O'Sullivan, *The Irish constabulary*, p. 60. **14** 'Royal Irish Constabulary', *Weekly Irish Times*, 24 May 1913. **15** Séamus MacDiarmada, ex-IRA, Bureau of Military History 1913–21, Witness Statement No. 768, pp 1–2.

and paraded publicly, were inspected by prominent national leaders, procured rifles and shotguns from Dublin and Cavan town, and produced buckshot ammunition.[16]

On the evening of Holy Thursday 1916, the leader of Belfast IRA sent a message to one of his trusted men, Seán McCormack, giving him authority to take charge of the Volunteers mobilizing for the Rising in Cavan. He was to oversee the distribution of shotguns in Ballinagh. McCormack boarded a train for Ballinagh on Easter Saturday but when he reached Portadown, orders were received that 'all is off'.[17] The Cavan Volunteers played no part in the Easter Rising but during the War of Independence, Ballinagh was the chief centre of IRA activities in the county.[18]

All is changed, changed utterly, 1916–22

At the time of the Easter Rising, Michael Lang was stationed in the Phoenix Park Depot as a sergeant in the RIC Reserve. He would surely have heard the sounds of bombardment coming from the city and, although I do not know for sure, I presume in view of its purpose that his unit was called upon to restore calm in the aftermath of the rebellion.

In September 1916, he was transferred to Longford town, having given 'every evidence of ability and tact' during his time in the Reserve, and he left 'with the sincere good wishes of [his] many comrades and friends'.[19] The following year, he moved to Granard Station in the north of the county. By then, there was a noticeable change in the mood of the people. Granard, like Ballinagh, was a hotspot of IRA activity. In April 1918, he was transferred back to the Depot where I expect he would have felt less on edge. Sergeant John Dillon also obtained a transfer, initially to Cavan town and subsequently to Killeshandra, where there was much less agitation than in Ballinagh.

In January 1919, the IRA declared its intention to use 'all legitimate means of warfare against the soldiers and policemen of the English usurper, and to slay them if it is necessary to do so'.[20] According to Richard Abbott's extensive research, the RIC suffered 493 fatalities between the Soloheadbeg ambush and the disbandment of the force in 1922.[21] Jim Herlihy places the death toll at 534 for the same period if non-political killings are also included.[22] Things were

16 Séamus O'Sullivan, ex-IRA, Bureau of Military History 1913–21, Witness Statement No. 393, pp 2–3. **17** Seán Cusack, ex-IRA, Bureau of Military History 1913–21, Witness Statement No. 9, pp 17–24. **18** MacDiarmada, BMH Witness Statement No. 768, p. 2; Patrick Caldwell, ex-IRA, Bureau of Military History 1913–21, Witness Statement No. 638, p. 18. **19** 'Royal Irish Constabulary: Notes and News', *Weekly Irish Times*, 2 September 1916. **20** O'Sullivan, *The Irish constabulary*, p. 283. **21** Richard Abbott, *Police casualties in Ireland, 1919–1922* (Cork, 2000), p. 7. **22** Jim Herlihy, *The Royal Irish Constabulary: a short history and genealogical guide* (Dublin, 1997), pp 151–2.

relatively quiet at the beginning but in 1920 the heat of battle was turned up. RIC shootings became everyday occurrences and not a week passed without several injuries and fatalities. The RIC as a police force was unsuited to dealing with guerrilla warfare. This was not what they had signed up for. They retired or resigned in their droves throughout 1920. Most left for fear of their lives or because of pressure exerted on them or their family members.

Sergeant Michael Lang would have been relatively safe in the barracks at the Phoenix Park although there was a risk of being tailed if he ventured into the streets of Dublin city. As an instructor in the Depot, the chances are that he was acquainted with some of the young policemen whose deaths he was reading of in the RIC weekly newsletter. In County Sligo and elsewhere, local branches of Sinn Féin were urging the parents of RIC men to send letters requesting their sons to resign. Michael Lang's mother died in July 1919 and his father was long dead, but he had a brother and sister still living in the home place and another brother and his family nearby. I am not aware if there was any IRA intimidation going on but it is a possibility. Even more likely though is that it was the disgraceful actions of the Black and Tans that ultimately influenced his decision to retire. The Tans were wreaking havoc in Sligo; one day my grandfather heard them coming in an angry mood and hid under Billa bridge (near Collooney) to avoid their wrath. For whatever reason, my great grand-uncle Michael Lang was one of seventy men who left the RIC in the first week of October 1920. John Dillon's brother-in-law, the aforementioned Constable Joseph McCormack, also retired that same week.

Turning then to John Dillon, he was in a very different and much more difficult quandary. Whereas Michael Lang was a single man, Sergeant Dillon had a wife and seven children to protect and provide for. When the War of Independence broke out in 1919, his youngest child was not yet two and the eldest was just fifteen. They were then all living in the barracks at Killeshandra.

In 1911, there were twenty-eight RIC stations in Cavan but ten years later just eleven remained in operation.[23] Several rural posts were evacuated in the early months of 1920 as part of the RIC's strategy to retreat into fortified towns. During Easter week of that year, the IRA destroyed hundreds of former RIC barracks around the country. For policing purposes, County Cavan was divided into the districts of Swanlinbar, Bailieboro, Virginia and Cavan. Killeshandra was in the latter district and it along with Ballinagh and Cavan town were the only three stations still occupied in that area in January 1921.

23 Based on analysis of 1911 Census on IrishConstabulary.com forum. (http://irishconstabulary.com/topic/621/Cavan) and list of RIC men serving in Cavan as of 1 January 1921 (FindMyPast.com, UK national archives series HO/184).

Arvagh re-opened the following month, having been successfully attacked by the IRA in September 1920.

Despite the resignations from the force, it is notable that of the 138 rank-and-file men listed in the January 1921 RIC register for County Cavan, 79 per cent were Roman Catholic. Another notable statistic is that the majority of the Cavan policemen who were eligible to be married were indeed so.[24]

There is a view in some circles that the RIC men who decided to stay in the force were 'spies and traitors' who sided with the enemy.[25] As attested by several sources, many of the men of the RIC, even though they may not have agreed with the tactics of Sinn Féin, were in favour of home rule or outright sovereignty. Most of those who opted not to stand down simply could not do so for economic reasons. The General Employment Agency that had been established by the Minister for Labour, Constance Markievicz, failed dismally in its efforts to find alternative employment for ex-RIC men who resigned.[26] Besides, what kind of police force would Ireland have had if all the Irishmen stepped aside? Utter lawlessness and chaos would almost certainly have prevailed. Fennell makes the point that during the War of Independence, the RIC acted as 'a restraint upon [the Black and Tans and Auxiliaries] and may have often saved the lives of people by privately communicating projected raids'.[27] Rather than castigating the Irishmen who continued to serve in the RIC, many of them deserve credit for faithfully honouring their oath to execute their peace-keeping duties 'without favour or affection, malice or ill-will' during those very difficult times. In numerous cases, RIC men or their family members discretely passed information to the IRA through priests and other trusted mediums, played dumb when asked by British officers to identify suspects, and used their good sense to defuse incendiary situations.[28]

Like everyone else, they could not have known what the future held but they must have realized that things could not continue as they were for much longer. For a number of reasons, the RIC was in an unsustainable situation as a police force by the end of 1920. First, its own members had been crying out for changes for several years. Sergeant T.J. McElligott, who served with my great grand-uncle Michael Lang in the RIC Reserve, founded the Police Union in 1918. The Union was supported by the majority of the rank-and-file men and called for disarmament, religious equality of opportunity and other major reforms. For his efforts, McElligott was isolated by the hierarchy and he

24 Based on analysis of list of RIC men serving in Cavan as of 1 January 1921 (FindMyPast.com, UK national archives series HO/184). **25** O'Sullivan, *The Irish constabulary*, p. 309. This term was used in an IRA HQ statement made in 1920. **26** J. Anthony Gaughan, *Memoirs of Constable Jeremiah Mee, RIC* (Cork, 2012), pp 137–8, 150. **27** Fennell, *The RIC*, p. 107. **28** For example, see Cormac Ó Comhraí, *Revolution in Connacht* (Cork, 2013), pp 75, 82, 90, 124.

resigned in 1919, subsequently bringing many more disillusioned men out with him.[29] Second, the composition of the RIC was no longer representative of the communities they policed. The thousands of Irishmen who resigned in 1920 were replaced in even greater numbers by ex-British army soldiers who were policemen only in name.[30] The force as a whole had therefore lost the consent of the people, even though many individual members were still well respected. Third, the passing of the Government of Ireland Act 1920 meant that the police force would inevitably be restructured when the country split into two separate jurisdictions.

Sergeant John Dillon was a wily and diplomatic operator, quite capable of reading the political situation. His utmost priority was to safeguard the welfare of his wife, son, and six young daughters. He was approaching the end of his police career and would have been keeping an eye on the future. He knew that if he kept his wits about him and sensibly controlled things within his own area, the storm would pass. There were eleven policemen stationed in Killeshandra in 1921: Sergeant Dillon, Sergeant Concannon and nine constables, most of whom had completed several years of service. Fortunately, of all the places to be during the War of Independence, Cavan was one of the safest counties and Killeshandra was one of the most peaceful places in Cavan. At the beginning of the conflict, some shots were fired when John Dillon was out on patrol one day. The barracks in which he and his family lived was reinforced with sandbags, barbed wire and shutters but in general life was unperturbed and continued as normal. Most of the barracks in west Cavan were attacked at some point but Killeshandra was spared.

The official Sinn Féin policy of social ostracism did not affect the Dillon family. Eileen Dillon had a small vegetable patch at the rear of the barracks and she also kept pigs, which she fed with slops willingly provided by the Killeshandra creamery. On a number of occasions, when word reached Killeshandra Station that certain men were to be picked up, my grandmother who was then just a young girl was dispatched to serve warning. The Black and Tans once took two men from the creamery into custody but Sergeant Dillon put a call through to Cavan town and intervened to effect their release.

Killeshandra was colonized by Scottish settlers during the Ulster Plantation. Three centuries later, the population of the area was three-quarters Roman Catholic and one-quarter Protestant. The town had a staunch unionist community and several of them were signatories of the Ulster Covenant. Twenty-three members of the local Church of Ireland died in the First World

29 T.J. McElligott, ex-Sergeant RIC, Bureau of Military History, 1913–21, Witness Statement No. 472. **30** C.J.C. Street, *The administration of Ireland, 1920* (London, 1921), pp 277–8.

War, including the rector's own son. The Killeshandra branch of the Ulster Volunteer Force was in possession of 114 rifles and ammunition, a vastly superior arsenal than the IRA in west Cavan had at its disposal.[31]

Importantly, relations between the Protestant and Catholic people were very good. As the rector put it in his address to the large 12th of July gathering in Killeshandra in 1920, 'if the cow of a Roman Catholic took sick, a Protestant would sit up all night to help his Catholic neighbour, and the Catholic, of course, would do the same ... we are all brethren and Irishmen'.[32] When the Ulster unionist leaders decided to support the Government of Ireland Act, the counties of Cavan, Monaghan and Donegal were severed from the other six of Ulster. The Protestant community of Killeshandra was conscious for some years beforehand of their likely exclusion from a partitioned Ulster. They therefore adopted a pragmatic attitude of minding their own business and avoiding political trouble. For their part, although many of the Roman Catholic clergy in Cavan openly supported Sinn Féin, they were also unequivocal in their condemnation of IRA violence against the RIC. [33]

Three RIC men were killed in Cavan during the War of Independence – one in Swanlinbar in December 1920 and two in Arvagh in May 1921 – compared to twelve in the neighbouring county of Longford.[34] A major reason for this difference is that the Cavan IRA lacked organization and leadership.[35] In the 1918 general election, Peter Paul Galligan of Sinn Féin was elected unopposed in West Cavan. He was described as 'one of the most dangerous men in the rebel movement' but spent most of the period from 1919 to 1921 in prison.[36] In 1920, the IRA leadership sent Joseph McMahon to 'liven up the area' but shortly after he arrived, he accidentally killed himself when testing a bomb.[37]

In the main though, the war in Co. Cavan was fought not with guns and bombs but by other means. The local IRA could not have won a direct military battle against the crown forces.[38] Instead, Sinn Féin's objective was to bring British administration to its knees by disrupting the systems of justice, commerce, transport and communications. Evacuated RIC barracks were destroyed to prevent them being used again. Roads were blocked and trenched to render them impassable by motorized vehicles. The drivers of the Cavan and

31 Dublin Castle Records, UK National Archives. 1917 CO 904/29: Returns of arms in possession of Irish, National and Ulster Volunteers. **32** 'Killeshandra Twelfth meeting', *Anglo-Celt*, 17 July 1920. **33** J.A. Donohue, 'The impact of the partition crisis on Cavan and Monaghan 1914–1926' (MA, Maynooth University, 1999), pp 8–34, 59. **34** Herlihy, *The RIC*, p. 456; Abbott, *Police casualties in Ireland*, pp 166, 227–8. **35** MacDiarmada, BMH Witness Statement No. 768. **36** Kevin Galligan,, *Peter Paul Galligan: one of the most dangerous men in the rebel movement* (Dublin, 2012), p. 29. **37** MacDiarmada, BMH Witness Statement No. 768, p. 2; Seán Sheridan, ex-IRA, Bureau of Military History 1913–21, Witness Statement No. 1613, p. 10. **38** Galligan, *Peter Paul Galligan*, p. 35.

Leitrim Railway refused to carry crown forces. Telephone lines were cut and mails were seized. Messages were intercepted by post office employees working on behalf of the IRA. People refused to pay taxes and license fees. Local authority records offices were burned. The legitimacy of crown courts was denied and preference was given to republican courts.[39]

Even though it was an outpost company of the Ballinagh Battalion, there was very little aggressive IRA activity in Killeshandra. They raided the creamery in early 1920 to steal bicycles so that the IRA Volunteers could swiftly move around.[40] A cryptic note printed in the local newspaper in May 1921 stated that 'unknown men have again visited houses about Killeshandra and carried off arms and ammunition',[41] which might be a reference to IRA raids on Protestant homes.[42] From August 1920 onwards, a major element of the IRA campaign in Killeshandra was the enforcement of the Belfast boycott. Businesses were ordered by the IRA to entirely stop trade with suppliers of goods from Belfast and Lisburn as a response to the unfair treatment of Roman Catholics in those towns. Despite concerns being raised that an indiscriminate economic blockade would harm those whose plight it was intended to resolve, it proceeded.[43] A bread van owned by Inglis and Company, a large Belfast bakery, was held up and burned in Killeshandra in April 1921. Sergeant Dillon was handed a threatening notice which had been served upon John Storey, a local Protestant shopkeeper aged in his sixties: 'your turn next, clear out, IRA'. Next to this note, Mr Storey found a tin of petrol.[44] It was stated in court that this act was committed by outsiders because no local would do such a thing to one of his neighbours.

A truce was agreed, to the relief of all, in July 1921 but the Belfast boycott remained in place. By September 1921, the RIC County Inspector reported that it 'has been so bad at Belturbet, Killeshandra and Bailieboro, that fairs and markets at those places have almost died out. The country people find it more convenient to transfer their custom to towns where there are few shopkeepers etc. on the [Belfast] Boycott black list.'[45] John Dillon's time in Killeshandra was by then nearly at an end. He was promoted to the rank of head constable in October and transferred to Galway. On his departure, in appreciation of the impartial manner in which he had executed his duties and held the community

39 Sheridan, BMH Witness Statement No. 1613, p. 9; Donohoe, 'The impact of the partition crisis on Cavan and Monaghan', pp 49–53. **40** Sheridan, BMH Withness Statement No. 1613, p. 4. **41** 'Killeshandra raid', *Anglo-Celt,* 24 May 1921. **42** Galligan, *Peter Paul Galligan,* p. 31; Donohoe, 'The impact of the partition crisis on Cavan and Monaghan', p. 43. **43** Donohoe, 'The impact of the partition crisis on Cavan and Monaghan', pp 72–97. **44** 'Cavan Qr. Sessions: Malicious Injuries Claims', *Anglo-Celt,* 16 April 1921. The 'Mr Storey' referred to in the report was identified as John Storey, a shopkeeper in Killeshandra town, using the 1911 census. **45** RIC County Inspectors Monthly Report of Outrages, Cavan, September 1921. Dublin Castle Records, UK National Archives.

together, the people of Killeshandra organized a function in his honour and presented him with a gold watch and chain.

As a head constable, John Dillon's duties mainly involved winding down the force. He spent a month in Galway city, then another in Westmeath and then on to Collooney, Co. Sligo, where he used to march the RIC men up the street to Mass on Sundays. Among the parishioners in weekly attendance at Collooney services was my grandfather. He did not then know that this man in charge of the local RIC would in time become his father-in-law. That fine church in Collooney was reluctantly bombarded by General Seán Mac Eoin during the Civil War because its steeple was occupied by IRA snipers.[46] By a turn of chance, my grandfather became good friends with Seán Mac Eoin and John Dillon when their paths crossed again in Longford a few years later. John Dillon ended up in the RIC Clerical Company at Dublin Castle in 1922. He and his wife stayed in the castle on the night before it was handed over to the incoming troops of the Irish Free State.

Life after the RIC

In 1922, the RIC was disbanded and replaced by the new Civic Guard. Thousands of former policemen faced uncertain futures with no place to go. Many chose or were compelled to leave the Free State and went to Northern Ireland, Britain, or other foreign shores. Others stayed on, living out the remainder of their lives in relative anonymity.[47] Only a few former members of the RIC were admitted into the new police force.

When he left the RIC in October 1920, what was Michael Lang to do? He was still a young man, just forty-six years-of-age. His decision to exit the police force meant that his income was now reduced by almost half but that was enough to satisfy his modest needs. Going back home to Sligo was not an option because the county was in a very disturbed state and, even after the truce, several ex-RIC men were ordered to leave Sligo by the IRA on pain of death.[48] In any case, there was nothing much for him to return to. Instead, he took up residence in the Brazen Head Hotel in Lower Bridge Street, Dublin.

It seems an unusual place for an ex-RIC man to go because that particular hostelry, which is reputed to be the oldest in Ireland, had long associations with revolutionaries going back to the times of Robert Emmet and the United Irishmen. Several witness statements from the Bureau of Military History refer to IRA deals being brokered there and it was a favoured meeting place of

46 M. Farry, *The aftermath of revolution: Sligo, 1921–23* (Dublin, 2000), p. 78. **47** John Reynolds, 'Divided loyalties: the Royal Irish Constabulary in county Tipperary, 1919–1922' (PhD, University of Limerick, 2013), p. iii; Brewer, *The RIC*, p. 12. **48** Farry, *The aftermath of revolution*, p. 165.

Arthur Griffith and other Sinn Féin activists.[49] Just two months after Michael Lang moved in to the Brazen Head Hotel, on the night of 19 December 1920, a brigade of British soldiers forcefully charged through the front door in a raid for arms and wanted persons. They took the names of the proprietor and twenty male residents, several of whom were ex-RIC men.[50]

Eighteen months later, as dawn broke on 28 June 1922, the Free State army attacked the Four Courts with eighteen-pounder guns located at Winetavern Street and Lower Bridge Street, just a few yards from the front door of the Brazen Head Hotel. The Civil War had commenced. Just six years after the Easter Rising, the streets of Dublin were again being turned into battle zones. What must the ex-RIC men staying in the hotel have thought of the chaotic situation unfolding before their eyes?

Having been a policeman for twenty-six years, Michael Lang spent the remaining twenty-eight years of his life as a lodger in the Brazen Head Hotel. I do not know if he ever took up employment again or how often, if ever, he ventured back to Sligo. My aunt, who was eleven years old when he died, remembers visiting him in the 1940s with her father who was then a Garda stationed in Meath. She remembers her granduncle as a very correct and immaculately presented man who was always generous to his family. She also remembers seeing the other ex-RIC lodgers in the lounge area, just sitting there reading the newspapers.

The impression that emerges is of a group of men who were so accustomed to the daily regimen and rituals of barrack life that they were institutionalized. Goffman's definition of a 'total institution' is 'a place of residence and work where a large number of like-minded individuals, cut off from the wider society for an appreciable period of time, together lead an enclosed, formally administered round of life'.[51] Much of Michael Lang's time in the police force was spent in environments that fit in with this definition. Little wonder then that he and the other ex-RIC bachelors found solace in each other's company at the Brazen Head Hotel. Sadly, it seems that quite a few of them were estranged from their families and came to lonely endings. My great grand-uncle died in 1948 and was laid to rest in Glasnevin Cemetery.

John Dillon's story is rather different. With the gratuity that he received upon retirement, he purchased a farmhouse in Co. Longford. There are several references in the literature to ex-RIC men and their families being harassed and intimidated in rural Ireland in the early years of the Free State, yet here is an example of a former head constable, who served right through the War of

49 For example, see Bureau of Military History 1913–23 Witness Statements Nos. 30, 707 and 1244.
50 FindMyPast.ie, 'Easter Rising and Ireland under martial law, 1916–1921' records collection.
51 Quoted in Malcolm, *Irish policeman,* p. 92.

Independence, choosing to set up home in the heart of one of the most active IRA territories in the whole country. Not just that, but one of his daughters was on very friendly terms with a brother of General Seán Mac Eoin, potentially with an eye to marriage. John Dillon was very well received by the local people, often being invited to sing on stage at community occasions. How can this be explained?

One key factor was that John Dillon's wife was a native of the area and her family had assisted the IRA during the war. The parish priest, Canon Patrick Markey, was president of the local Sinn Féin branch. In November 1920, a constable was shot near the parochial house in Clonbroney on the orders of Michael Collins.[52] Two lorries of Black and Tans arrived at Canon Markey's door to interrogate him. He denied any knowledge of IRA activities and was sentenced to death. Before departing, the District Inspector gave him permission to go back into his house and he escaped down a hidden laneway. The sixty-one-year-old priest went on the run and Seán Mac Eoin moved him from place to place during the harsh winter of 1920/1. Notably, one of the places that he hid was in the home of the Collum family in Drumlish, John Dillon's wife's people. Two daughters from that household, my great-grandmother Eileen and her sister Agnes, married RIC men but it was still a safe house from the Black and Tans. Seán Mac Eoin had been the officer in charge of the IRA 1st Midlands Division, which included West Cavan, so he would probably have also known some of the inner details of John Dillon's work in Killeshandra. John Dillon and his family therefore had nothing to fear in Longford. Canon Markey survived the War of Independence and in the years that followed, he officiated at the weddings of four of John Dillon's daughters, including that of my grandmother and grandfather. My grandmother only ever spoke of her years in Cavan and Longford with fondness. I do not believe that at any time she or any member of her family experienced any ill will.

Conclusion

The majority of the combatants during the War of Independence were decent men and women who stood firm to their loyalties. Roadside monuments throughout Ireland stand as sombre reminders of those terrible times, many of them bearing inscriptions in memory of IRA soldiers or members of the National Army. Yet who dares to speak of constables James McDonnell and Patrick O'Connell who were fatally wounded at Soloheadbeg in the opening

52 General Seán Mac Eoin, ex-IRA, Bureau of Military History 1913–21, Witness Statement No. 1716, pp 108–10; Francis Davis, ex-IRA, Bureau of Military History 1913–21, Witness Statement No. 496, pp 18–19.

volleys of the war? At the time, their deaths sparked public outrage but the IRA were unapologetic and the Irish Free State was quick to turn its back on the RIC after 1922. Not alone were former policemen effectively debarred from re-admission into the Garda Síochána but those who resigned from the RIC because of their nationalist sympathies were awarded lesser pensions than those who stayed until disbandment; several successive governments failed to rectify that injustice.[53]

In 2009, a memorial garden for the Garda Síochána, Royal Irish Constabulary and Dublin Metropolitan Police (DMP) was opened in the grounds of Dublin Castle and in 2016, a remembrance wall was erected in Glasnevin Cemetery to honour all those who died during the Easter Rising, including seventeen policemen. These are important symbolic gestures of reconciliation. Another was the decision of the Irish postal service to issue a series of definitive stamps marking the 1916 rebellion, one of which features the unarmed DMP Constable James O'Brien who was the first fatality of the Rising.

The essential dilemma surrounding police casualties of the War of Independence is that it is not possible in all cases, as Pádraig Ó Ruairc has suggested, for 'a clear distinction [to] be drawn between those who served in the RIC as policemen as we understand that role today, protecting and serving society, and those who were involved in the very worst aspects of the British military campaign'.[54] Therefore, to erase from our national memory the perpetrators of atrocities, it seems that we must also condemn to oblivion the names of those who behaved honourably. Unfortunately, there is still a stigma attached to the RIC that impedes proper discourse of the War of Independence. It was with no small amount of trepidation that I delved into my family past, not knowing what I might uncover. As the son of a Garda sergeant, maybe it is easier for me to feel empathy towards the RIC rank-and-file than if I had come from a different background. My childhood home was an old RIC barracks which was originally constructed sometime about 1840. That grand old building had a character of its own. Growing up there, I often wondered about its past. It is no coincidence that many of the published histories of the RIC are the works of members of An Garda Síochána, whose perspectives are naturally compassionate towards their predecessors.

As stated at the outset, I felt a particular urge to discover what I could about my namesake Sergeant Michael Lang. That personal name has been passed down through several generations of our family, each of us called after

53 Gaughan, *Memoirs of Jeremiah Mee*, pp 284–7. **54** 'To remember or commemorate? Pádraig Óg Ó Ruairc on the RIC Memorial', *The Irish Story*, 3 September 2012, http://www.theirishstory.com/2012/09/03/ric-memorial/ accessed 1 June 2017.

the previous bearer. We are linked together by a chain across time. Not alone did they all share the same name but the last three Michaels before me all followed each other down the same walk of life by joining the Irish police force, the most recent of whom was my late uncle Michael who performed for many years as a tenor with the Garda Síochána band. And so, on a trip to Dublin in the summer of 2016, I decided to make a detour to Glasnevin Cemetery before returning home. As I entered the main gate, a guide dressed in military regalia was about to lead a group of visitors on a tour of the famous patriot graves. I was tempted to join them but stuck to my personal mission. Among the verdant shadows of the oldest section of the cemetery, I eventually found what I was looking for: a modest headstone, eroded by the passage of time, marking my great grand-uncle's final resting place. To see his name – my name – etched on the slab stirred a peculiar reaction within me. He was no celebrity or hero, just the son of a peasant farmer who chose to join the RIC for genuine reasons, like John Dillon and so many others of their generation. In the distance, the tour guide was passionately bellowing out a re-enactment of Pearse's oration: 'the fools, the fools, they have left us our Fenian dead'. In that surreal moment, I felt at ease in the company of a long-forgotten Sligo man who lies there in a communal plot alongside the ordinary working-class people of Dublin city.

Acknowledgments

I am grateful to my aunt, Moira Hunt (née Lang), for sharing her knowledge of our family history with me and helping to fill in the gaps in my recollections of stories that I had originally heard from my grandmother Kathleen Lang (née Dillon) many years ago.

Cantans intra et extra Chorum: Patrick and Francis Shaw

OLGA COX CAMERON & JOHN COX

As Ireland waved the tricolour in the centenary commemorative ceremonies for 1916, our family could not but ruefully look over its shoulder at our grandfather, Patrick Shaw, Cumann na nGaedheal TD for Longford-Westmeath (1923–33), who wrote to the king in 1916 to apologize for the Rising, and at our uncle Francis Shaw SJ who marked the 1966 celebrations with a strongly worded revisionist paper on the Rising that *Studies* declined to publish until after his death in 1970.

In this chapter we collate family memories of these two relatives, father and son, and test the extent to which it is valid to speak of inter-generational transfer. The wheel of life, like that of fictional form, operates as difference in repetition. Patterns recur but are transmuted by new shapes, and what we encounter in family history as elsewhere is always what *Finnegans wake* describes as 'the seim anew'. On the face of it Patrick's life does not seem to have been echoed by that of Frank. A colourful character, given to high living and the flamboyant gesture, our grandfather's exploits do not come to mind when looking at the very austere portrait of Frank at the *1916 Portraits and Lives* exhibition in Kilmainham Gaol, in which he was the only person featured who was not a direct participant in the Rising. The differences between the two men leap to the eye even in their degree of family presence. Frank was much loved and much talked of in the family, while the doings of our grandfather, in particular his gambling and womanizing, inspired a deeply reticent silence in his children.

However, the stories told and the stories silenced are what form the warp and weave of family identity, and we have been able to draw on interviews with a number of cousins who remember our grandfather. Almost all of them remember our uncle Frank well so we have also been able to amplify the useful information about him in the Jesuit archive and to fill out the background to its contents. As a collation of family memories and stories, this chapter cannot aspire to absolute reliability. It simply addresses a not so simple question: to what extent was Frank Shaw his father's son?[1]

1 Published biographical sources for both men are very limited, and there is no biography of Patrick. For Frank see Francis Finegan, 'Fr Frank Shaw', *Irish Province News* (Apr. 1971), pp 76–9, and Patrick Maume, 'Fr Francis Shaw and the historiography of Easter 1916', *Studies*, 103 (2014/15), pp 530–51. The

Patrick Shaw

It would doubtless come as a surprise to Patrick Walter Shaw (1874–1940) to find himself playing second fiddle to his son Frank, as is the case in this chapter, given that he himself had a prominent and colourful life and was not lacking in vanity. Born in 1874 as the fourth son of Joseph and Elizabeth (neé Doyne) in a family of eight, he reaped the benefits of his mother's business acumen. She was the driving force behind the purchase of a number of shops in Mullingar from 1878 onwards, initially a grocery but also a drapery, ironmongery, jewellers and pub. A street adjacent to these shops became known as Shaw's Lane. Little is known of Patrick's early life but he received his secondary education at Castleknock College, another sign that he came from a well-off family, even though his father died in his early forties when Patrick was young. The ironmongery and hardware business was assigned to Patrick and provided his income. It seems he rarely, if ever, worked inside the shop, leaving its running to a Mr Coleman among others, although he was to be seen outside, greeting customers.

Patrick married Minnie Galligan, eldest daughter of Hugh Galligan, Oldcastle, and they had their own family of eight, including Francis (Frank) who was born in 1907 as the fourth arrival. The marriage appears to have been an unlikely one in terms of personalities. Minnie was deeply religious while Patrick, although an orthodox Catholic, led an ostentatious lifestyle. Family sources reveal a man with a passion for outdoor pursuits, notably horseracing, fishing, hunting and shooting. His obituary notes that he was regarded as one of the best shots in Ireland and won the national Clay Pigeon Shooting Championship in 1901. He owned twenty-three horses, one of them named Belsize after the family home he bought in Mullingar in 1909. Frank shared his father's love of fishing and shooting, citing lots of time spent on these activities while convalescing at Belsize in summer 1932. Lavish food and wine were on the menu when the Shaws entertained guests on a frequent basis.

Patrick owned the first car in Mullingar and also the first radio, the latter attracting townspeople to Belsize to listen to Sunday matches, gathered under the sitting room window. Patrick's vanity was indulged by jewellery and he liked to wear diamonds. Belsize seems to have been a bustling home, a haven of middle-class comfort. Patrick was the dominant figure, with Minnie very much in the background. Although quiet, Minnie was also prominent in Mullingar and her funeral was recorded as the largest in the town for several years.[2] The relationship between Patrick and Minnie was not very close and he

Jesuit Archives in Dublin are the primary source of unpublished material about Frank (IE IJA/J451).
2 *Westmeath Examiner*, 16 Mar. 1940.

socialized more with others, having a reputation as a womanizer. At home he chose typically to eat alone, although in good style with dinner accompanied by wine and sometimes champagne.

Patrick and his five brothers represented a bastion of middle-class respectability in Mullingar in the early twentieth century. The businesses purchased by their mother provided a solid foundation for James and Thomas, who was also a County Councillor. Edward and Joseph were solicitors, while Richard owned over 500 acres of land. They engaged in similar pursuits to Patrick and even today the website of J.A. Shaw Solicitors in Mullingar notes that Edward favoured fishing and shooting over the practice of law.[3] Wheatley describes the Shaws as 'the Mullingar family most closely tied to the clergy', instancing a huge clerical presence at Richard's funeral in 1910, with thirty priests on the altar.[4] Most of the brothers were highly active in various local enterprises and Wheatley asserts that they 'were members of just about every society and public committee going'.[5]

The Shaws, notably Thomas, Edward and Patrick, navigated the Westmeath political landscape with a pragmatic, even opportunistic, neutrality. They did not appear to align directly with the Redmondite Irish Party, although they ultimately nailed their colours clearly to its mast, and managed to maintain an accommodation with supporters of the nationalist dissident from that party, Laurence Ginnell from Delvin, such that their influence grew steadily. Patrick was a particular beneficiary, becoming chair of the Mullingar Town Commissioners in 1911 and securing election to Westmeath County Council in 1914, ultimately rising to vice-chair in 1920. He was also chair of the Westmeath Board of Health.

The outbreak of the First World War brought the Shaws out strongly in support of John Redmond's advocacy in September 1914 that the Irish Volunteers should enlist in the British army. Others, including Ginnell, saw this as treachery and a major split in the Volunteers ensued. Patrick was active at recruitment rallies in 1915 and 1916 and his position hardened at the time of the Rising. His opposition to the Rising was clear and during Easter week at a meeting he chaired of the Mullingar Town Commissioners he proposed the formation of a volunteer corps to assist the authorities in dealing with the crisis.[6] The *Westmeath Examiner* reports that in early May he telegraphed the UK *Daily Mail* to the effect that 'We have no rebels in Mullingar. All the men are fighting at the front'.[7] Furthermore, in an action known only within the

3 jashaw.ie/about/, accessed 10 June 2017. 4 Michael Wheatley, *Nationalism and the Irish Party: provincial Ireland, 1910–1916* (Oxford, 2005), p. 123. 5 Ibid., p. 124. 6 Pádraig Ó Snodaigh, *Two godfathers of revisionism: 1916 in the revisionist canon* (Dublin, 1991), p. 35. 7 *Westmeath Examiner*, 13 May 1916.

confines of his own family, he wrote a letter to the King to apologize for the Rising. Patrick's hostility to the Rising did not go unnoticed locally and our cousins Frank and Buddy Shaw report a story that during a later Dáil election campaign someone painted a question on walls around Mullingar: 'Where was Shaw in 1916?'. This did not trouble Patrick who paid someone to paint 'Fairyhouse! Where else?' underneath. One can see how Frank might have formed less than favourable views of the events of Easter 1916.

Wheatley observes that the Shaws did not belong to any political movement 'until Patrick's adherence to Sinn Féin in 1921'.[8] His attitude to 1916 and subsequent membership of Cumann na nGaedheal would have put him firmly on the pro-Treaty side of the party but his actions in the period beforehand graduated from political pragmatism to a risky patriotism. Family members recall that during the War of Independence he provided Michael Collins with a safe haven at Belsize, hiding him in the pantry for a number of nights when he was being pursued by the Black and Tans who threw a grenade at the house and blew up the monkey puzzle on the front lawn. Collins expressed his gratitude in a letter that Patrick subsequently kept framed on the dining room wall. On an earlier visit Collins addressed a rally on a chilly night in Mullingar and Patrick lent him his overcoat. After Collins' assassination the coat was returned and Denis Shaw recalls that his father Paddy, son of Patrick, said he reverently examined it for the bullet holes that would indicate that Collins was wearing it at the time of his death.

Patrick's change in outlook in the period around the War of Independence needs to be seen in perspective. Membership of Sinn Féin seems surprising but might be born of the same kind of pragmatism that enabled the Shaw brothers to work with Laurence Ginnell previously. Opportunism was a likely factor as the Home Rule party had been decimated by Sinn Féin in the 1918 election and only held six seats. Sinn Féin would have offered Shaw better prospects for local advancement and he may have felt more closely aligned with its moderate wing under Arthur Griffith. His concealment of Collins could reflect his susceptibility to the dramatic action, despite the risks involved. Also, he was not alone in taking this kind of action and another example is known in which the Sinn Féin TD Kevin O'Higgins was sheltered while on the run by P.J. Meehan, the Home Rule MP whom he had defeated in the 1918 election.[9]

This phase proved to be a temporary dalliance politically as the end of the Civil War saw Patrick join the new Cumann na nGaedheal party. He stood as a parliamentary candidate in the Longford–Westmeath constituency in 1923

8 Wheatley, *Nationalism and the Irish Party*, p. 124. **9** Patrick Meehan, *The members of parliament for Laois and Offaly (Queen's and King's Counties), 1801–1918* (Portlaoise, 1983), p. 80.

and was a TD for ten years, securing election on four occasions, including top position in the poll twice in 1927.[10] Known sometimes to have skated to the Dáil along the Royal Canal in icy conditions, he was a regular contributor and spoke on 340 occasions, ranging from 61 in 1924 to 14 in his final year, 1932. The range of topics on which he spoke crossed a broad spectrum from school meals for children and payment of unemployment grants for road works to finance and housing bills. There was a noticeable clustering of contributions around topics closer to his own interests than those of the majority of constituents, for example betting tax receipts, the horse-breeding industry, fisheries and game preservation bills and the trapping of foxes. A debate in 1931 on the funding of Fisheries and Gaeltacht Services afforded him the opportunity to make a long-winded speech in which he informed members, by reading from a newspaper report, that he had caught a record number of fifteen trout on Lough Ennell in May that year.

Overall, Patrick, while never becoming a minister, seems to have made a solid contribution to his party and his country. He showed a loyalty to the government, which was attacked by Professor William Magennis who, in a tirade against Shaw in early 1927, described him as 'such a minion of the Government, that they could do no wrong according to him'.[11] A tendency to toe the party line is apparent in his Dáil contributions but this would have been appreciated in Cumann na nGaedheal as it took on the challenging task of government after the Civil War. Although elected again in 1932, he decided not to contest the snap election called by de Valera in 1933. His obituary attributed this to pressure of business, but a letter from Frank states that he had stood only reluctantly in 1932 and that he did not do so in 1933 due to ill health.[12] The same obituary referred to failing health for some years and Patrick seems to have had a quiet retirement until his death at Belsize in October 1940.

Minnie's death in March 1940 greatly affected him and his own death a few months later was hastened by remorse according to the family. The clergy attended his funeral in force, along with many others, including a number of TDs. Interestingly, as seems to have been the tradition at the time, the *Westmeath Examiner* cited his sons but not his daughters as chief mourners, reflecting appropriately in this instance his male-dominated household.[13]

What did others think of Patrick? There were mixed views of him. Servants at Belsize were very loyal towards him and he enjoyed strong

10 Mel Farrell, '"Few supporters and no organization"? Cumann na nGaedheal organization and policy, 1923–33' (PhD, NUI Maynooth, 2011), pp 122–61. eprints.maynoothuniversity.ie/4072/1/%27Few_supporters_and_no_organisation%27Cumann_na_nGaedheal_organisation_and_policy%2C_1923-1933.pdf, accessed 10 June 2017. **11** *Westmeath Examiner*, 26 Feb. 1927. **12** *Westmeath Examiner*, 21 Sept. 1940. **13** Ibid.

popularity among the locals as he was well read and good company. The only two grandchildren born in his lifetime, Mary and Rosemary, remember him with great affection – a gramps who met the tiny Mary halfway between her house and his and walked together with her downtown to the ironmongery. Rosemary's memories are similar, someone lavish with ice cream and small sums of money and affection for the little girls. His own children are considerably more reticent. Most of them never spoke of him at all, a collective silence which is in itself significant. In later years, Violet, who lived into her nineties, affected complete amnesia about her childhood. Only Paddy, a gentle affectionate man, again in later years said outright of Patrick that he was self-centred, arrogant and treated Minnie badly. From Frank we have not a word.

Francis Shaw

Born in 1907, two years before the family moved into the beautiful Belsize, Frank would have been nine in 1916. We know from family lore that Patrick certainly told Minnie, who may also have told the children, about his letter to the King apologizing for the Rising. Did the children, including Frank, register the extent of his political *volte face* over the next few years? With the exception of his eldest daughter Dot (Kathleen) whom he adored and who often dined alone with him, Patrick's opulent lifestyle does not appear to have included much time with his children.

Like Dot, Frank's health was a worry from very early on. This was a family haunted by the spectre of tuberculosis (TB). While stories abound about Tom, the eldest, and the other wild uncontrollable boys in this very patriarchal household, Frank is never included. During his delicate childhood he would have seen his older sister sent off to various sanatoria in Switzerland, ultimately to no avail, while at home, his own recurring bouts of TB meant that he could not follow in his father's footsteps and be educated at Castleknock College. Instead he was sent to the Carmelite school in Terenure where it was possible for him to have his own room and not share in dormitory life. Decades later in a tribute to Johann Kaspar Zeuss, another Celtic scholar afflicted with lifelong TB, he perhaps heard echoes of his own childhood when he wrote: 'He was serious minded ... did not play games and was of excellent conduct'.[14]

Was Frank his father's son? In terms of inter-generational transfer it is not hard to see how Patrick's Redmondite and Home Rule politics influenced Frank's stance in his famous article on 1916.[15] Patrick's clericalism allied with

14 Francis Shaw, 'Johann Kaspar Zeuss', *Studies,* 43 (1954), p. 195, www.jstor.org/stable/30098542, accessed 10 June 2017. 15 Francis Shaw, 'The canon of Irish history – a challenge', *Studies,* 61 (1972), pp 113–53, www.jstor.org/stable/30087966, accessed 10 June 2017.

Minnie's marked piety, may also be visible in some of Frank's more Catholic writings. Frank's lifelong passion for shooting, fishing and indeed gambling, are very clear heritages from his father, but less evidently than these external traces Frank's character and temperament bear witness in a different form to a deeper identification with certain salient aspects of his father. Patrick was possessed of both combativeness and a certain stylistic flair. He was not easily intimidated as is obvious in his response to the scrawled electoral question 'Where was Shaw in 1916?'. And behind what looks like pragmatic opportunism he must have been susceptible to the lure of the heroic gesture. Otherwise, would he have hidden Michael Collins long enough to alert the Black and Tans in a houseful of children?

However, the very first thing we know for sure about Frank is that by the age of eleven his most defining feature is already visible. This was memorably summed up for us by a younger Jesuit in the phrase '*Cantans extra chorum*' (Singing outside of the choir). Unlike his politically-minded father, Frank was always more likely to be singing outside of rather than along with the choir. The Shaws, while considering themselves Irish, were markedly anglicized, exhibiting all the features excoriated by Douglas Hyde in his famous broadside.[16] Most of the work in the house, including child-rearing, was done by servants. A number of cousins claim not to have known their parents since they were 'brought up by maids'. Shooting parties were organized for winter Sundays, with the men decked out in knickerbockers and returning in the evening to a sumptuous dinner. The girls played piano and sang Gilbert and Sullivan. Irish music and the Irish language were the domain of the lower orders. Our mother Olive, the youngest, clung to these attitudes all her life, priding herself on not understanding Irish. None of her siblings had the least interest in the language or showed any sign of having lived through the Gaelic Revival (in contrast to our father's family where his mother would promise: 'If you are good today I will teach you some Irish').

It comes therefore as a surprise to see Frank's name in the *Westmeath Examiner* in July 1918 as a winner of prizes for excellence in Irish at the Mullingar Feis. The first recorded prize is for solo singing. Four years later, home on holidays from boarding school, he won three prizes in the under-16 category: First Prize for Irish Elocution, and First Prize for reciting Canon O'Leary's Irish Catechism. No second prize is recorded so perhaps Frank was the only Mullingar boy interested in this pious exercise! He also won Second Prize, beaten by a girl, for Irish speaking. No other member of the family

16 Douglas Hyde, 'The necessity for de-anglicising Ireland' in D. Kiberd and P.J. Mathews (eds), *Handbook of the Irish Revival: an anthology of Irish cultural and political writings, 1891–1922* (Dublin, 2015), pp 42–6.

features in any of the surprisingly varied categories – one could win a prize for the best darn! But no Shaw of our mother's generation would have dreamed of attending, still less participating in, a Feis. It is of course not impossible that by 1918, the politically astute Patrick saw the advantage of having a young son with Gaelic League leanings. However, everything points to Frank starting to sing outside of the family choir.

One of the epigraphs of Frank's controversial article about 1916, submitted to *Studies* in 1966, was a quote from Michael Collins, defining Irish nationality. At one level this is surprising, since by most accounts Collins was a far more ruthless revolutionary than Pearse. But Collins was the family hero. Frank was probably in boarding school when, in the incident described earlier, the monkey puzzle at Belsize was blown up by the Black and Tans, as he very likely also was on the occasion of Collins' earlier visit when Patrick lent him his coat. But Frank could not have missed seeing what the end of the War of Independence meant to Patrick. In July 1921 his youngest sister was born in Belsize and three days later Patrick named her Olive Truce to celebrate the cessation of hostilities. Patrick rarely failed to step up to the mark with stylistic flair. His son was not altogether unlike him.

Why did Frank choose to enter the Jesuits? There is no record of this decision. Politically it would keep him on the paternal side of the tracks since the Jesuits were known to favour home rule, and University College Dublin (UCD) would for many decades be Redmondite in sentiment. Even the main repository of his published work, the Jesuit journal *Studies*, was 'born in the intellectual and social world of Home Rule Ireland and for much of its history was part of the UCD/Cumann na nGaedheal/Fine Gael nexus'.[17] In 1924, at the age of seventeen he began his novitiate in Tullabeg, an institution that scandalized the Shaws by its austerity. It would seem that Frank to some extent set out to alleviate this state of affairs. His niece Mary Counihan recalls how he commissioned his sister, Dorothy, Mary's mother, to make a hundred pots of blackberry jam for them. He himself got out his gun and his fishing rod to provision the dinner table.

Anyone who saw Frank, especially in later life, will recall a gauntness that seemed incompatible with normal functioning, let alone with enjoying life. He was about six foot four, weighed just seven stone had longish black hair falling into his eyes, a pale gaunt face, black glasses and wore the long black soutane of the Jesuits with its floating wings. To the unwary he was an apparition. His nephew Edward recalls being too awed to greet Frank in UCD as he wafted

17 Barra Ó Seaghdha, 'History as a moral tale', *Dublin Review of Books,* 19 (2012), www.drb.ie/essays-/history-as-a-moral-tale, accessed 10 June 2017.

spectrally by. Other family stories underwrite this other-worldliness. His niece Mary recalls meeting him one day in Dublin on O'Connell Street. As they were parting after a pleasant chat Frank asked if Mary had noticed which way he had been going: if towards the GPO (General Post Office), then he had already had lunch, if not, he had not yet eaten! But this may not have been asceticism. Another niece, Olivia, remembers that while he was acting president in UCD she was, aged twelve, commissioned to bake a tray of meringues for him every week, brought to Dublin by her father Paddy, Frank's younger brother. Frank, in appreciation, had a UCD scroll made out for her, awarding her an honorary degree in meringue baking!

His gothic appearance and sometimes overly pious pronouncements belied an energy and a *joie de vivre* that in Patrick had expressed itself via twenty-three race horses and a lavish lifestyle incurring debts that it would take his son Paddy thirty-five years to pay in full. In Frank one can see something of this *élan vital* in his forceful intelligence, his vigorous writing style, his giftedness as a teacher as well as in his Shaw passion for the sporting life. His constant ill health impinged far less than it should have on these activities. His nephew Frank accompanied him on many of his shooting expeditions where, as Mary Counihan remarked, he was happy to lie all night in a wet field in soaking clothes in order to bag a pheasant. The family was very well aware that being hospitalized for TB, as he often was, in no way prevented him from leaving his bed without permission to go shooting. A member of the public wrote to the Jesuit Father Provincial to complain of Frank walking the streets of Dublin in his soutane with a shotgun under his arm. Frank was unperturbed, suggesting that he could make it look more like a crozier so people would think he was a foreign bishop.

Recurring TB and a passion for the outdoor life seem unlikely bedfellows but they mark, in almost equal measure, his early and indeed all of his life as a Jesuit. While he was studying theology in Valkenberg his eldest sister Dot died of TB in 1931, aged twenty-eight. Frank was not allowed home for her funeral which was attended by President Cosgrave and huge swathes of clergy. One year later Frank was sent home himself with TB from Bonn where he had been studying Old Irish under Rudolf Thurneysen. He had tried to conceal this illness from his parents but rather unusually the Jesuits sent him back to Belsize to recover. It must have been a sad household, with the much-loved Dot recently dead and the youngest boy Vincent already ill (he too would die of TB just over a decade later). And now Frank too was at home with the same disease. Unlike many families the Shaws never made a secret of this terrible spectre stalking their children. The sadness and worry is visible in letters written by both Minnie and Patrick to the Father Provincial at this time.

Frank's letter requesting a few more weeks at home is perhaps deliberately upbeat so as to reassure his Superior, and lists fishing in Lough Ennell and shooting parties as part of his regimen of recuperation. One year later he would have TB again, and so it would go on with depressing regularity.

It is likely that his early independent pursuit of Irish determined his career path. Fr Lambert McKenna SJ, himself a distinguished Celtic scholar, urged him in this direction and by the relatively young age of thirty-four Frank was Professor of Early and Medieval Irish in UCD, a position he held until his death in 1970. Looking at his remarkably prolific career, given his near invalidism, one can recognize some of the ingredients which would create the explosion caused by his highly revisionist paper about 1916, 'The canon of Irish history'.[18] If Patrick could be combative when challenged, this was Frank's default position and was perhaps not entirely devoid of the arrogance, which was one of his father's character traits. As his obituary says, 'Frank was an intelligent man and could not fail to realize the fact. He was also a born dialectician and enthusiastically defended the weaker case in any argument'.[19]

Also, while being considerably more conservative than he himself may have appreciated, he had a horror of the mindless complacencies of the *status quo*. He wanted his writings on St Patrick to provide 'a jolt to our accepted ideas'.[20] He approved Pope John XXIII's dislike of 'sacred cows' and his war on 'the twin dragons of pious pusillanimity and curial caution'.[21] He strongly endorsed Fr Paul Walsh's suspicion 'of anything that came to him second-hand' and he thrilled to Zeuss' great achievement in single-handedly re-constructing the grammatical structure of the Celtic languages without trusting to books and without ever coming into contact with anyone who knew these languages.[22] *Cantans extra chorum*, these were Frank's heroes. But, as with his Redmondite stance in the 'Canon', there were also choirs to which he loyally belonged, and in which he loudly sang.

His field was Celtic Studies. As has been well documented, historically the term 'Celtic' bifurcated, first into a domain of research that was for many years led by continental scholarship and was mainly philological and grammatical in its focus. The second, and much more pervasive, turn was into a hugely

18 M. Proinséas Ní Chatháin, 'The academic and other writings of Rev. Professor Francis Shaw, SJ', *Studies*, 60 (1971), pp 203–7, www.jstor.org/stable/30088714, accessed 10 June 2017; Shaw, 'The canon of Irish history', *Studies* 61 (1972), pp 113–53, www.jstor.org/stable/30087966, accessed 10 June 2017. **19** Francis Finegan, 'Fr Frank Shaw', *Irish Province News* (Apr. 1971), p. 79. **20** Francis Shaw, 'St Patrick: a study in missionary achievement', *Irish Monthly*, 58 (1930), p. 132, www.jstor.org/stable/20518705, accessed 10 June 2017. **21** Francis Shaw, 'John XXIII: anniversary', *Studies*, 53 (1964), p. 114, www.jstor.org/stable/30088823, accessed 10 June 2017. **22** Francis Shaw, 'Father Paul Walsh: the scholar', *Studies*, 30 (1941), pp 447–8, www.jstor.org/stable/30098142, accessed 10 June 2017.

popular late romantic literary movement, spearheaded by Matthew Arnold and best known here in Yeats' *Celtic twilight.* Like Cúchulainn holding back the waves, Frank spent enormous amounts of time and invective in establishing the claims of serious scholarship against the tide of what he called the 'idiotismus' of the 'Celtomaniacs'.[23] This was an inherited irritant but not less vigorously endorsed for that. It is visible in the 'Canon' in his undermining of Pearse's cult of Cúchulainn.

The other choir in which he loyally sang was orthodox Catholicism. His era was that of the 'Church triumphant' with priests feeling entitled to pronounce definitively on matters of which they knew almost nothing. The back page of Frank's pamphlet *Gone with the wind: a commentary* lists other recommended works: *What a girl should know, Domestic virtues, Can I keep pure?*[24] All were authored by priests. For Frank there was the added layer of the Shaws' profound respect for the clergy, Minnie's daily mass-going and his younger sisters' marriages which were brokered by a priest. He would not hesitate to instruct the Catholic laity about the viewing of a film and unsurprisingly, if bizarrely, in the 'Canon', he could imagine as an ancient tradition the Irish people accepting 'loyally the serious guidance of the Church to which they belonged'.[25]

That he was not all that keen himself on accepting serious guidance is evident from some of the incidents the Jesuit Archives records.[26] In 1936, he explains assertively to the Father Provincial why he is at the centre of a public row following his condemnation of compulsory Irish at a meeting of UCD's Literary and Historical Society. In 1938, he is again arguing with the Father Provincial, pushing for the publication of one of his writings. In 1946, Frank is objecting to Archbishop McQuaid's insistence that he personally should read Frank's talks on Raidió Éireann ahead of the broadcast. And when *Studies* refused to publish his inflammatory article in 1966 he had a hundred copies typed up and quietly circulated in Dublin where it became a badge of honour in intellectual circles to have read it. The Jesuits' wish to assert copyright prompted its publication in *Studies* in 1972.

Where did Frank stand politically? The 'Canon' renders very visible his Redmondite leanings but there, as in his other work, Patrick Maume's observation that his political and religious convictions overlapped with his scholarly preoccupations is entirely accurate.[27] The world in which he taught and

23 Shaw, 'Johann Kaspar Zeuss', p. 203. **24** Francis Shaw, *Gone with the wind: a commentary* (Dublin, 1942). **25** Shaw, 'The canon of Irish history', 118. **26** Irish Jesuit Archives. IE IJA/J451 (Papers of Fr Frank Shaw SJ, 1907–1970). **27** Patrick Maume, 'Fr Francis Shaw and the historiography of Easter 1916', *Studies,* 103 (2014/15), p. 536, www.jstor.org/stable/24347848, accessed 10 June 2017.

studied, UCD, and the journal *Studies* were Redmondite and Fine Gael in orientation, and against this background his political DNA may not have seemed particularly visible to him. The only time we hear of him overtly donning the paternal mantle is recorded in an entertaining note in Maume's article: 'ex-Chief Justice Thomas Finlay recalled that, when he was a Fine Gael candidate in Dublin South Central in the 1954 general election, Fr Shaw asked hospital patients whom he visited to vote for Finlay'.[28]

It is reasonable to see two other 'political' interventions prior to the 'Canon' as fuelled by Frank's commitment to Celtic and, in particular, to Irish Studies. The row provoked in 1936 by his opposition to compulsory Irish, referenced earlier, is a case in point. In the other instance, regarding his 1934 article on Yeats and the *Celtic twilight*,[29] Roy Foster is somewhat unfair in locating it within the orbit of the scurrilous anti-Yeats campaign waged by the *Catholic Bulletin* and similar publications.[30] Frank's focus here is not on, as with these others, the un-Irishness of Yeats but the un-Irishness of Yeats' Celtic Twilight phase. He is provoked more by the appropriation of Celtic mythology by those unversed in the original texts than by vituperative Catholic nationalism. He acknowledges Yeats as the greatest poet of the Celtic Twilight and is specific in objecting not to the poetry *per se* but to 'the movement' spearheaded by Yeats promoting the view that Celtic, and especially Irish, literature is predominantly shadowy and dreamy and not, as in Frank's experience, full of life and action. He would not have agreed with Seamus Deane that 'an idea of tradition and continuity so vague as Ireland's needed all the dimness it could get'.[31] It is the dreaminess that irks Frank most, 'the mooning and moping among the fairies'.[32] In Frank's assessment 'The inhabitants of Mr Yeats' other-world may, I think, be conveniently divided into three classes: those who are just emerging from a Druid swoon, those who actually are in a Druid swoon, and the rest – those who at a moment's notice may go off into a Druid swoon'.[33] He takes wicked pleasure in juxtaposing Yeats' injunction to dream and an Old Irish warning: 'gazing at glowing embers is one of the worst things for the body of man!'.[34]

Others had noted that in Yeats' Celtic Twilight phase, Irish legends and sagas provided a framework for oriental theosophy. Frank, as a Celtic scholar, uses his expertise to copperfasten this assertion. But Frank's own title for the 'Canon' was 'Cast a cold eye …' (altered to its present title by the editor, Fr Roland Savage). And the final sentence of the original circulated typescript is

28 Ibid., p. 546. **29** Francis Shaw, 'The Celtic twilight', *Studies*, 23 (1934), pp 260–78, www.jstor.org/stable/30095144, accessed 10 June 2017. **30** Roy Foster, *The Irish story: telling tales and making it up in Ireland* (London, 2001), p. 90. **31** Seamus Deane, *Celtic revivals: essays in modern Irish literature, 1880–1980* (London, 1985), p. 21. **32** Shaw, 'Celtic twilight', p. 266. **33** Ibid., p. 273. **34** Ibid., p. 269.

also Yeatsian; 'Kathleen Ní Houlihan has settled down; she has no longer the "walk of a queen" which drove men to desperate deeds; her love affair with the hungry outlaw on the little hills would seem to be over'.

But it is his best-known work that best illustrates the intrication of his scholarly work with his religious and political affiliations. The 'Canon' is still in the top ten most frequently downloaded articles in *Studies* between 2009 and September 2016, a notable feat more than forty years on, and it generates more queries than any other article in the journal. A sizeable body of criticism and commentary on it exists, summarized by Maume among others, to which the family would be incautious to add as we lack the necessary historical expertise.[35] Frank's purpose was to de-mythologize the heroes of 1916, in itself striking since many of his other writings show him to be very susceptible to the heroic gesture, but of course he was consciously or unconsciously echoing his father's disapproval of the Rising. However, as his critics were quick to recognize, in setting out to de-mythologize, it is all but impossible not to re-orient the exposed fictions in the prism of one's own mythology. Reading the 'Canon' and its critics in light of each other in this regard is interesting.

There is also the tone of the article to consider. In much of his earlier work Frank, regardless of his admiration or annoyance, is at pains to present a fair picture. In writing of his heroes Thurneysen and Zeuss he acknowledges the off-putting turgidity of their style. In critiquing Yeats' *Celtic twilight* he repeatedly honours him as a very great poet, while in his pamphlet on *Gone with the wind* he is so impressed by the beauty and the force of both the film and the book that the orthodox sermonizing is continually punctured by this praise. In the 'Canon' he tries to do the same, repeatedly honouring Wolfe Tone's fearless honesty, but somehow his polemic tone overrides this attempt and creates an impression of harsh attack. This in its turn roused a counter attack in his critics. He was known to be a genial man and his obituary states that when he was well enough to attend community recreation, he radiated sheer delight.[36] This geniality and a certain playful sarcasm are missing in the 'Canon'. Indeed a year later the Jesuits refused publication in the *Irish Times* of an article by Frank on the grounds that it was unnecessarily harsh. Some frustration with their earlier refusal to publish the 'Canon' may have been at play with Frank and he may not have been as accepting of that decision as is reported by the editor in the introduction to the published version. Or a long life of physical pain was perhaps catching up with him. And another of the family spectres had begun to haunt him: addiction. Frank was addicted to painkillers in the final decade of his life.

35 Maume, 'Fr Francis Shaw and the historiography of Easter 1916', pp 540–2. **36** Finegan, 'Fr Frank Shaw', p. 79.

Patrick and Francis Shaw.

But undoubtedly, given the enduring status of this first foray into revisionism Frank hit a nerve in the Irish psyche and said something of what needed to be said. What would he have made of the furore it generated? It is hard to imagine him backing down. For better or for worse, like his father painting his flamboyant response to the graffiti questioning his credentials, Frank Shaw would have stood his ground. And Patrick, although generally more comfortable singing within the choir, *cantans intra chorum,* would have been proud of him.

Acknowledgments

We wish to express our sincere thanks to all the relatives we spoke to for their generously given time, documentation and hospitality and for the many valuable insights noted in the text, supplemented by other helpful observations by John and Rosemary Fagan and Ann Downes. Those interviewed were: Denis Shaw, Edward Shaw, Olivia Dunne, Buddy Shaw, Frank Shaw, Rosemary Shaw and Mary Counihan. We are also indebted to Damien Burke, the Irish Jesuit Archives, and Dr Martin O'Donoghue, NUI Galway.

Contributors

CIARA BOYLAN is a Postdoctoral Research Fellow at the Child and Family Research Centre, NUI Galway, working in the area of empathy, social values and education. She holds a doctorate in modern Irish history. Her research has focused on the history of education and childhood in Ireland, educational policy and empathy education.

TOM BOYLAN is Emeritus Professor of Economics at NUI Galway. He is a former Dean of the Faculty of Arts and was the first Dean of Research for the University. He was a member of the Higher Education Authority for ten years. He has published widely in the areas of econometrics, philosophy and methodology of economics, post-Keynesian economics, and the history of Irish economic thought.

BERNADINE BRADY is a lecturer at the School of Political Science and Sociology, NUI Galway and a Senior Researcher with the UNESCO Child and Family Research Centre. Her research explores how community, school, family and service provision influence outcomes for young people.

ANNE BYRNE is a sociologist drawn to narrative inquiry and the relation between predecessor and successor stories in early twentieth-century Ireland. Her interest is in the past and present as modes to anticipate human futures, and she has published work on identities and their complexities and how our stories make us.

SARAH-ANNE BUCKLEY is lecturer in history at the NUI Galway. Her research centres on the history of childhood and youth in Ireland. Author of *The cruelty man: child welfare, the NSPCC and the State in Ireland, 1889–1956* (Manchester, 2013), she is President of the Women's History Association of Ireland, Chair of the Irish History Student's Association and co-director of the Irish Centre for the Histories of Labour and Class.

JOHN CANAVAN is a senior lecturer at the School of Political Science and Sociology, NUI Galway and Associate Director of the University's UNESCO Child and Family Research Centre, part of the Institute for Lifecourse and Society.

JOHN COX is University Librarian at NUI Galway. A native of Delvin, Co. Westmeath, he has worked in research libraries throughout his career, and has a particular interest in digital libraries, including leadership of the digitisation of the Abbey and Gate Theatre archives at NUI Galway.

OLGA COX CAMERON is a psychoanalyst in private practice in Dublin. She lectured in psychoanalytic theory and in psychoanalysis and literature at St Vincent's University Hospital and Trinity College from 1991 to 2013 and has published numerous articles on these topics in national and international journals. She is the founder of the annual Irish Psychoanalysis and Cinema Festival.

MICHAEL DOLAN, recently retired, has forty years experience as a director of Dolan Brothers, a large manufacturing business based in Dublin. For many years, he has maintained am interest in Irish history generally and in the period of the revolutionary years (1914–23) in particular.

PAT DOLAN holds the UNESCO Chair in Children, Youth and Civic Engagement. He is founder and Director of the Institute for Lifecourse and Society (ILAS) and the UNESCO Child and Family Research Centre at NUI Galway. He has published extensively over many years in a wide range of books and journals and his major research interests are civic engagement in children and youth, family support, youth mentoring models, empathy education and adolescents' resilience and social networks.

DAITHÍ FALLON grew up in Castlerea, Co. Roscommon and is an engineer living in Cork and Head of the Department at Cork Institute of Technology. Daithí graduated with a BE (1985) and MEngSc (1987) in industrial engineering from University College Galway.

ENDA FALLON grew up in Castlerea, Co. Roscommon. He is a graduate of University College Galway (BE 1984, MEngSc 1987) and is currently employed as a senior lecturer in industrial engineering at the same University. He has taught and published widely in ergonomics and human factors engineering.

RÓISÍN HEALY is Lecturer in Modern European History at NUI Galway. Her most recent publications include *Poland in the Irish nationalist imagination, 1772–1922: anti-colonialism within Europe* (London, 2017), *Small nations and colonial peripheries in World War I* (Leiden, 2016) and *The shadow of colonialism on Europe's modern past* (Cambridge, 2014).

JIM HIGGINS is Heritage Office with Galway City Council. He is a graduate of NUI Galway, completing his PhD there about the medieval and late medieval funerary sculpture of Galway city, and has published widely on the archaeology of Galway city and county.

MICHAEL LANG is a senior lecturer in business information systems within the J.E. Cairnes School of Business & Economics at NUI Galway. His principal research interests are business systems analysis and design, database technologies, and information privacy and security. He also has a keen interest in Irish history, heritage and genealogy studies, has published a number of articles on local history and was nominated for a GAA MacNamee Award in 2015 for his work in researching the history of Gaelic games in his home parish in south Mayo.

CHRIS MCNAIRNEY was born in 1956 and grew up on the Falls Road, Belfast, and later Andersonstown. He was educated at St Malachy's College before going to Queen's University, Belfast where he took a degree in psychology and later to the University of Ulster where he studied HR management. Before taking up a post in NUI Galway in 1997 he was the Head of Personnel in Queen's University.

DOROTHY NÍ UIGÍN is í Riarthóir Theagasc na Gaeilge in Acadamh na hOllscolaíochta Gaeilge í an Dr Dorothy Ní Uigín. Tá suim aici i dteagasc agus i sealbhú teangacha agus sa litearthacht acadúil, agus tá spéis ar leith aici i stair na hiriseoireachta agus na meán Gaeilge.

LIAM Ó hAISIBÉIL is a Lecturer in Irish in the School of Languages, Literatures and Cultures at NUI Galway, where he teaches courses in onomastics, medieval Irish literature, early Modern-Irish and the indigenous arts. His primary research areas involve Irish place-names and surnames.

CIAN Ó NÉILL is currently pursuing an MPhil in modern Irish history at Trinity College Dublin. His current research interest is Irish nationalist activity in Germany during the First World War, and he has previously published work on armed robbery in Dublin during the Irish Civil War. He graduated with a BA in history from UCD in 2015.

GEARÓID Ó TUATHAIGH is Emeritus Professor in History at NUI Galway and former Vice-President of NUI Galway. He has written and contributed to numerous publications and is a former member of the USA-Ireland Fulbright

Commission. He has been Visiting Professor/Distinguished Lecturer in numerous universities and is currently a member of the Council of State.

NIAMH REILLY is Established Professor of Political Science and Sociology at NUI Galway. She co-edited *Religion, gender and the public sphere* (London, 2014) and authored *Women's human rights: seeking gender justice in a globalizing age* (London, 2009). Niamh is currently preparing a monograph on the political and social thought of Tom Kettle.

ANGELA SAVAGE was born in Ballisodare, Co. Sligo, obtained a BSc degree from UCG and a PhD in chemistry from UBC. Following postdoctoral work in Vancouver and in Germany, she returned to a lectureship in UCG in 1983 and was awarded a Personal Professorship for research in glycoscience. She retired in 2008.

DR MICHELINE SHEEHY SKEFFINGTON recently took early retirement from the Botany Department, NUI Galway, where she taught plant ecology from 1980. She is currently engaged in a campaign, supported by students, staff and many others, to redress the gender imbalance in senior posts in NUI Galway.

ANTONY WHEATLEY BSc (Hons), PhD, was born in Cork and educated in Dublin. Following graduation from Trinity, he held academic position at universities in South Africa, Switzerland, New Zealand before returning to NUI Galway in 2009, where he is Professor of Physiology. He has a keen interest in Irish history, especially the 1916–22 period.

Index

by Conor Reidy